W9-AQW-298

A Note from the Author

Dear Reader,

Thank you for choosing 40 Digital Photography Techniques, 2nd Edition.

If you are new to digital photography or if you have taken digital images without understanding how a digital camera really works, this book will be great for you. We will start with an introduction to the digital camera before moving on to its more advanced features. For film camera owners, this book also contains a brief comparison of film and digital cameras to help build on existing knowledge and let you make a smooth transition from film to digital.

For digital camera owners, this book will teach you a lot more than your camera manual. It describes 40 techniques for achieving specific results, using a combination of technical skills, art theories, and traditional photography know-how. Whether you enjoy taking pictures of people, landscapes, or any other subject, this compact little book is filled with plenty of examples and ideas. This book will also show you how to transfer, print, and share your images on the Internet.

In this second edition, a number of changes and additions have been made. At the end of every chapter, you will find a checklist to recap the techniques described in the chapter. With topics ranging from general shooting tips to advanced techniques, the checklists make a great reference and provide a quick refresher course. If you haven't yet purchased a digital camera, the checklist on buying a camera that is right for you will be a great resource. This checklist will help you select a camera with the features you want, without buying into features that you don't really need.

This edition includes two new techniques—wedding photography and action photography—to help you capture life's important moments. This edition contains hundreds of example images and suggestions to help you make the most of your digital camera. You will quickly discover that you can create fantastic results with standard digital cameras. Have fun!

John Kim

Contents

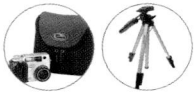

Introduction | Getting to Know Your Digital Camera 6

Comparing a Digital Camera with a Film Camera 8
Structure and Basic Functions 11
Choosing the Right Digital Camera 18
Accessorizing Your Digital Camera 21
Camera Care 24
Checklist: Buying a Digital Camera

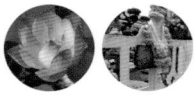

Chapter 1 | The Basics of Taking Photos 28

1 Preparing to Shoot 30
2 Preventing Camera Shake and Blurring 32
3 Adjusting Image Size and Quality 37
4 Locking a Focus 40
5 Using Lenses 42
6 Controlling Exposure 48
7 Composing a Shot 53
Checklist: Photo Basics

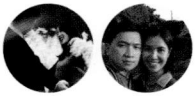

Chapter 2 | Exploring More Advanced Features 60

8 Working with Light 62
9 Using Flash 67
10 Creating Black-and-White and Sepia Images 72
11 Shooting Close-Ups of Small Objects 76
12 Taking Continuous Shots 81
13 Taking Action Shots 86
14 Using White Balance 89
Checklist: Advanced Features

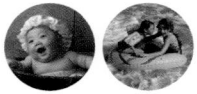

Chapter 3 | Photographing People 96

15 Taking Better People Photos 98
16 Changing the Camera Distance and Angle 104
17 Using Selective Focus 106
18 Photographing Children 109
19 Shooting Self-Portraits 113

20 Using Light 117
21 Manipulating Filters 120
22 Photographing Weddings 124
Checklist: Photographing People

Chapter 4 | Shooting Landscapes **128**
23 Landscape Photography Essentials 130
24 Vacation Photos 135
25 Rainy Day Photos 139
26 Snowy Day Photos 142
27 Night Photography 144
28 Capturing Sunrises and Sunsets 148
29 Creating Panoramas 152
Checklist: Shooting Landscapes

Chapter 5 | Experimenting with Common Themes **158**
30 Photographing Food 160
31 Taking Product Shots 163
32 Photographing Cars 167
33 Photographing Architecture 170
34 Taking Photos in a Museum or Art Gallery 173
35 Photographing Pets 177
36 Animal Shots in the Zoo 180
Checklist: Shooting Common Themes

Chapter 6 | After the Photo Shoot **184**
37 Transferring Images to the Computer 186
38 Organizing and Managing Images 191
39 Developing Photos 195
40 Creating a Web Photo Gallery 200
Checklist: After the Photo Shoot

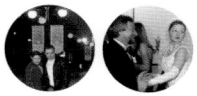

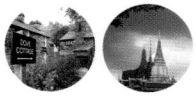

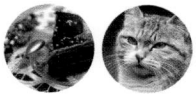

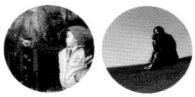

40 Digital Photography Techniques

40 DIGITAL PHOTOGRAPHY TECHNIQUES

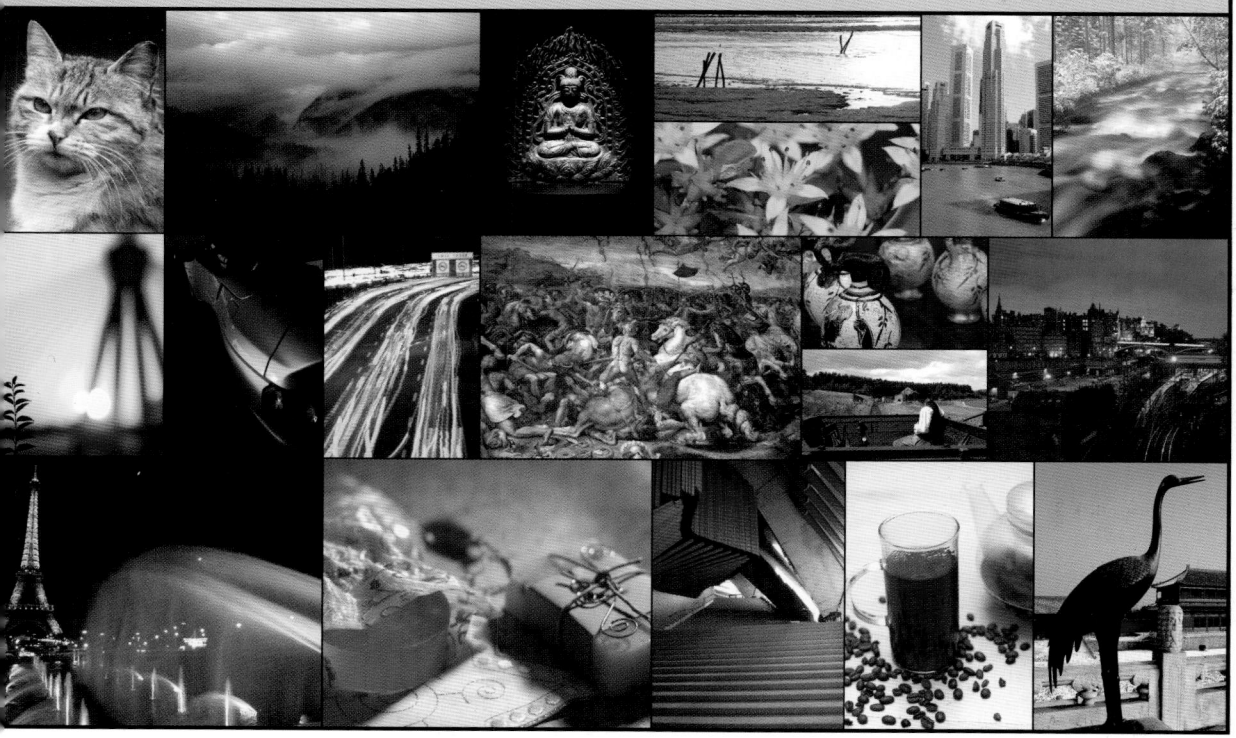

Y.
BOCA RATON PUBLIC LIBRARY
BOCA RATON, FLORIDA

Copyright © 2007 YoungJin.com Inc., 997-10 Daechi-dong, Gangnam-gu, Seoul 135-502, Korea. World rights reserved. No part of this publication may be stored in a retrieval system, transmitted, or reproduced in any way, including but not limited to photocopy, photograph, magnetic, or other record, without the prior agreement and written permission of the publisher.

ISBN: 978-89-314-3369-2

Printed and bound in the Republic of Korea.

How to contact us

E-mail: support@youngjin.com
feedback@youngjin.com.sg

Address: YoungJin.com
997-10, Daechi-dong, Gangnam-gu
Seoul 135-502, Korea

Credit

Production Manager: Suzie Lee
Developmental Editor: Rachel Lake, Publication Services, Inc.
Project Manager: Lorie Donovan, Publication Services, Inc.
Editorial Services: Publication Services, Inc.
Book Designer: Litmus
Cover Designer: Litmus
Production Control: Jay Won, Misook Kim

Notice of Rights
All rights reserved. No part of this book may be reproduced or transmitted in any form by any means, electronic, mechanical, photocopying, recording, or otherwise, without the prior written permission of the publisher.

Trademarks
Many of the designations used by manufacturers and sellers to distinguish their products are claimed as trademarks. Where those designations appear in this book, and YoungJin.com Inc., was aware of a trademark claim, the designations appear as requested by the owner of the trademark. All other product names and services identified throughout this book are used in editorial fashion only and for the benefit of such companies with no intention of infringement of the trademark. No such use, or the use of any trade name, is intended to convey endorsement or other affiliation with this book.

Notice of Liability
The information in this book is distributed on an "As Is" basis without warranty. While every precaution has been taken in the preparation of the book, neither the author nor YoungJin.com Inc., shall have any liability to any person or entity with respect to any loss or damage caused or alleged to be caused directly or indirectly by the instructions contained in this book or by the computer software and hardware products described in it.

Introduction

Getting to Know Your Digital Camera

The first goal of this book is to help you understand how a digital camera works. As you may be more familiar with the traditional film camera, we will start by comparing digital cameras with film cameras. Although digital cameras and film cameras are different, they share many similarities.

In this chapter we will also look at the structure and basic functions of a digital camera, and how to choose and accessorize one. So, whether you just bought your first digital camera or are planning an upgrade, this chapter contains the essential information you need.

I Comparing a Digital Camera with a Film Camera

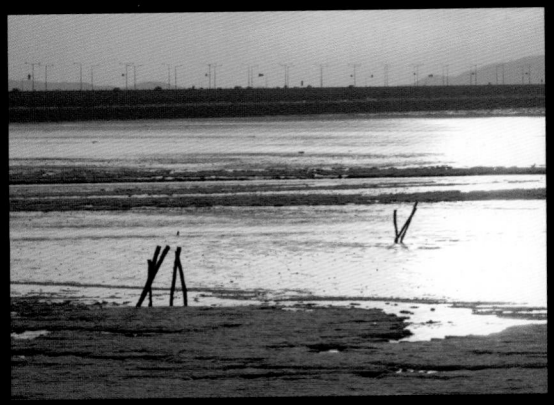

Photography has been around for a long time. The first photograph was made in 1826, and there have been many technological advances to produce smaller and better film cameras since. But these advances were incremental; with the invention of the digital camera we witnessed the first photography revolution, making the leap from film to digital in the last century.

The Key Difference

The following figures show you how film and digital cameras record images. As you can see, the two diagrams are nearly identical. The only difference is that light entering a digital camera hits the CCD (Charge-Coupled Device) rather than film. As mentioned earlier, a film camera and a digital camera share many similarities, so if you know how to use a film camera, you will have no problem operating a digital one.

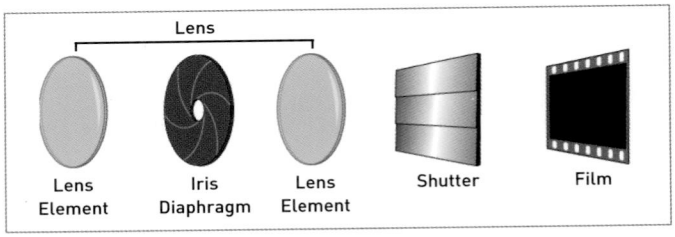

▲ A film camera.

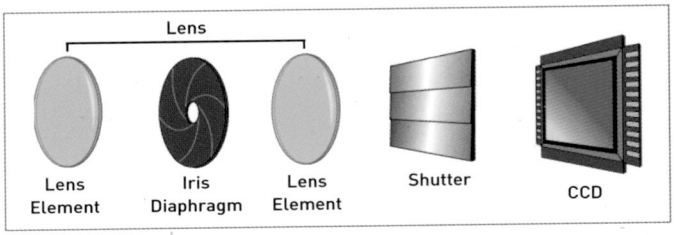

▲ A digital camera.

About the CCD (Charge-Coupled Device)

The CCD found in a digital camera is a light-sensitive semiconductor composed of millions of tiny dots known as pixels (short for picture elements). A 4.0 megapixel camera, for instance, has a CCD that comprises 4,000,000 pixels. When light hits the CCD, each pixel is converted into an electrical charge that corresponds to a color in the color spectrum. The film used in traditional cameras is a light-sensitive emulsion that records images through a chemical reaction.

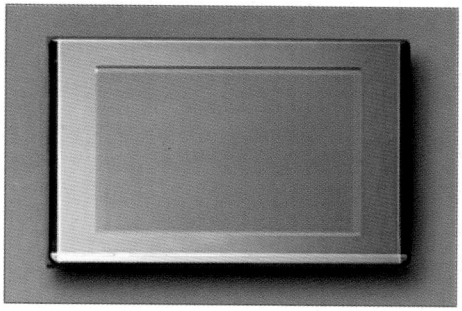

▲ A CCD.

CMOS (Complementary Metal Oxide Semiconductor)

Some digital cameras use a CMOS (pronounced see-moss) instead of a CCD. As the technical difference between the two is too advanced (and too dry) for this book, all you need to know is that the CMOS records images in the same way as the CCD.

Digital Camera Advantages and Disadvantages

Advantages of the Digital Camera	Disadvantages of the Digital Camera
No need for film.	A digital camera is more expensive than a film camera that produces similar results.
Minimize mistakes. • You can check your photos right after you take them and try again.	Higher energy consumption. • Battery drains more quickly, especially in cold weather.
No need for a scanner. • You can transfer digital photos directly to a computer without losing quality. • You can easily share your photos through e-mail or on the Internet.	Time delay. • Startup delay. A digital camera takes longer to start up. • Image capture delay. After taking a shot, some digital cameras will take up to a few seconds to record the image. As it records, you can't take another shot. This can be a problem for action shots.
Flexible printing costs. • You can choose to print only the best images.	There's a limit to the image size you can develop.
It is easier to store, organize, and search for photos.	Poor lighting will produce noise (unwanted specks, grain, etc.) in the image.
The quality of the photos won't degrade with time or as additional copies are made.	The product life cycle is very short, so finding compatible accessories can be a problem if the camera has been on the market for awhile.

Other Advantages of the Digital Camera

One of the best things about digital cameras is their small size. Digital cameras can be made smaller than film cameras because the CCD is smaller than a roll of film. Because of this, there is a trend to equip laptops, cell phones, MP3 players, and even watches with small and compact digital cameras.

Another advantage of the digital camera is that it can be easily coupled with other electronic products since it is a digital device. The most popular combination is between digital cameras and camcorders. You can take still shots with digital camcorders or record movies with a digital camera. The camcorder feature in most digital cameras lets you shoot 3-second to 3-minute movies. Some of the latest digital cameras are equipped with full camcorder functionality.

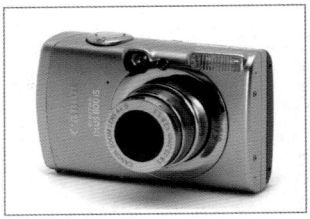

▲ The Canon Powershot SD700 IS (digital camera).

II Structure and Basic Functions

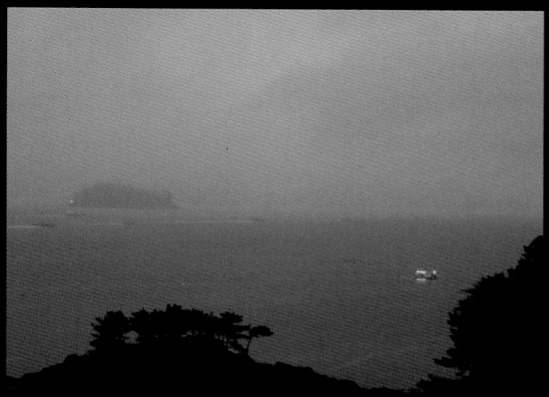

Before you can shoot good photos, you need to know your camera well. Many people shoot photographs without first understanding the capabilities or limitations of their equipment. They sometimes underestimate or try to stretch their camera's capabilities.

Main Features

Refer to your camera manual, especially the specifications page, for specific information about your camera.

▶▶▶ CCD

Many novice photographers think that the number of pixels on the CCD is the only factor to consider in terms of picture quality. The size of the CCD is just as important. What we are seeing on the market now are digital cameras with even more pixels, while the size of the CCD itself remains pretty much the same.

The reason for this phenomenon is that the CCD is the most expensive element in a digital camera, so increasing its size will increase costs significantly. Since CCDs are costly, many companies try to squeeze more pixels into CCDs to reduce costs. But this causes pixels to overlap, lowering the quality of individual pixels and creating a lot of noise. This is why bigger CCDs are found only in a few high-end digital cameras, while most manufacturers push their cameras along the megapixel line.

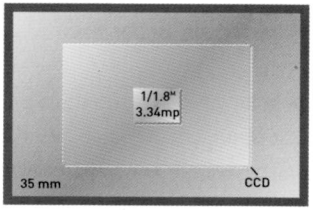

▲ Comparing the size of the CCD on a consumer camera (1/1.8 ″) with the CCD on a high-end camera and a 35 mm film.

tip As a guide, look for cameras with a CCD that is at least 1/1.8 inches with more than 2.0 megapixels.

▶▶▶ File Formats

When saving images on a digital camera, you will be asked to choose a file format. Here's a run-down of the formats available:

- JPEG: JPEG (Joint Photographic Experts Group) is the name of the organization that developed this file format. One of the biggest advantages of JPEG is that it can compress image data at a ratio of 20:1 or higher, resulting in small file sizes that are great for the Web. The downside of this popular format is that it uses a lossy compression scheme: It throws away image data during compression. Therefore, each time you open and resave as a JPEG, some data gets lost and the image degrades further.
- TIFF: This is another popular file format. When saving as a TIFF, you can select no compression to maintain image quality or LZW compression, which is a lossless compression scheme, to minimize damage. Although the difference in quality between JPEG and TIFF images cannot be seen on the small LCD monitor, it becomes obvious when the images are printed. The no-compression TIFF format is a better choice for printing, but it does not create small file sizes like JPEG.
- RAW: As the name implies, the RAW file format saves images in their raw, unprocessed form. Images are saved in this format on the camera before they are saved as JPEG or TIFF.

Most entry-level cameras support only JPEG, while average to high-end cameras support JPEG and TIFF or JPEG and RAW.

▶▶▶ Image Resolution

This refers to the image size in pixels. The average range is from 640 × 480 pixels to 2272 × 1704 pixels. Most cameras support a few sizes, and it is a good idea to buy a camera with more choices (such as higher resolution). However, remember that the larger the pixel size, the bigger the file size.

▶▶▶ JPEG Compression Levels

Choose from Super-Fine, Fine, or Normal compression levels when saving photos in JPEG format. Most photographers set compression to Super Fine (the lowest compression rate) for better image quality. However, you should note that a low compression rate produces a bigger file size.

▶▶▶ Lens

The lens used in a camera is a major factor in determining camera quality and price. Leading camera manufacturers, such as Nikon, Canon, and Olympus, use their own lenses in their cameras. Other brands, like Sony, Casio, and Panasonic, use third-party lenses.

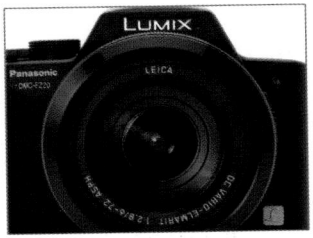

▲ Leica is a renowned lens maker whose lenses are often used in cameras other than their own.

What Is Focal Length?

The focal length of a lens is the distance between the lens and the point where the incoming light rays focus behind the lens. The focal length is measured in millimeters. If the lens length is not fixed (a zoom lens, for example), you will see the focal length expressed as a range in the camera's specifications. A short focal length is used when zooming out to wide-angle shots, while a long focal length is used when zooming in on subjects for close-ups (telephoto).

What Is 35 mm Camera Equivalent?

In your camera's specifications, you will probably see the words *35 mm film equivalent* followed by your camera's focal length range. This means that a lens with a focal length of 7.1 mm to 21.3 mm on a digital camera, for example, will produce results that are equivalent to a lens with a focal length of 35 mm to 105 mm on a 35 mm film camera.

▶▶▶ Zoom

In general, digital cameras support two different types of zooms: optical zoom and digital zoom. Optical zoom is achieved by using the camera lens, while digital zoom works by taking a part of an image that has been shot and enlarging it. Digital zoom works in the same way as the zoom tool in photo editing programs. Every time you use digital zoom, the resolution of the image goes down. In contrast, there's no loss of resolution when you use optical zoom. The digital zoom function is of little use most of the time, so beware of advertising hype that focuses on the digital zoom capability.

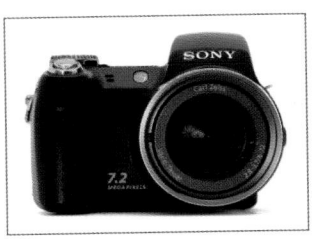

▲ The Sony DSC-H5 uses a 12× optical zoom lens.

▶▶▶ Focusing Range

This refers to the range within which the camera can focus on a subject. Most cameras can focus to a distance of infinity, so the main concern is how close the camera can focus. This factor determines if you can take extremely close shots of small objects such as flowers or insects. Most cameras can focus from a minimum distance of 1 cm to 10 cm.

▶▶▶ Aperture

Behind the lens is an iris diaphragm (illustrated on page 8). Adjusting the size of its opening controls the amount of light passing through to the CCD. The size of this opening is the aperture. The iris diaphragm is so called because its overlapping blades work like the iris of the eye.

▶▶▶ Shutter Speed

For film cameras, this refers to the length of time the shutter stays open to let light into the camera. Most digital cameras, however, do not actually use a physical shutter to control exposure time. They use an electronic switch to tell the camera how long to keep the CCD turned on. Shutter speed is measured in fractions of a second.

▶▶▶ Exposure Control

Exposure refers to the amount of light that the CCD or film receives for a shot. Two factors control the exposure of an image: shutter speed and aperture. If you have an automatic camera, the camera will set the exposure automatically for you. Depending on your camera, you may have the exposure compensation feature, which lets you modify the exposure automatically set by the camera. Some automatic cameras also have Scene modes—a set of pre-programmed settings recommended for specific situations.

For semiautomatic or manual cameras, you have more control because these cameras have Shutter Priority, Aperture Priority, or Manual modes. In Shutter Priority mode, you set the shutter speed and the camera chooses the aperture setting. It's the other way around in the Aperture Priority mode. In Manual mode, you set both the shutter speed and aperture.

▶▶▶ Sensitivity

This refers to the sensitivity of the CCD when it receives light. Sensitivity is rated in ISO. A low ISO rating means that it is less sensitive and needs more light to expose an image properly. When you shoot a subject at ISO 100 or lower, your image will look softer. Conversely, a high ISO means that you will need less light. Unfortunately, a raised ISO rating only boosts the electronic signal from the shot and this can create graininess in your images. The most common ISO ratings are from ISO 100 to ISO 400, but high-end cameras can have a rating of up to ISO 3200.

▶▶▶ Flash

The built-in flash that comes with a digital camera can usually light up to a distance of 9–10 feet (3 meters). Some digital cameras use an infrared sensor to determine the distance between the camera and the subject and adjust the flash intensity according to that information. Check your user's manual to find out the exact flash coverage. It is important to know this to illuminate your subjects properly.

▶▶▶ Continuous Shot Function

This feature, which is found in most digital cameras, enables you to take a few continuous shots by pressing the shutter release button only once.

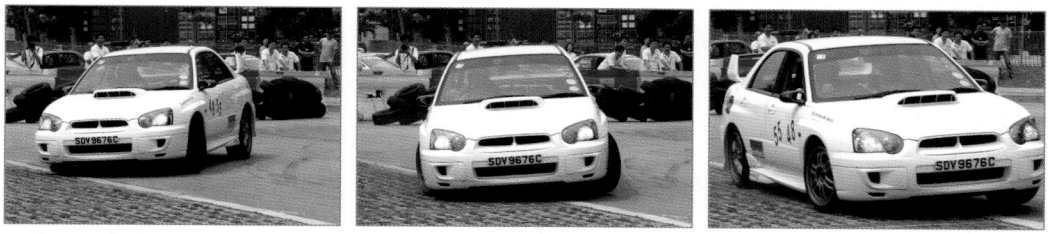

▲ Consecutive images taken with the Continuous Shot function.

▶▶▶ Movies

Except for a few high-priced cameras, most digital cameras can only record a 30-second movie when the image resolution is set to 640 × 480 pixels. If the image resolution is lowered to 320 × 240 pixels, you can record for about three minutes.

▶▶▶ Viewfinder/LCD Monitor

One common problem with using the viewfinder is a discrepancy between what you see in the viewfinder and the final photo. This is because the viewfinder shows the image from a slightly different viewpoint than what is actually captured on the CCD. As this problem usually occurs while shooting close-ups, you should use the LCD (liquid crystal display) when shooting at close range. The LCD shows you the current camera settings and a preview of the image. You can also review images that have been taken.

▶▶▶ Storage Media

The most popular choice for image storage is a CompactFlash (CF) card, which can store up to 12GB of data. On cameras that support the Type II CF card, a microdrive that has a capacity of up to 8GB can be used. Other memory cards include Sony's Memory Stick, which, unfortunately, can only be used with Sony cameras and some Samsung cameras. It is also more expensive.

SD and xD-Picture cards are currently getting a lot of good reviews. These cards are being hailed as the "memory cards of the future" because their physical size is getting smaller, even as their memory capacity gets bigger. Select a memory card that is compatible with your camera. Check that you have at least 128MB of memory. Even with 128MB of memory, you can only store about 40 images at a resolution of 6 megapixels in JPEG format.

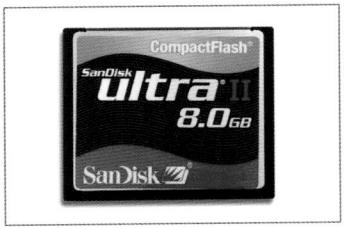

▲ An 8GB CompactFlash card.

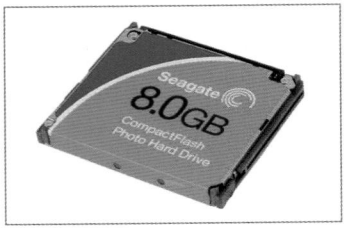

▲ The Seagate 8GB microdrive.

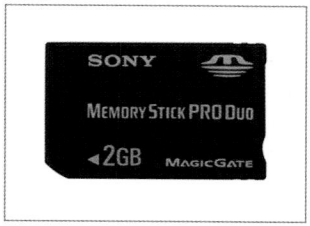

▲ Sony's Memory Stick PRO DUO.

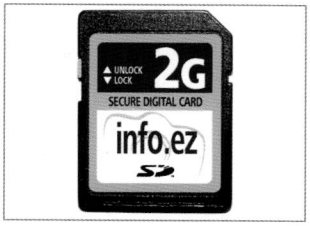

▲ The 2GB SD card.

▶▶▶ Power Sources

A digital camera is composed of many electronic parts. These parts, coupled with frequent use of the LCD monitor, can drain the camera's batteries very quickly. The problem is even more acute in cold weather.

The current trend is to create digital cameras that use only rechargeable lithium ion batteries. These batteries are long lasting by digital camera standards, but they are also more expensive. However, there are some cameras on the market that use both lithium and alkaline batteries. With such cameras, you can use alkaline batteries when the lithium ones fail.

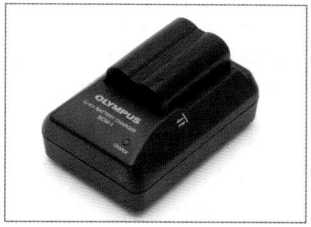

▲ Olympus's lithium ion battery pack and charger.

▶▶▶ Dimensions and Weight

A small and light digital camera is obviously the first choice for portability. However, it can be difficult to hold such cameras steady while taking pictures, and you could end up with blurry images.

III Choosing the Right Digital Camera

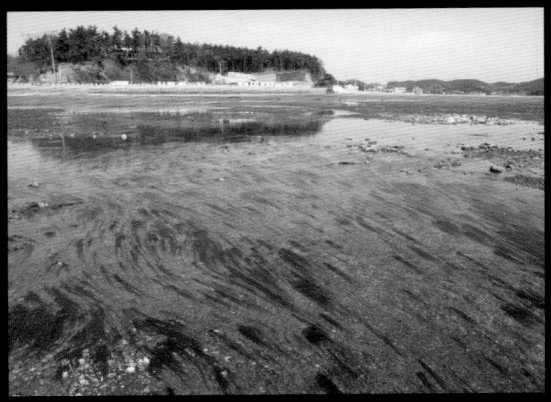

Now that you know what makes up a digital camera and how it works, let's look at choosing the right camera. Even if you already have a digital camera, the information in this section could help you in making your next purchase. Three of the most important factors in purchasing a camera are cost, portability, and features.

Automatic Cameras

Most fully automatic digital cameras have a resolution of around 1.0 to 3.0 megapixels and no manual exposure control. The camera determines the settings for you automatically, so all you need to do is press the shutter release button.

Other cameras that fall into the automatic digital camera category are new models that have Scene modes, such as Portrait mode. Each of these modes is a collection of pre-programmed settings that are suitable for specific kinds of shots.

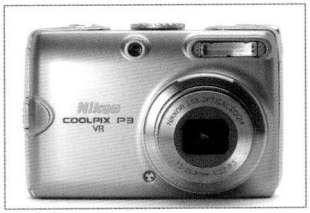

▲ Nikon Coolpix P3 VR.

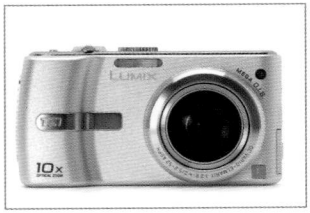

▲ Panasonic Lumix DMC-TZ1.

Semiautomatic and Manual Cameras

These digital cameras usually have a resolution between 6.0 and 10.0 megapixels and allow you to manually set exposure and focus. You will find Shutter Priority, Aperture Priority, and Manual modes on these cameras.

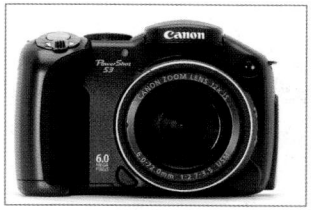

▲ Canon Powershot S3 IS.

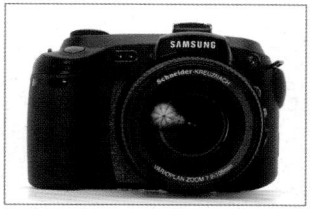

▲ Samsung Pro-815.

tip Prices for digital cameras have fallen recently, so beginners should feel comfortable buying a camera in this category. Once you have some control over exposure, you can take better and more creative pictures.

SLR Digital Cameras

SLR (single-lens reflex) cameras are top-of-the-line cameras used by professionals and have a resolution ranging from 6.0 to 20.0 megapixels. Besides manual controls, one of the best things about these cameras is that you can change and use a variety of different lenses. These cameras are expensive and not really necessary for photography hobbyists.

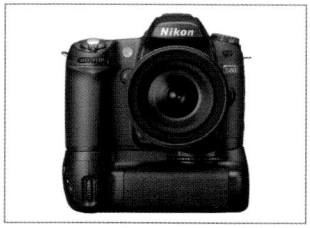

▲ Nikon D80.

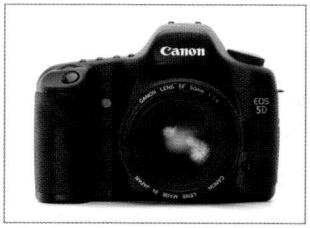

▲ Canon EOS 5D.

Grip Cameras

Cameras with grips are gaining popularity as they are easier to hold steady, especially if the camera is heavy. However, this is largely a matter of personal taste. There are some who think that such cameras don't feel right in their hands. The best way to find out if you will like such a camera is to try it at the store.

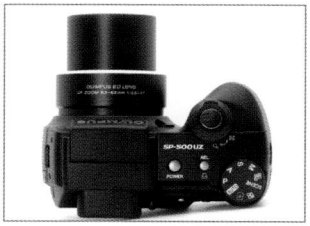

▲ Olympus SP-500 UZ.

Special Cameras

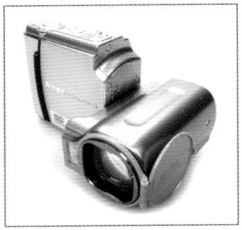

▲ Nikon Coolpix S4 with rotating lens.

There are tiny cameras on the market that are extremely portable. But they also have very low resolution, so you may end up with images that you can't print at a decent size.

How Many Pixels Do You need?

As a general guide, you need a resolution of 300 pixels per inch for photographic quality prints. If, for example, you want to print your images at 4R (4 × 6), you should preferably have a resolution of 1,200 (i.e. 4 × 300) × 1,800 (i.e. 6 × 300) or 2.2 megapixels.

If you enjoy taking pictures of yourself and your companions, a camera with a rotating lens or LCD is a must. Just rotate the lens or LCD 180° to point at yourself, check your image in the LCD, and click. Such cameras are also great for making overhead or tight shots.

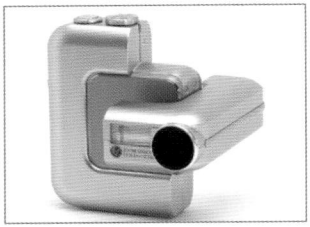

▲ Nikon Coolpix SQ with rotating lens.

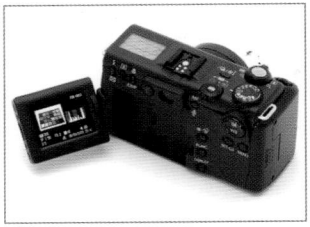

▲ Canon Powershot G-5 with rotating LCD .

Faulty Pixels

Always check that the camera does not produce faulty pixels. There are two kinds of bad pixels: dead pixels and hot pixels. Dead pixels, like the name suggests, are no longer working and therefore appear black. Hot pixels, on the other hand, receive the wrong electronic signals, displaying as white or other color pixels.

The problem can be with either the LCD or CCD. You can check the LCD visually to see if it is responding to the electronic signals correctly. The problem is more serious if the camera has a faulty CCD that's sending the wrong signals, because a faulty CCD affects the picture. If you have already bought the camera, ask for a replacement. Although manufacturers have different exchange policies, most will let you exchange the CCD at least twice and the LCD at least three times.

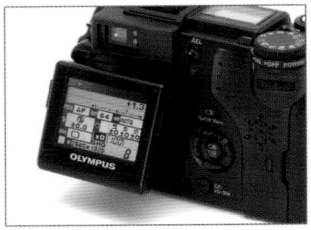

▲ A faulty LCD can be detected right away.

IV Accessorizing Your Digital Camera

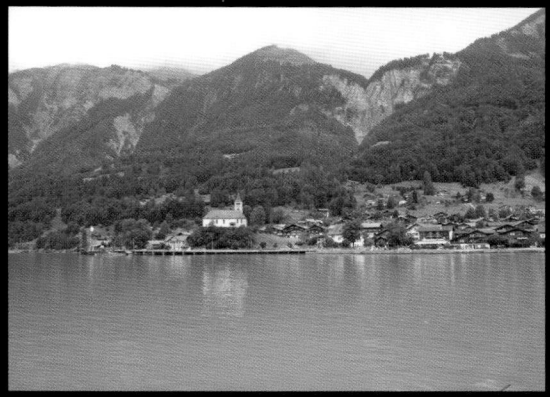

Once you start taking photos, you will begin seeing photo opportunities in many different locations and situations—some of which can be rather challenging. There are many accessories that can help you take better pictures, or at least make the process easier, but unnecessary items will only weigh you down. Let's take a look at some common accessories.

Essential Accessories

▶▶▶ Memory Card

Top on the list is an additional memory card. Most digital cameras come with a 16MB to 32MB memory card. However, you will likely require an additional 256MB to 512MB memory card.

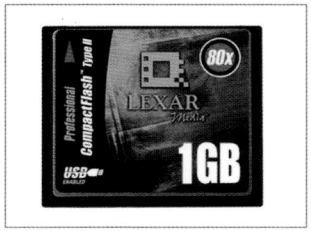

▲ 1GB CF card.

▶▶▶ Battery

You will likely drain your battery while shooting outdoors, so it is advisable to have a reserve battery on hand. If the camera comes with a non-rechargeable battery, you should consider buying a rechargeable battery pack and a rapid charger, which will be more cost-effective and convenient in the long run.

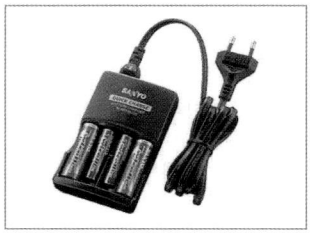

▲ A rapid charger.

▶▶▶ Tripod

Although the tripod is an important camera accessory, many avoid using one because it is cumbersome. Tripods are commonly used for taking portraits and shots in low-light conditions, such as at night, and indoor shots so as to prevent camera shake. Get a light-weight yet sturdy tripod, and if you are worried about bulkiness, get a mini-tripod.

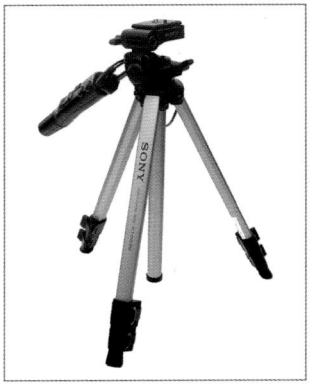

▲ Sony's basic tripod.

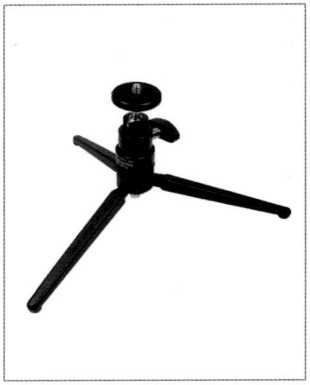

▲ Mini-tripod.

▶▶▶ Camera Bag

Although a portable bag may come with the camera, buy a padded one for greater shock absorption. In addition, consider buying a waterproof camera bag or one that has a waterproof cover for those rainy days.

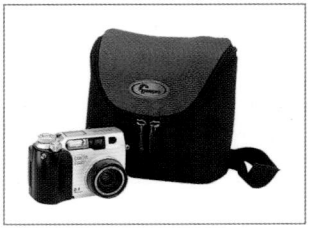

▲ Lowepro's digital camera bag.

Other Accessories

▶▶▶ Filter

Generally speaking, you can attach filters to your lens to create special effects if you have a mid- to high-end digital camera. Even though photo editing software can create these effects easily, some photographers prefer to use filters so that they can visualize the results in the viewfinder. Some of the filters available are polarizing filters, color-warming filters, and star filters.

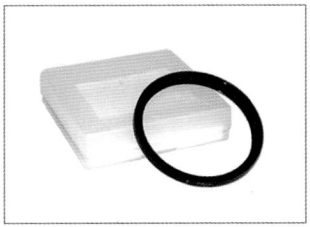

▲ UV filters correct for ultraviolet light, which can result in a bluish cast.

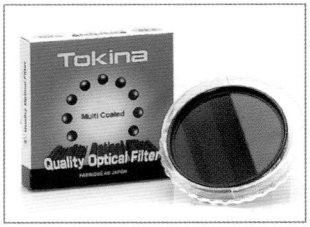

▲ Polarizing filters eliminate surface reflections and enhance tint contrast.

▶▶▶ Conversion Lens

This is placed over the camera's fixed lens to create a variety of effects. Some conversion lenses include the wide-angle conversion lens and the telephoto conversion lens.

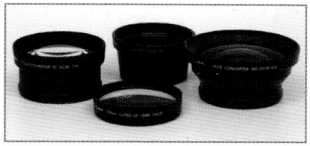

▶ Conversion lenses.

▶▶▶ Lens Adapter

You may need a lens adapter to attach a filter or conversion lens.

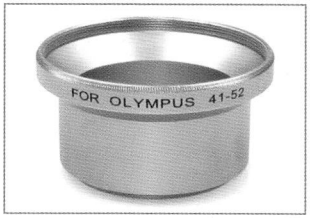

▶ Olympus lens adapter.

▶▶▶ Card Reader

Although you can transfer images from your digital camera to the computer via the USB cable, this transferal method will drain the batteries of your camera and you can't use your camera while it is transferring images. A more convenient method is to use a card reader. If you have a number of devices, such as a PDA (personal digital assistant), that use storage media cards, you should get a multiple card reader that will read a variety of cards.

First, remove the memory card from your camera and insert it into the reader. Next, connect the card reader to the computer with a USB cable. The computer will recognize the card reader as an external cache, allowing you to transmit your pictures easily.

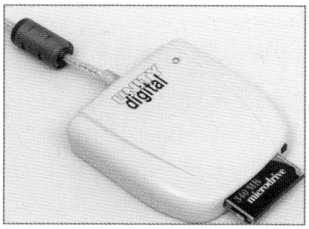

▲ Using the card reader to transmit pictures.

▶▶▶ External Flash

Most digital cameras come with a small, built-in flash. However, there may be times when the built-in flash is not bright enough, and you may need to use an external flash, or strobe. Some cameras have a hot shoe to which you can connect the strobe.

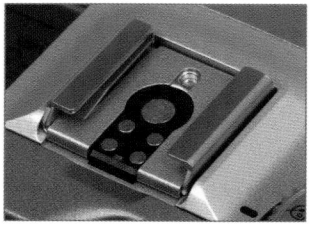

▲ The hot shoe.

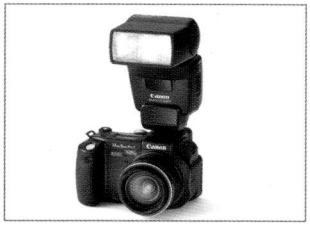

▲ Strobe connected to the hot shoe.

V Camera Care

A digital camera is a sophisticated device made up of very small, sensitive electronic components. Even minute particles like dust, moisture, and salt can damage your camera permanently. On one hand, it is important that you keep your camera clean and free from harmful particles. On the other hand, excessive cleaning can damage its parts. Since neither excessive nor inadequate care is desirable, let's learn to provide the right level of care in this section.

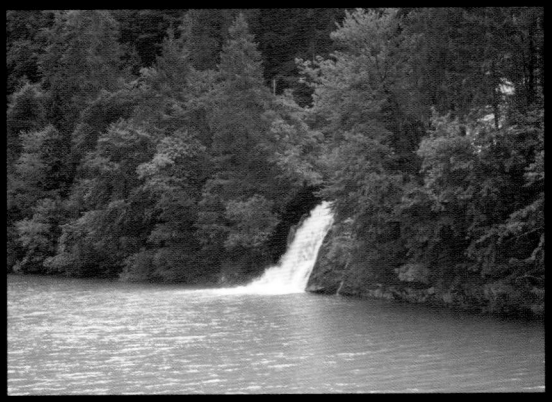

Dusting the Camera

Before and after using a camera, use the blower (air brush) to remove dust. If the blower is not effective, use a soft brush or a lens pen. Fingerprints and other foreign matter on the lens can be removed gently using a lens cleaning cloth. Because lenses have a multi-layer coating on the surface for reducing internal reflection, you need to clean gently since excessive rubbing or wiping can wear the coating out. Unless absolutely necessary, you should refrain from touching the lens in any way. A little dust on the lens will generally not affect your photos, so don't worry about it too much.

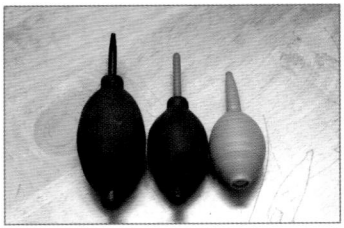

▲ Blowers.

Removing Excess Moisture

Always store your camera in a cool, dry place. You should never store your camera in direct sunlight. Mold can form on camera lenses left in humid conditions. Once in a while, you should take your camera out of storage to air it. The best thing to do is to use your camera frequently.

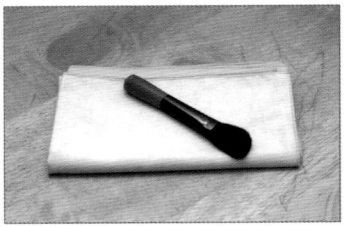

▲ Lens brush and lens cloth.

Cleaning the Lens

Frequent cleaning is not desirable as this can wear off the anti-reflective coating on the lens. If you must clean the lens, follow these steps:

▶▶▶ Using the Blower

Blowing on the lens with your breath can get saliva and condensation on the lens, which is why it is recommended that you use a blower. In most cases, this is all you need to do to clean and take care of the lens.

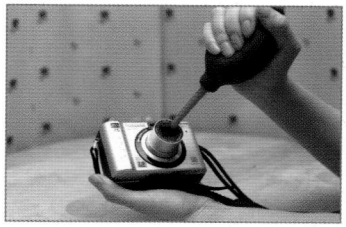

▲ Using the blower .

▶▶▶ Using the Lens Brush

Sometimes there are a few stubborn specks of dirt that refuse to budge when using the blower. In such cases, you can use a soft lens brush.

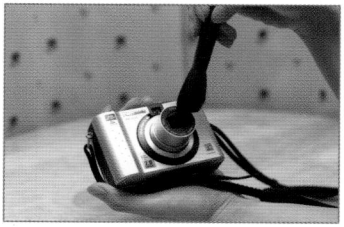

▲ Using the lens brush.

▶▶▶ Using the Lens Cloth

To remove fingerprints and other foreign matter from the lens, wrap a lens cloth lightly around your finger and gently wipe the lens, using a circular motion. If this doesn't work, take your camera to the nearest service center.

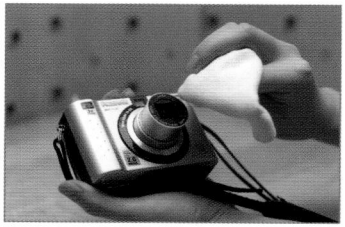

▲ Using the lens cloth.

Watch Where You Place Your Fingers!

Our fingers have small traces of perspiration on them, which is why touching a lens leaves behind small amounts of moisture and salt residue. You should always be careful not to touch the camera lens.

Camera Care Under Other Situations

▶▶▶ At the Beach

Sea air contains salt particles, which can seriously damage your camera. The salt will cling to the digital camera, both inside and out, causing corrosion. Should this happen, use a slightly damp cloth to wipe off the salt residue from the outside of the camera and then go over it again using a camera cloth. It's best to avoid exposing your camera to sea air for long periods of time.

▶▶▶ If Your Camera Gets Wet

A wet digital camera can be dangerous. You should remove the battery before you do anything else. Do not switch on the camera in an attempt to see if it is broken. Use a cloth to wipe the water off the camera body and take it immediately to a nearby service center. If you drop your camera in the sea, rinse the camera with drinking water to remove the salt residue before taking the camera in for repairs.

▶▶▶ In Winter

The camera's battery drains quickly at low temperatures. If you keep the battery warm before using it (by keeping it in your pocket, for example), you can extend the battery life. Another problem is water condensation. If you bring your camera indoors after using it out in the cold, water will condense on both the outside and inside of the camera. To prevent this from happening, place the camera in its bag before bringing it inside. This allows the camera to gradually adjust to the higher room temperature.

Checklist: Buying a Digital Camera

- √ For both urban and rural landscapes, you will need a wide-angle lens or a conversion lens (35 mm or wider film equivalent, preferably 28 mm) in order to fit the entire scene into your picture.
- √ To take photographs of objects that you cannot approach, such as wild animals, you will need a camera lens with six times optical zoom (35 – 210 mm or longer). Alternatively, you can buy a telephoto conversion lens to beef up an existing camera's telephoto capability.
- √ If you take many indoor shots, the manual white balance feature is useful for removing the color cast from indoor lighting.
- √ For indoor pictures of a group of people standing, you will need an external flash gun or strobe that can illuminate up to 13 feet (4 meters) or farther. You should first check if your camera has a hot shoe to which you can attach the external flash unit.
- √ To capture a freeze frame of fast-moving subjects such as toddlers, you will need an automatic camera with a Sports Scene mode. For really fast-moving objects such as cars and athletics at sporting events, you will need a camera with very large aperture (*f*/2.8 to *f*/2.0) and a fast shutter speed (1/250 second or faster). To consistently take good action shots, you will need a semiautomatic camera that lets you set the shutter speed. Note that it is hard to take action shots with automatic cameras.
- √ For self-portraits, a rotating lens or LCD will let you compose and take pictures of yourself without having to ask someone else to take the shot.
- √ To shoot close-ups of small objects such as insects and flowers, look for a camera with a minimum focusing distance of 4 cm or less.
- √ It is a good idea to buy an additional memory card. As a guide, if your camera has a resolution of 4.0 megapixels, you should consider getting a 256MB memory card (stores approximately 140 images).
- √ To take pictures of a city at night, you will need a tripod and a cable release or a camera with a remote control. This will keep the camera steady during long exposures.
- √ For easy beach, snow, or sky shots, purchase a camera with these modes, the exposure compensation feature, or the ability to adjust exposure manually.
- √ The product life cycle for most cameras is two years, so don't overbuy. To print an 8R photo, you will only need a camera with a resolution of 4.0 megapixels. For beginners, it is best to start with an affordable automatic or semiautomatic camera before moving on to pricier cameras. After you've had some experience with photography, you will know the type of photographs you are likely to take and can then decide whether you need certain camera features.

40 Digital Photography Techniques

The Basics of Taking Photos

Chapter 1

As in any field of study, you will save time and get the best results if you learn the right techniques first. In this chapter, we will look at photography basics, such as preparing for a shoot, taking care of a digital camera, holding a camera and keeping good posture, adjusting image size, using lenses, locking a focus, controlling exposure, and composing an image.

01 Preparing to Shoot

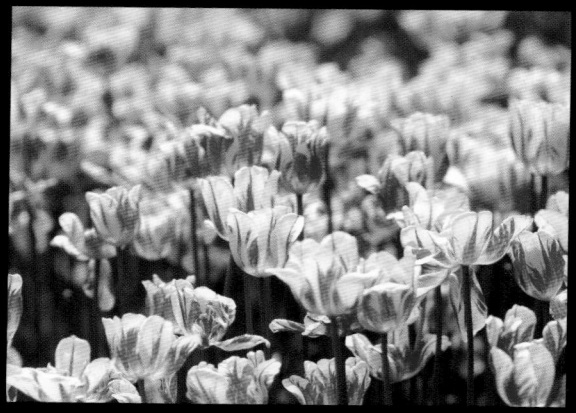

The only way you will take better photos is with practice. To get enough practice, you must always have the camera by your side. The camera has to be kept in top working condition so that you won't miss a practice opportunity or ruin any shots. Before you run out the door with your camera, let's go over some pre-shoot checks in this section.

Gather Your Equipment

First of all, your battery must be ready, because the digital camera is an energy guzzler. If you are using a rechargeable battery, you will need to charge the battery to full power. This will probably take about two hours. If you are using regular alkaline batteries, take some extras along.

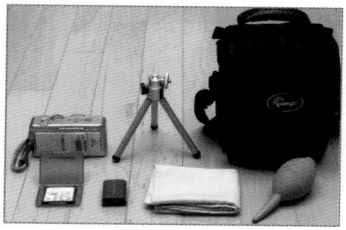

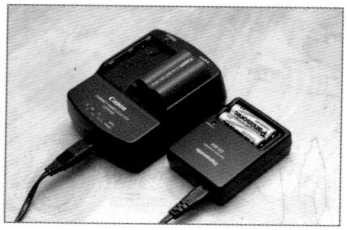

▲ Get in the habit of charging your batteries.

Next, check that the lens is clean and that there is nothing physically wrong with the camera. Also make sure that you have inserted the memory card. People who use a memory card reader often forget that they have left their cards in the reader. Don't head out to your photo opportunity with a digital camera that can't store photos.

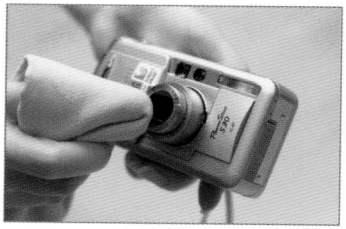

▲ If the lens is dirty, clean it gently.

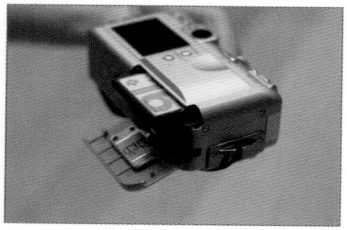

▲ Make sure that the memory card is in the camera.

Finally, check that the camera straps are secure. If not, you run the risk of dropping and breaking your camera.

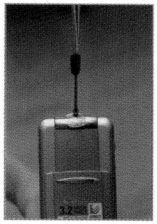

▶ Check that the camera straps are not loose.

When you have completed the checks, it is time to pack your equipment (camera, lens cleaning cloth, blower, extra memory card, mini-tripod, and so on) into the camera bag. It is a good idea to include a desiccant (containing a chemical drying agent) to absorb excess moisture and keep your equipment dry. Your lens will get moldy and the electronic parts will malfunction if your camera is kept in a humid environment.

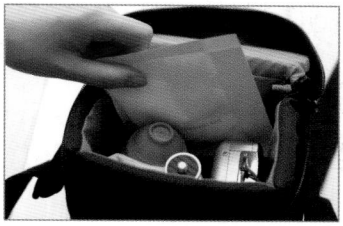

▲ Professional photographers keep their equipment in a dry box, but for hobbyists, a desiccant will do.

Planning the Shoot

Before you start shooting, think about the photos you are going to take, and be specific. Instead of stopping at "I'm going to take a photo of my family today," think about how and what kind of family photos you want to take. When you have a plan, you are less likely to miss golden moments.

Most people take more pictures when they use a digital rather than a film camera. Because of this you may end up taking many similar shots, and few meaningful ones, if you don't have an action plan in mind.

02 Preventing Camera Shake and Blurring

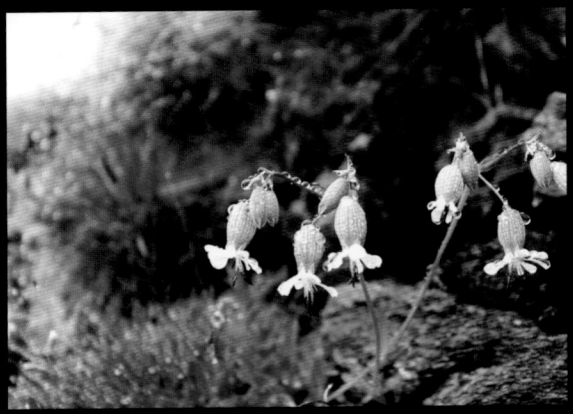

The secret to non-fuzzy photos lies in your grip and stance. Knowing how to hold and stand with a camera is important in combating even the slightest camera shake, After mastering posture, we will look at how to adjust your camera's settings to reduce blur and snap sharper images.

Getting Familiar with the Camera

Most people hold their camera with the left hand and use the right hand to press the shutter and adjust other functions. There are many buttons on the back of the digital camera, but you will probably use only a few of them.

Check your camera's manual to get familiar with the buttons, and remember to press them lightly but firmly.

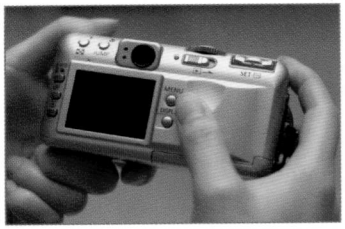

▲ Familiarize yourself with the buttons and functions on your camera.

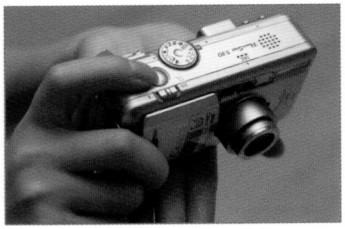

▲ Hold the camera steady and press the shutter lightly.

Getting a Good Grip

Place your left palm at the base of the camera. Use your right hand to hold the camera, or the grip, and place your right index finger lightly on the shutter. Exert a stronger grip with your left hand. If you hold the camera with a strong right-hand grip, you may move the camera when you press the shutter button. One reminder, though: always keep your fingers clear of the flash, autofocus window, and lens.

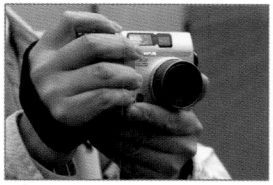

▲ Put one hand through the camera strap's loop and rotate your wrist to wrap it around for a safe grip.

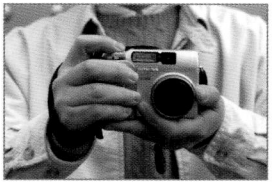

▲ For cameras with grips, use your right hand to hold the grip and your left hand to support the base of the lens lightly.

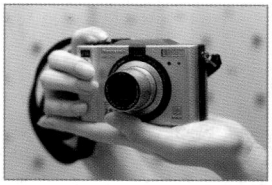

▲ For cameras without grips, use your left palm to support the camera.

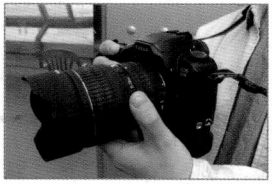

▲ If you are using a large lens, use your left hand to hold the lens.

Practicing the Right Stance

Adopting the right stance can prevent blurring the image, lower the risk of dropping the camera, and reduce fatigue during long photography sessions.

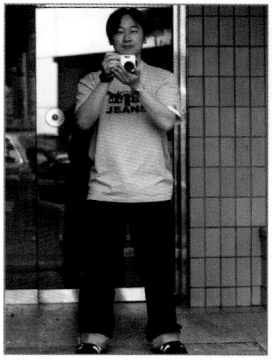

▲ In the basic stance, keep both arms close to your body and spread your legs shoulder-width apart for balance.

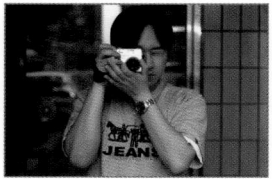

▲ For horizontal photos, keep both arms close to your body.

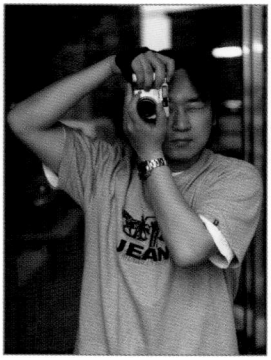

▲ For vertical photos, make sure your fingers do not cover the lens or the built-in flash.

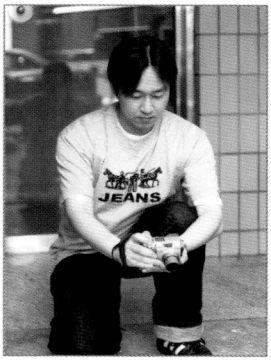

▲ When taking photos of subjects lower than you, squat down to their level and use your knees to support yourself.

Trying Other Positions

If you are sitting down, raise one knee and use it to support your elbow. If you need to get even lower to take the photo, sit cross-legged on the ground and support your elbows on your knees.

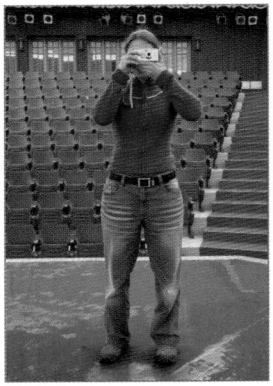

▲ Keep your back straight and your arms close to your body.

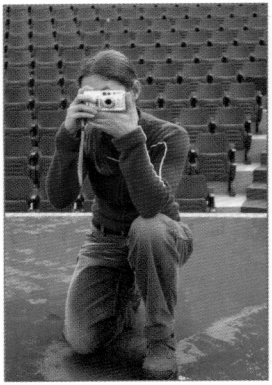

▲ Raise one knee and use it to support your upper body.

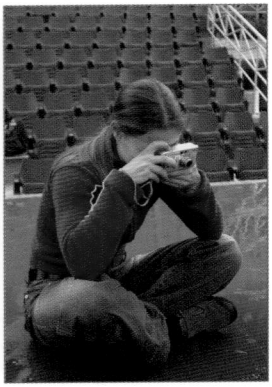

▲ Sit cross-legged to take low shots.

Using the LCD

When you use the LCD, the camera is held away from your body. Because the camera does not have the added support of your body to help stabilize it, blur becomes a bigger issue.

The LCD stance: Use your left hand to support the camera and your right hand to press the shutter. You should not grip the camera too tightly. In addition, keep the camera as close to your body as possible and tuck your elbows in for more support.

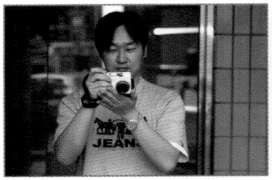

▲ Using the LCD for horizontal shots.

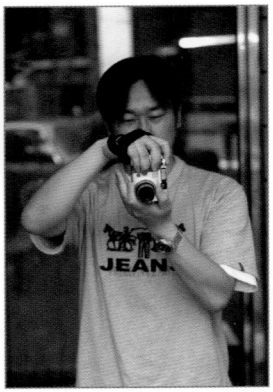

▲ When taking vertical shots, make sure your photo is level.

When taking vertical shots through the LCD, check that your fingers are not covering the built-in flash. You probably won't make the mistake of covering the lens with your hand because, if you do, you will see it on the LCD. This is one advantage of using the LCD rather than the viewfinder.

Regulating Your Breathing

Hold your breath as you press the shutter button, as the subtle movements of your breathing can produce blur in your photos. You should also get into the habit of pausing slightly after shooting an image, as moving immediately after releasing the shutter can also blur your pictures.

Using Objects for Support

One of the best ways to prevent camera shake is to use a tripod, but if you find it troublesome to carry one, you can use other objects at the shoot location for support. This technique is useful for preventing blur when you use a shutter speed of up to 1/20 second.

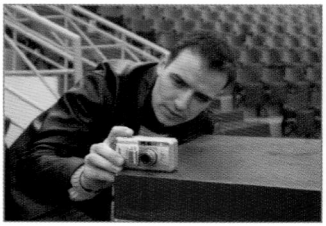

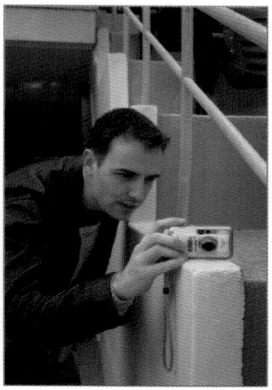

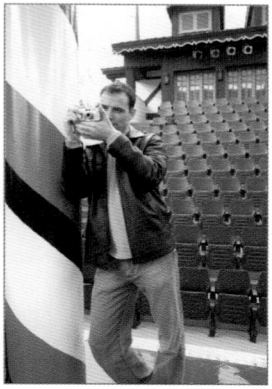

▶, ▶▶ Using other objects as a substitute tripod.
▶▶▶ Using the wall.

Using a tripod

Sometimes there are no objects on location that you can use for support. To be sure that you get sharp images all the time, use a tripod.

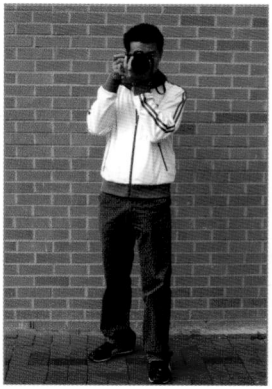

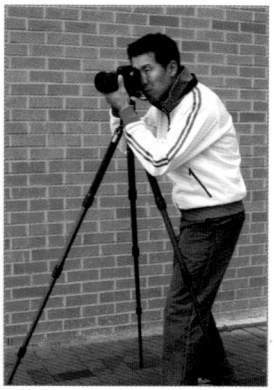

▶ A proper stance and the use of a tripod are essential for preventing motion blur in photos.

Other Ways of Reducing Blur

▶▶▶ Shutter Speed

A fast shutter speed will diminish blur and appear to freeze action, while a slow shutter speed will capture even the slightest movement as blurred streaks. If you are using an automatic camera, you should note that some of the Scene modes, such as Night Landscape and Fireworks Show, use slow shutter speeds and are more prone to blur. When using such Scene modes, it is best to use a tripod or some form of support, as camera shake becomes more obvious.

▶▶▶ Flash

When synched to work with the shutter, the flash can also reduce blur and appear to freeze action. This option is not available on most automatic cameras.

▶▶▶ Lens Type

When you use a telephoto lens (to zoom in), a slight camera movement will translate into a huge blur in the image because you are zooming in on a small section of the view. The same amount of camera movement will be less obvious when using a wide-angle lens. If you have a semiautomatic camera, you can set a fast shutter speed when using telephoto lenses to combat blur. With an automatic, you should keep your camera steady and use an external support.

03 Adjusting Image Size and Quality

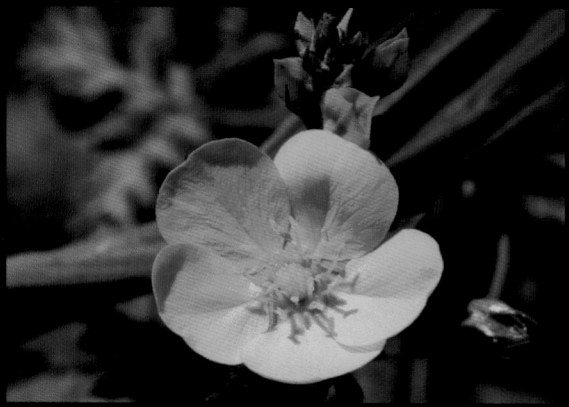

Unlike a film camera, a digital camera lets you change the size and resolution of your photos as you take them. Surprisingly, most camera owners don't know how to use these features to their advantage. In this section, we will learn about image sizes and resolutions.

Image Size or Resolution

Image size and *image resolution* mean the same thing on a digital camera. An image resolution of 1600 × 1200, for example, means that the image is recorded with 1600 pixels across the width and 1200 pixels down the length. So a photo shot with a bigger image size is recorded with more pixels and will print at a better quality.

▶▶▶ Pixels and Maximum Image Size

The maximum image size you can take with your digital camera depends on the number of pixels your camera has, as outlined in the following table:

Pixels	Maximum Image Size
2.0 million	1600 × 1200
4.0 million	2272 × 1704
6.5 million	3072 × 2048

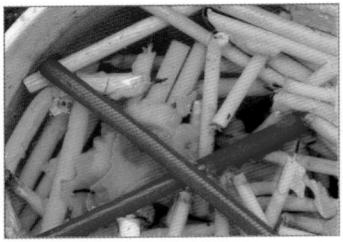

▲ Resolution: 1600 × 1200; file size: 1119KB.

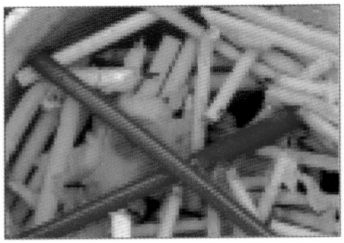

▲ Resolution: 800 × 600; file size: 434KB.

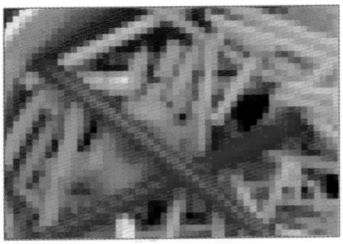

▲ Resolution: 400 × 300; file size: 134KB.

▶▶▶ When Do You Need High-Resolution Images?

Before taking large or high-resolution images, you should consider the capacity of your memory card because these images take up more memory and limit the number of photos you can take. However, there are some instances when you should take high-resolution images.

- If you need to develop photos that are 8 × 10 or larger.
- If you need to take a close-up but your camera's zoom cannot work at that distance. In such a scenario, you can shoot a high-resolution image, use the crop tool in a photo editing program to crop it to size, and blow it up to look like a close-up.

▶▶▶ When Can You Take Low-Resolution Images?

Generally, it is a much better idea to take images at high resolutions and scale them down later than to take low-resolution shots up front. But if quality is not a major concern and quantity is, then these are some situations when you may wish to use low resolution:

- If you have limited memory, as low-resolution images require less memory.
- If you are taking photos for the Internet, you can take images at 800 × 600 pixels or less. Since you probably want fast downloading speed, you should keep image resolution small.

Using the Continuous Function

When you take continuous shots using the Continuous function, the images are stored temporarily in the camera's buffer memory, which is small in most popular digital camera brands. Therefore, only low-resolution images are taken with the Continuous function.

Image Quality

Images are compressed as they are saved on the memory card in order to reduce the memory they use. The most common file format is JPEG, which uses a lossy compression method. Most cameras offer two (Basic or Fine) or three (Normal, Fine, or Super Fine) different levels of image quality. When you set a high image quality (Super Fine), the camera will use a low rate of compression. Conversely, a high rate of compression creates a low image quality (Basic).

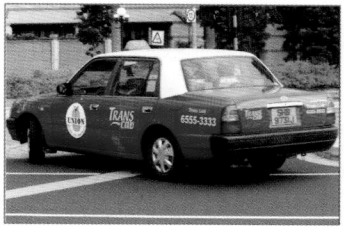

▲ Image quality: Super Fine.

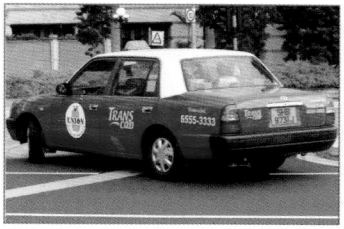

▲ Image quality: Fine.

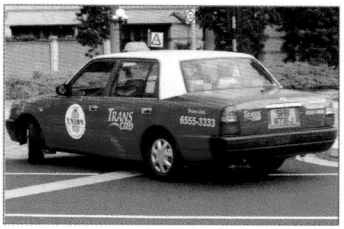

▲ Image quality: Normal.

Changing Image Size and Quality

In most cameras, the Menu button will let you control the image size and quality. The figures on the right show you how to change the image size and set the image quality to Super Fine. As every camera model is different, refer to your camera manual for specific instructions.

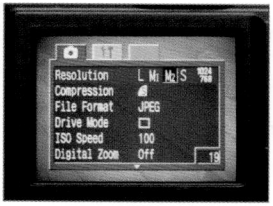

▲ This camera offers four different image sizes to choose from.

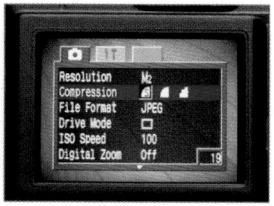

▲ This camera has three levels of image quality.

04 Locking a Focus

A camera's autofocus (AF) system works by automatically focusing on the object in the center of the viewfinder. If you press the shutter-release button while your subject is positioned off-center, your subject will be out of focus, as the camera is automatically set to focus and expose for the object in the center. To focus and expose an off-center subject correctly, you will need to use Focus Lock, a system for telling the camera where to focus.

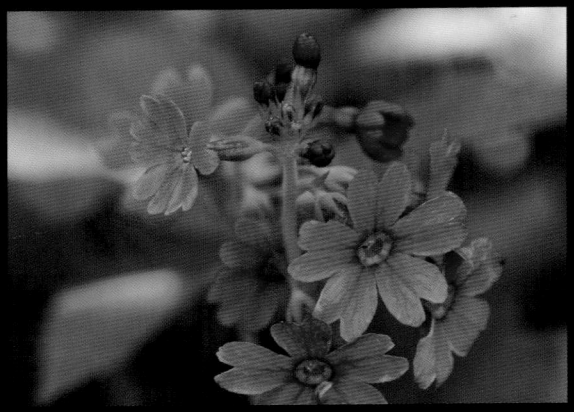

Using Focus Lock

First, position the subject in the center of your viewfinder. Next, press the shutter-release button halfway to lock the focus on your subject. As you press the button, you will hear a click or see the focus indicator (most likely a green dot) light up on the LCD.

While still holding the shutter halfway, reposition the subject so that it is off-center on your LCD. Be careful that neither you nor your subject move from your original position as you recompose the shot. Finally, press the shutter all the way down to take the picture. By locking the focus first, your subject will be in focus even though it is not centered. As you won't be taking only subject-centered images, practice this technique so that you can compose freely while still keeping your subject in focus.

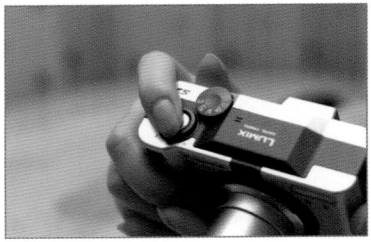

▲ Press the shutter-release button halfway to lock the focus, and keep your finger in this position.

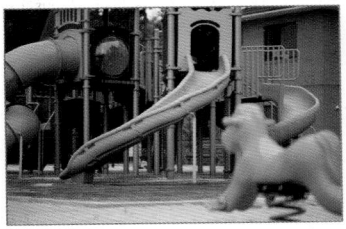

▲ Photo taken without using Focus Lock.

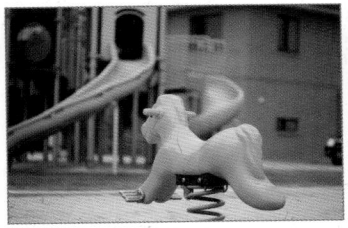

▲ Position the subject in the center and press the shutter-release button halfway to focus on the subject.

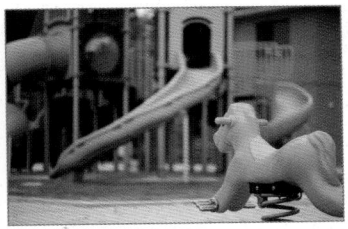

▲ Recompose the shot and press the shutter-release button all the way down to take the photo.

Adjusting Exposure Using Focus Lock

When you lock the focus on a subject, the camera is also set to expose properly for it. In other words, if you lock the focus on a very bright subject, the camera will underexpose the shot in order to expose the subject correctly. The effect of doing this is to make the entire photo appear slightly darker. Conversely, if you lock the focus on a very dark subject, the camera will overexpose the shot and this will make the photo appear slightly brighter.

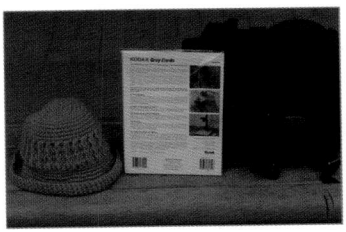

▲ Underexposing the photo by locking the focus on the brightest area.

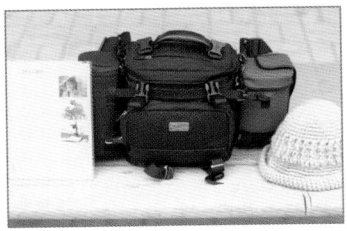

▲ Overexposing the photo by locking the focus on the darkest area.

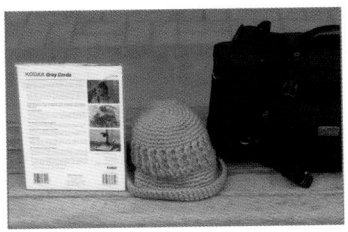

▲ Exposing the picture correctly by locking the focus on a suitable area.

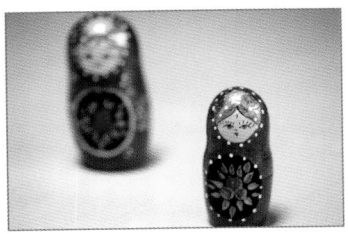

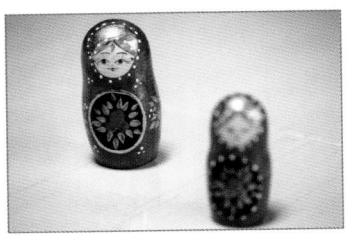

▶ Using the Focus Lock function, you can choose which subject to focus on.

05 Using Lenses

The earliest camera was the pinhole camera, which was just a black box with a pin-sized hole in one side. Pinhole cameras did not use lenses to help them focus light rays, so the images produced were rather blurry. But since lenses were incorporated into camera design, things have been very different. Today, there are countless types of lenses that can be built into digital compacts or attached to SLRs.

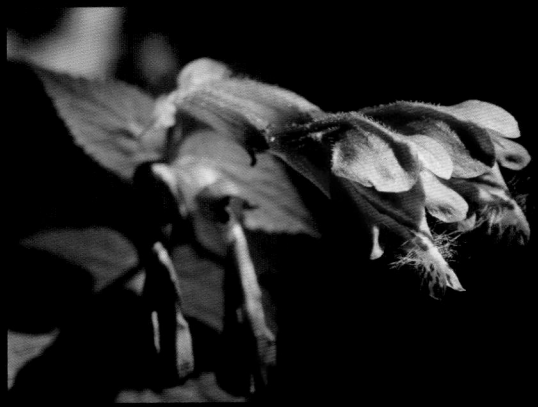

About the Lens

The term lens refers to a transparent substance, usually glass, used in optical devices to change the convergence of light rays. In photography, these pieces are known as lens elements. Lens can refer to a single lens element or groups of these elements. Inside a lens, you will also find an iris diaphragm that controls the amount of light entering the camera.

▶▶▶ Aperture

As explained in the introduction, the aperture is the size of the opening created by the iris diaphragm.

When you open up the aperture, you let in more light. The aperture of a lens is measured on a scale of f-stops, or f-numbers, that are fractions of the focal length of the lens. A large aperture would have a small f-number, while a small aperture would have a large f-number.

Understanding the Terminology of Lenses: An Example

Olympus Super Bright Zoom Lens Olympus uses the term *Super Bright* to describe lenses with a large maximum aperture.

AF Zoom The camera's zoom lens is capable of autofocusing.

7.1–21.3 mm These numbers represent the focal length range of the lens. This digital range is equivalent to a focal length range of 35–105 mm on a film camera. Note that the maximum focal length of 21.3 mm is three times that of the minimum focal length of 7.1 mm. So another way of describing the focal length range of a camera like this one is to say that it has a 3× optical zoom.

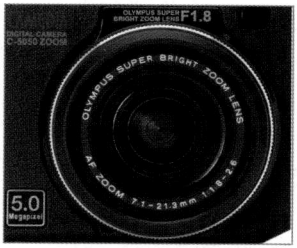

▲ Olympus C-5050 lens.

1:1.8–2.6 These numbers indicate the range in aperture size. An aperture size of *f*/1.8 is considered very large for popular digital cameras. For most of us, an aperture of *f*/2.8 or smaller is good enough.

Zooming Effect

If you zoom while using a slow shutter speed, you can create a zooming effect, as shown below. First, set a slow shutter speed. When the shutter is open, zoom into a target while keeping your camera steady.

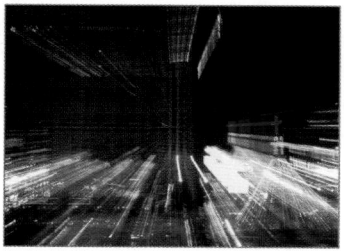

▲ A zooming effect.

With an automatic camera, you can achieve the same effect by using the Night Landscape Scene mode, which uses a slow shutter speed.

▶▶▶ Angle of View

The amount of a scene that can be recorded by a lens is called the angle of view. The angle of view depends on the focal length of the lens. A wide-angle lens, as the name suggests, has a wide angle of view, meaning that it can record much of the scene before it. A telephoto lens, on the other hand, has a narrow angle of view and is used for zooming in on subjects at a distance.

In general, lenses with a focal length between 14 mm and 50 mm (film camera equivalent) are considered wide-angle lenses. Those with focal lengths around 50 mm are standard lenses, while lenses longer than 50 mm are telephoto lenses. If you have a 3× zoom lens with a focal length of 35 – 105 mm, it simultaneously serves as a wide-angle (35 mm) lens, a standard (50 mm) lens, and a telephoto (105 mm) lens.

The following photos show the same scene shot with different lense lengths. Observe how the focal length affects how small or large the subject appears.

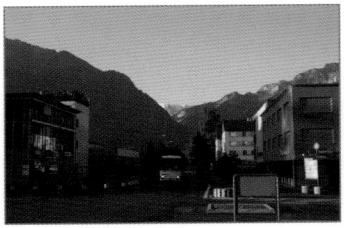

▲ Focal length: 30 mm.

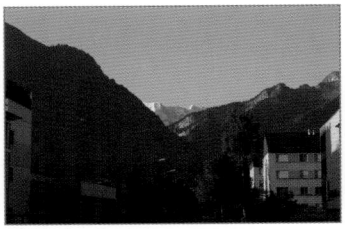

▲ Focal length: 50 mm.

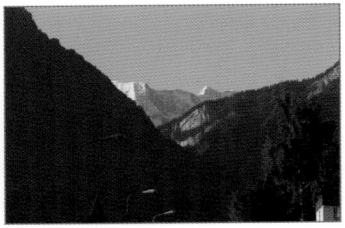

▲ Focal length: 100 mm.

▶▶▶ Perspective

Changing the focal length not only changes how much of the scene you capture, but also changes the perspective. Your subject can seem nearer or farther away from other elements in the shot depending on the lens you use. When you use a telephoto lens, the perspective is compressed and your subject will appear closer to the background. In contrast, your subject will appear to be farther away from the background if you use a wide-angle lens.

▶▶▶ Depth of Field

Depth of field, also known as depth of focus, is the range of distance in which you can keep the scene sharply focused. When describing depth of field, we say it is either deep or shallow.

In the photo on the left, both the objects and the background are brought into focus, so we say that it has a deep depth of field. In the other photo, the middle object is in focus while everything else is blurred, so this photo demonstrates a shallow depth of field.

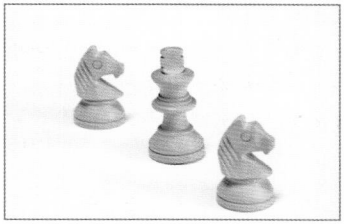

▲ Deep depth of field.

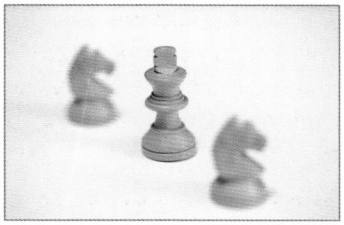

▲ Shallow depth of field.

Changing the Depth of Field

You can change the depth of field by adjusting the aperture. A large aperture creates a shallow depth of field, while a small aperture creates a deeper depth of field. The results will appear quite different. This is covered in greater detail later in the chapter.

Another way of controlling the depth of field is to change the lens. You will get a shallow depth of field when you are close to your subject and a deeper depth of field when you are farther away. In the same way, telephoto lenses (or maximum zoom on your camera), with their long focal length, have a shallow depth of field, while wide-angle lenses, with their short focal length, have a deeper depth of field.

In addition, you need to remember that the range of focus in front of and behind a point of focus is unequal. About 1/3 of your depth of field is in front of your point of focus, while 2/3 of it is behind.

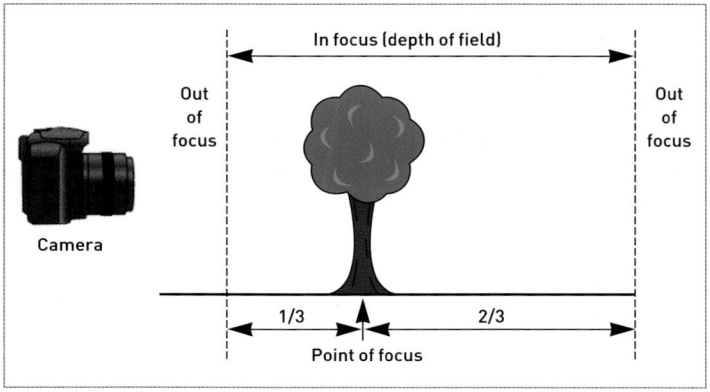

Choosing Between Wide-Angle and Telephoto Lenses

▶▶▶ Wide-Angle Lens (Zoom-Out)

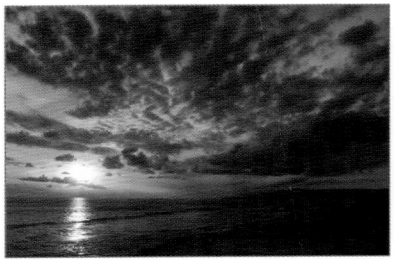

▲ A wide-angle lens is great for shooting scenery.

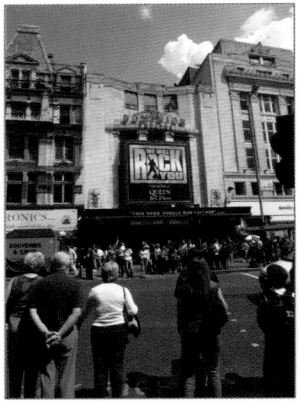

▲ Shooting objects or buildings with a wide-angle lens exaggerates perspective and makes them look more majestic.

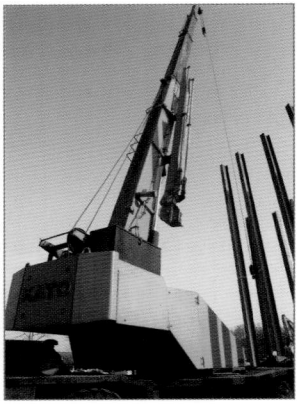

▲ This lens creates a deep depth of field that allows both the subject and the background to remain in focus.

▶▶▶ Telephoto Lens (Zoom-In)

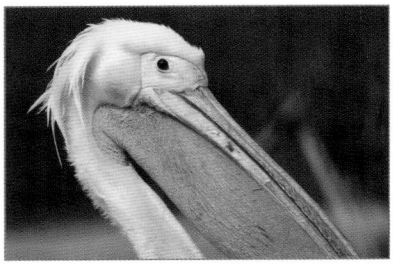

▲ A telephoto lens is a must for taking photos of subjects that you can't approach.

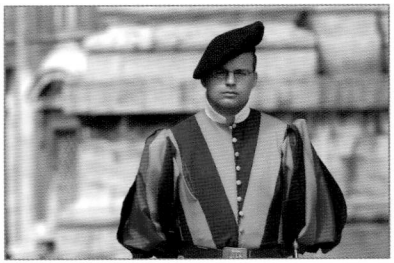

▲ A shallow depth of field gives emphasis to the subject by bringing it into focus against a blurry background.

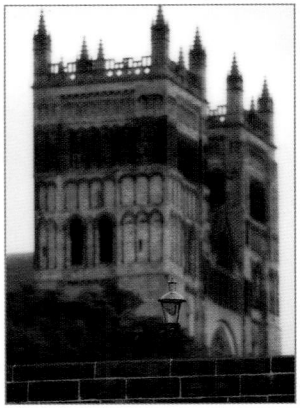

▶ A telephoto lens compresses perspective and makes subjects, such as landmarks in the distance, appear closer than they really are.

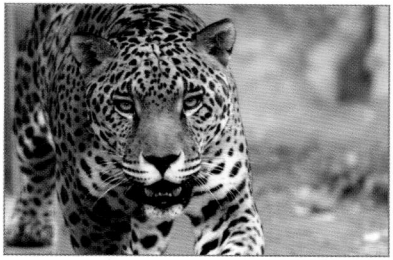

▲ It helps to remember that in addition to the background, a telephoto lens will also blur out the foreground elements. In this shot, the cage wires in the foreground are blurred out.

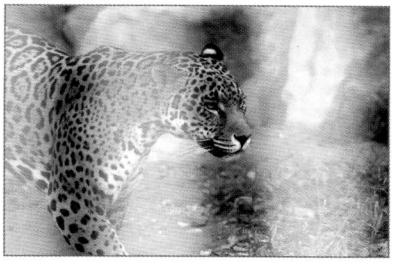

▲ If you don't zoom in enough, the cage wires become more obvious.

06 Controlling Exposure

In this section, you will learn to adjust the exposure on an automatic camera with the Exposure Compensation feature, or on a semiautomatic camera the Shutter Priority or Aperture Priority mode. Even if you can't adjust the aperture or shutter speed on your camera, this chapter will help you understand how your camera arrives at the automatic settings and what happens in the Scene modes.

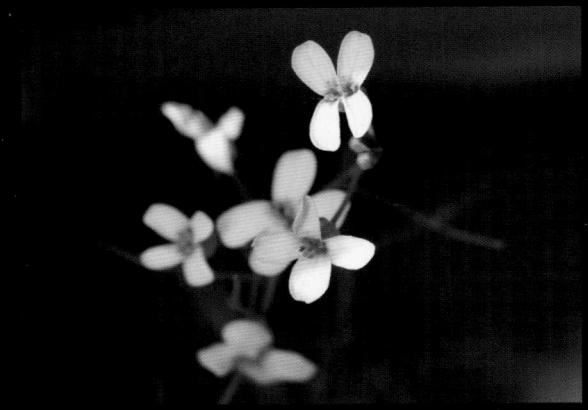

What Is Exposure?

Exposure refers to the total amount of light that hits the CCD on a digital camera or the film on a traditional camera. An image is said to be overexposed when the CCD receives too much light, and underexposed when it receives too little. Changing the aperture or shutter speed will alter the exposure, but these two methods produce slightly different results.

Adjusting Exposure with Exposure Compensation

Also known as EV (exposure value) adjustment, this feature lets you modify the automatic exposure set by the camera up or down a few levels. A value of 0 represents the exposure suggested by the camera. Select the + values (for example, +0.3, +0.7) to increase the exposure and make the image brighter, or the – values (for example, –0.3, –0.7) to decrease the exposure and darken the image.

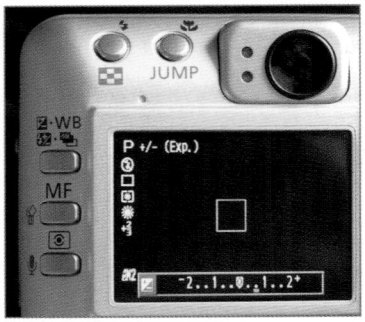

▲ The Exposure Compensation menu.

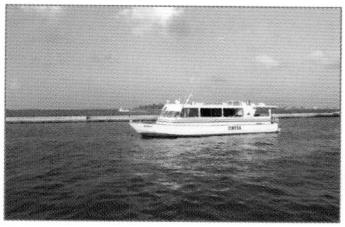

▲ Original exposure at 0.

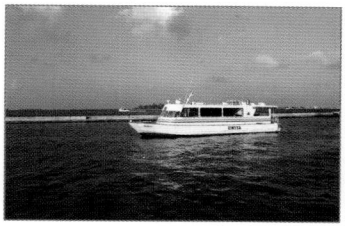

▲ Correct exposure at −0.3.

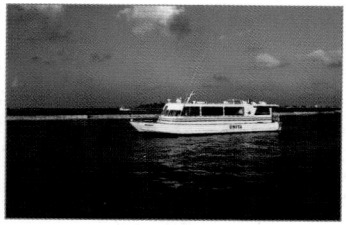

▲ Underexposed at −0.1.

Adjusting Exposure with ISO

Another way of adjusting the exposure on a consumer camera is to change the sensitivity of the CCD to light. Check if your camera supports manual ISO adjustment. If it does, increase the ISO when shooting in low-light conditions so that the image needs less light to be properly exposed. If it doesn't, use additional light sources (candles, flashlight, for example) to brighten up the location. Conversely, use a low ISO, turn off the lights, or provide some shade when shooting in a very bright location.

Adjusting Exposure with Aperture

Recall that aperture is measured on a scale of f-stops or f-numbers, and the smaller the f-number, the bigger the aperture. The stop numbers are *f*/1.0, *f*/1.4, *f*/2, *f*/2.8, *f*/4, *f*/5.6, and so on. The interval between each stop is known as one stop.

The size of the aperture or the amount of light passing through it doubles every time we stop up (use a smaller f-number). Conversely, it reduces by half as we stop down (use a larger f-number). At an aperture of *f*/4, for example, the amount of light passing through the lens is half of *f*/2.8 but twice as much as *f*/5.6. Lenses with a big maximum aperture are expensive. Most consumer lens apertures may not open wide enough to work well in poorly lit areas.

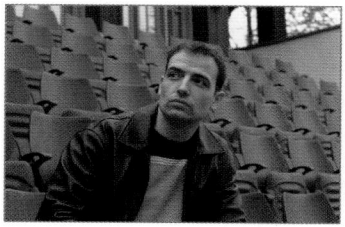

▲ Underexposed at *f*/5.6: amount of light halved.

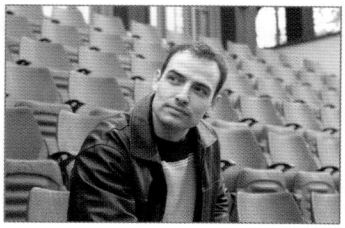

▲ Correct exposure at *f*/4.

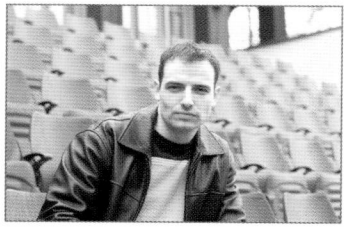

▲ Overexposed at *f*/2.8: amount of light doubled.

When to Use Aperture Priority Mode

When adjusting exposure in the Aperture Priority mode, you should note that opening up the aperture has the effect of making the depth of field in the image more shallow, causing a loss of detail in the image. The reverse is true when closing the aperture.

▶▶▶ Shallow Depth of Field

To emphasize a subject by bringing it into focus while blurring the background, set the camera to Aperture Priority mode and open up the aperture to create a shallow depth of field. You can get a similar effect by selecting the Portrait mode on an automatic camera.

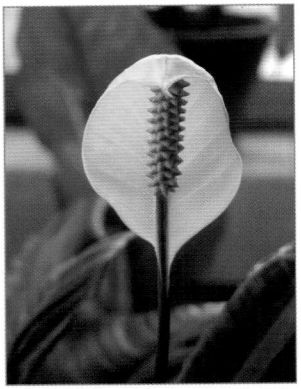

▲ Exposure set to *f*/1.8 at 1/250 second.

▶▶▶ Deep Depth of Field

To make sure that the entire image is sharply focused (especially for scenic shots), use a small aperture to create a deep depth of field. When you use a small aperture, you have to use a slow shutter speed in order to expose the image adequately. The camera automatically adjusts these settings if you select the Landscape mode. A slow shutter speed will make the camera sensitive to movement, so the use of a tripod is recommended.

At times, you can't use a slow shutter speed but you need to have a large depth of field. For instance, you may be taking a shot of people standing at various distances from the camera who can't keep still. In such cases, you can still use a small aperture with a normal shutter speed, but you will need a very bright environment for correct exposure.

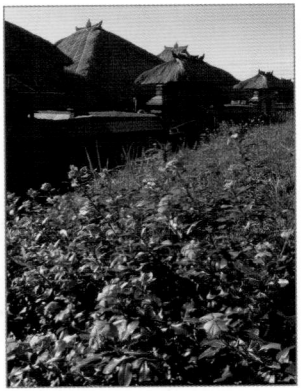

▲ Exposure set to *f*/8 at 1/50 second.

Adjusting Exposure with Shutter Speed

The shutter controls the length of time that light enters the camera. A fast shutter speed shortens the exposure time, reducing the total amount of light the CCD receives. On the other hand, a slow shutter speed increases the amount of light entering and is therefore ideal for low-light photography. The range of shutter speeds available is very wide. The more commonly used range is from 2 seconds to 1/500 second. Like aperture intervals, one shutter speed interval is equal to 1 stop. Similarly, a shutter speed of 1 second, for example, is twice as slow as a shutter speed of 1/2 second and lets in double the amount of light.

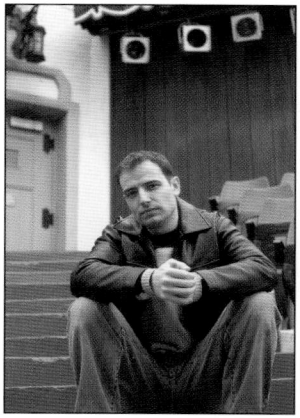

▲ Correct exposure at a shutter speed of 1/60 second.

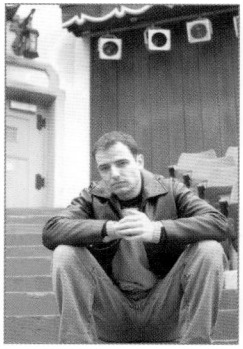

▲ Overexposed at a shutter speed of 1/30 second: amount of light doubled.

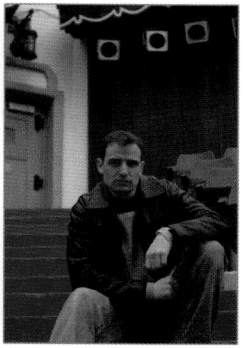

▲ Underexposed at a shutter speed of 1/125 second: amount of light halved.

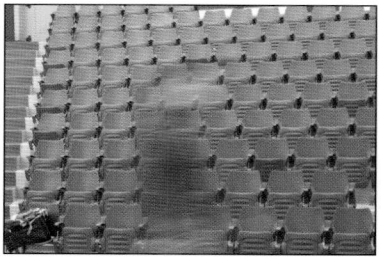

▲ Shot at a shutter speed of 1/2 second.

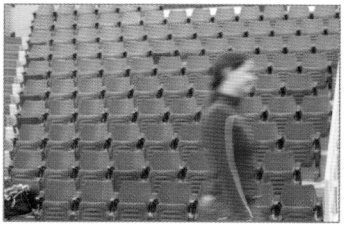

▲ Shot at a shutter speed of 1/30 second.

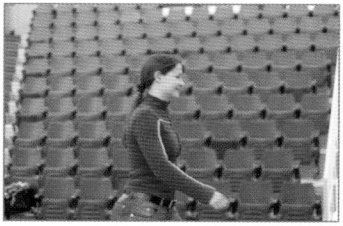

▲ Shot at a shutter speed of 1/125 second.

When to Use Shutter Priority Mode

Other than its effect on exposure, shutter speed has a tremendous impact on how movement is captured. A fast shutter speed can freeze a subject in motion, which is why you should use fast shutter speeds at sporting events. Using a slow shutter speed captures the motion of moving objects as light trails.

▶▶▶ Fast Shutter Speeds

Set the camera to Shutter Priority mode and use a fast shutter speed to freeze a subject in motion. If you have an automatic camera, you can switch to the Sports mode, which automatically sets faster shutter speeds.

As shutter speed increases, more light is needed to properly expose the image, so sunny days and well-lit surroundings, together with high ISO (light sensitivity) settings, are best for such shots.

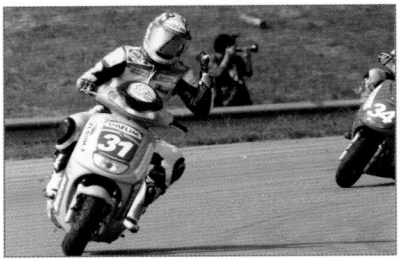

▲ Shutter speed of 1/500 second.

▶▶▶ Slow Shutter Speeds

Try a slow shutter speed to capture the motion streaks of vehicles at night. Remember to use a tripod to prevent camera shake. On an automatic camera, the Night Landscape or Fireworks Show mode will produce similar results. While in these modes, the camera uses a slow shutter speed, focuses at infinity, and turns off the flash.

When you use a slow shutter speed, the CCD receives a lot of light, so you should take these shots at night or in dimly lit surroundings to prevent overexposure.

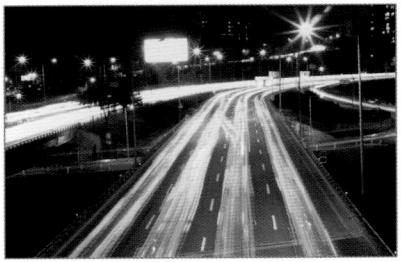

▲ Shutter speed of 30 seconds.

07 Composing a Shot

Composition, in both photography and art, refers to the way in which the elements that make up the work are arranged. While there are clear, technical instructions on how to use a camera, the interpretation of what makes a good composition is subjective. But while there may be no simple formula, there are some general guidelines, and dos and don'ts, that will help you compose a shot.

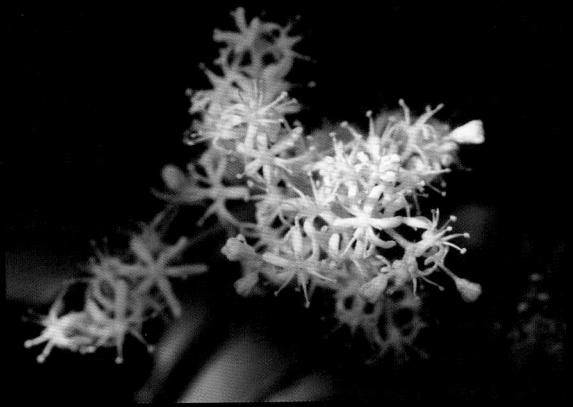

Subject Placement

▶▶▶ Place the Subject in the Right Spot

The subject need not be in the center of your photos all of the time. The subject can be in the center, but it can also be off-center for a completely different effect.

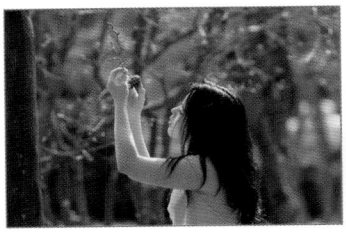

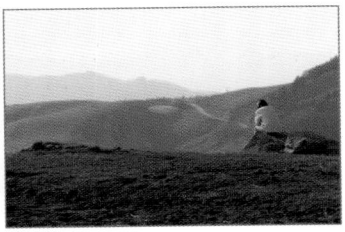

tip A well-composed image is one that complements the photographer's vision or perspective. For example, if your aim is to portray your subject in a favorable light, the composition should enhance your subject's positive characteristics.

▶▶▶ Avoid Interference

A common mistake made by beginners is concentrating on getting the subject right but forgetting everything else. Don't fall into that trap. Remember that in order to create a good composition, all elements in the photo must mix well. Before you press the shutter button, check that surrounding objects do not interfere with your main subject. This could include objects such as a lamp post or a tree branch, as demonstrated here.

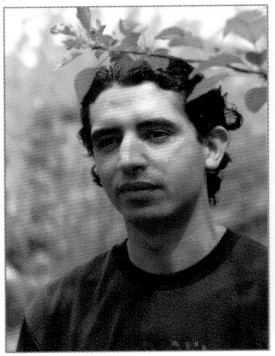

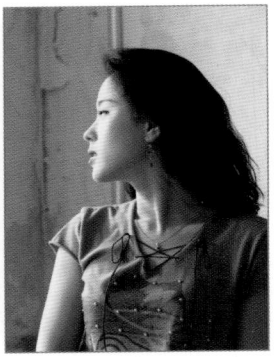

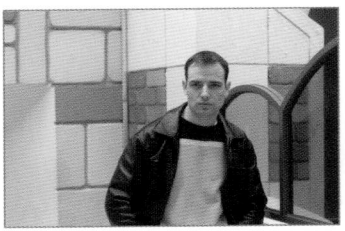

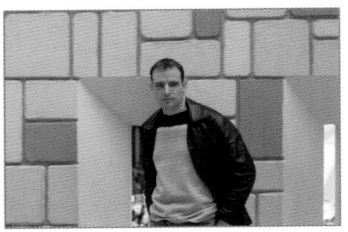

▲ In the original shot, the railing was distracting from the man, who is the main subject. The photo looks much better when the model moves away from the railing.

▶▶▶ Rule of Thirds

Essentially, the Rule of Thirds is about dividing the frame into thirds horizontally and vertically. As the rule goes, you will get a pleasing composition if you place your subject along the lines or the intersections of the lines. It is widely acknowledged among photographers that this "rule" is merely a guide, and may not work for all compositions.

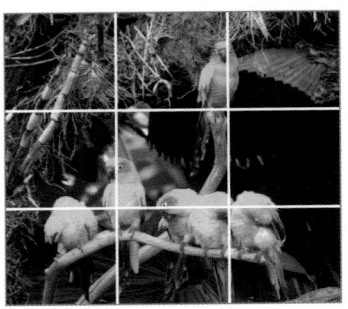

▶ Using the Rule of Thirds in this shot produced a pleasing composition.

tip Before taking a photo, think of how to organize your subjects in order to communicate your theme, and try to visualize the results. While composing an image, most photographers go through the process of repeatedly adding and removing elements before they finally settle on a particular composition. During this process, a photographer has to keep reviewing his vision of the final image. With practice, a photographer will be able to match his vision with reality more closely. Many well-composed shots, especially indoor ones, are not accidental; they were pre-visualized and shot as planned.

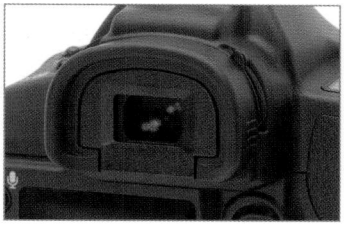

▲ You need to develop a "camera's eye" for seeing the world in order to pick out photo opportunities.

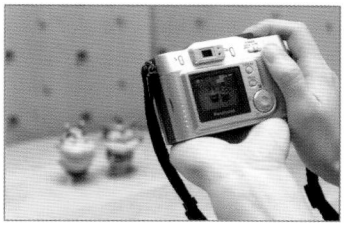

▲ The LCD on digital cameras makes it easier to compose a shot.

Horizontal or Vertical?

You can make the same photo look completely different simply by changing the orientation layout. The key is in choosing a layout that best highlights the subject's features and characteristics. Horizontal shots, in general, can give a sense of stability to the photo, while vertical shots are normally used to shoot tall scenes to give emphasis to height.

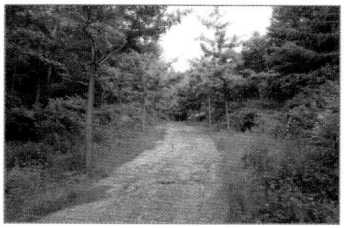

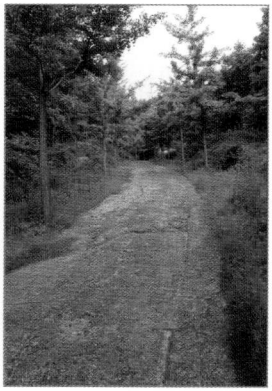

▶ A horizontal shot makes the forest look dense and enclosed, while a vertical shot includes less of the forest and more of the path and the sky, making the scene look more open and the perspective a little deeper.

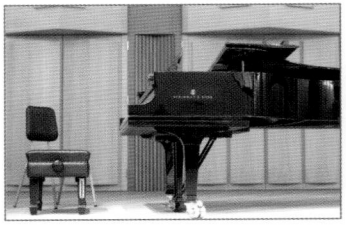

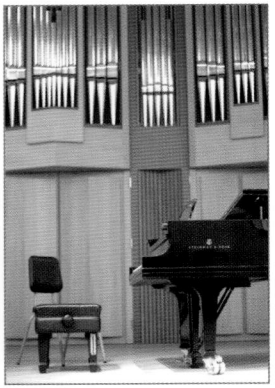

▶ The choice between a vertical and horizontal orientation here depends on whether the photographer wants to emphasize the chamber pipes or the grand piano.

Filling Up the Frame

A common mistake is to take the shot too far away from the subject. Try moving one step closer to your subject to give it more emphasis vis-à-vis the background. This will help to focus the viewer's attention on the characteristics and features of the subject. This technique will also remove a cluttered or dull background from the photo.

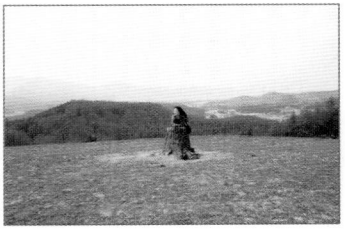

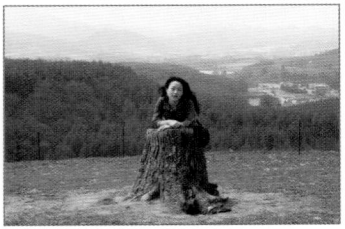

▲ From a long way off, the subject looks insignificant while the background looks featureless. Moving closer captures more of the detail in the subject and the background.

While sometimes you'll want to add elements to a scene, you should also remove unnecessary objects to keep the main point of interest on the subject. You can do this by physically removing the unwanted elements, moving closer, or shooting from a different point of view.

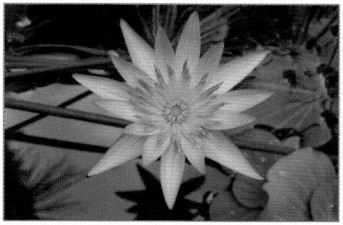

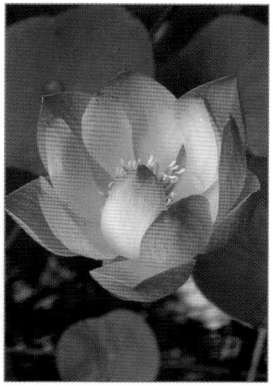

▲ Get closer to get more of the subject and less of the distracting background.

Leading Lines

The environment around us is composed of natural lines—the horizon, winding paths, straight roads, etc. By exploiting the existing lines in a scene, we can move the viewer's gaze across or deeper into the photo, making it a more dynamic and engaging work. These lines—known as leading lines—are often used to direct the viewer's eyes to the main subject.

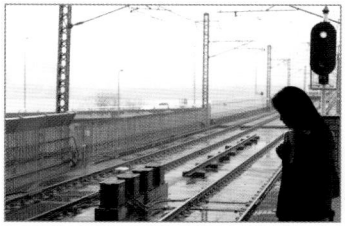

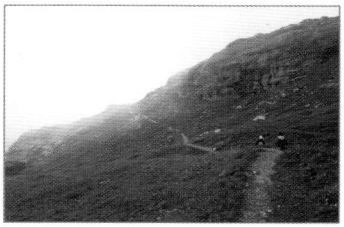

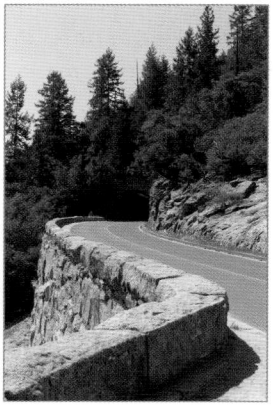

▲ Use leading lines to guide your viewer's gaze into the photo.

Experiment with taking a photo from high above or down below the subject for a fresh point of view. Even a photo of ordinary subjects can look extraordinary if shot from an interesting angle.

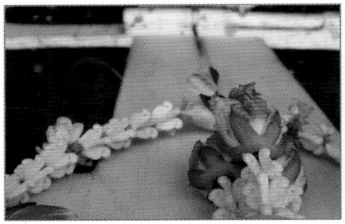

▲ A shot of the other side of the gate taken from the top.

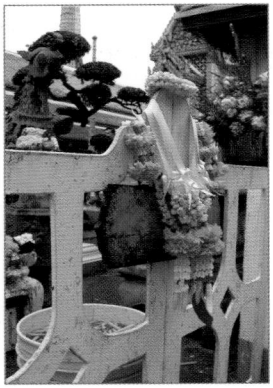

▲ A front shot of a gate.

Note

We've covered some common composition guidelines, but this does not mean that you should force all of your photos to fit into one of these forms. When composing a shot, it is more important that you evaluate the scene, the mood, and the moment before your eyes and explore compositions that will deliver the theme you have in mind.

In other words, how photos are composed is completely up to you. Instead of restricting your shots to the compositions discussed in this section, use them as a foundation for creating your own work.

For beginners, practice composing shots using inanimate objects because it will help you to develop a photographer's eye for good subject placement.

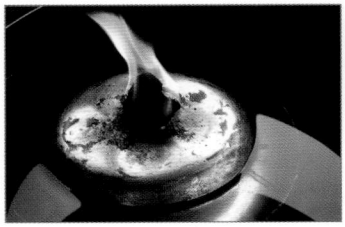

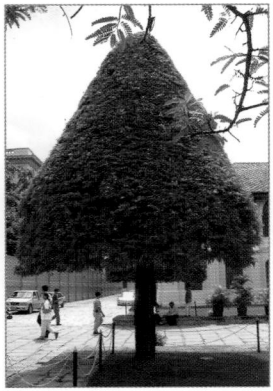

▶ Although these subjects are placed in the center and not 1/3 from the edge as spelled out in the Rule of Thirds, the compositions are still pleasing in their simplicity and balance.

Checklist

- √ Wrap the wrist strap around your wrist and get a good grip on the camera.
- √ Check that your fingers are not covering the lens or built-in flash.
- √ Adopt a steady posture, using other objects or a tripod for support if necessary.
- √ Use Focus Lock to focus on a subject that is not in the center of your viewfinder.
- √ Adjust the exposure using the Exposure Compensation feature if the image is too dark or too bright.
- √ If you have a semiautomatic camera, adjust the exposure by changing the aperture or shutter speed.
- √ Use a large aperture (small f-number) to blur the background.
- √ Use a small aperture (large f-number) to keep the entire image focused.
- √ Use a fast shutter speed to freeze action.
- √ Use a slow shutter speed to create motion streaks.
- √ Try positioning your subject somewhere other than the center of the frame.
- √ Check that surrounding objects do not interfere with your subject.
- √ Try using the Rule of Thirds.
- √ Fill up the frame with your subject.
- √ Look for leading lines in the scene.

40 Digital Photography Techniques

Exploring More Advanced Features

Chapter 2

Chapter 1 introduced many of the technical aspects of photography. In this chapter, we will explore the digital camera's more advanced features.

Some of these features, such as flash, close-ups, and continuous shots, are common to both digital and film cameras, while others, such as Black-and-White and Sepia modes and white balance, are unique to digital cameras.

08 Working with Light

The word photography means to draw a picture with light, and lighting is the most important element of photography. Since light is such a key element, we will examine the effects of light sources from different angles, at different times of day, and in different weather conditions, and learn to work with each lighting scenario. In this section, you will learn essential techniques for working with natural light, including light metering methods.

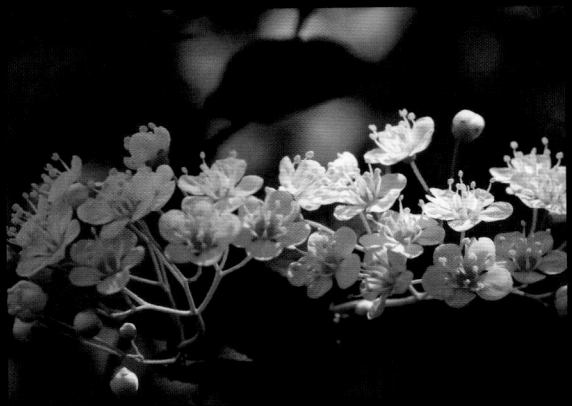

Angle of Light

Avoid taking photos with the light shining directly over a subject, as the harsh lighting will create strong highlights and deep shadows, resulting in a loss of detail. Light thrown at an angle from either side of the subject, or from behind the camera, is often easier to work with. When a subject is lit at an angle, you get a more three-dimensional effect.

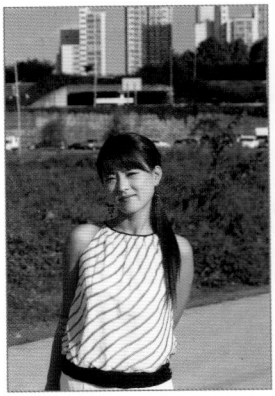

▲ A strong light source shining directly over the subject creates harsh shadows. In shots of people, this type of light source will deepen dark eye circles.

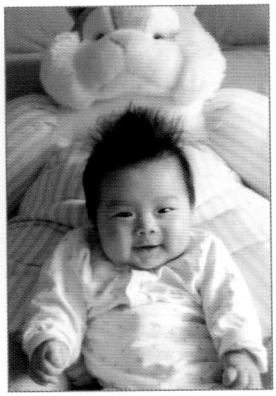

▲ Diffused light from both sides of the subject illuminates the subject's features.

▶▶▶ Backlighting

Another type of lighting condition to avoid is backlighting, where the light source shines from behind the subject, throwing the subject's features into shadow. Sometimes, these shots can't be avoided. For instance, you may want to take a photo of a friend standing in front of a landmark even though it is backlit.

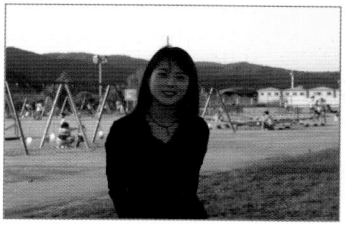

▲ Backlit photo taken with no flash.

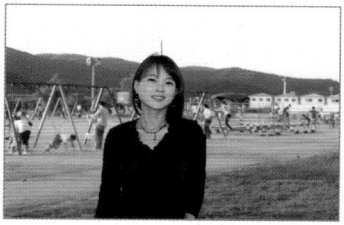

▲ Backlit photo taken with Fill Flash.

To make sure that your subject is not left in the shadows, select the Back Light or Fill Flash mode on your camera. The flash will fire automatically to fill in the shadows. If you can adjust the flash's intensity, lower it slightly for a more natural-looking photo.

tip A backlit scene is not necessarily a hopeless situation. If the subject is translucent, the light will shine through the subject. The subject will appear luminous and will not be underexposed. If the backlighting is soft and diffused and the background is unimportant, you can set the shutter speed and aperture to expose the subject correctly while overexposing the background. This method, which captures the subject details and foregoes the background image, may work better than using a flash because flash light is usually harsh and unnatural.

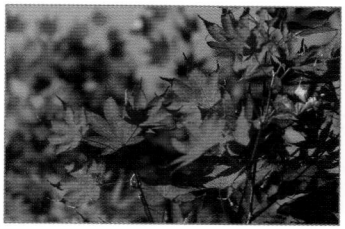

▲ As the light shines through the leaves, the veins on the leaves can be seen clearly.

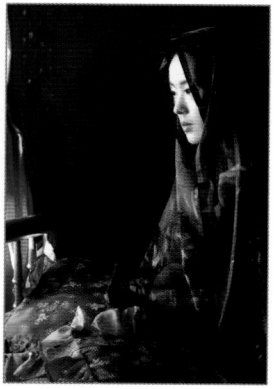

▲ The soft, diffused light from a window presented the perfect lighting conditions for this profile shot.

Light-Metering Methods

Light metering is a process of measuring the amount of light reflected off of your subject. Nearly all cameras have a built-in light meter, also known as an exposure meter, which measures light. Depending on whether you are using a manual or automatic camera, the camera will recommend or automatically set the exposure for you. There are three light-metering methods:

- Matrix Metering: The entire picture in the viewfinder is split into segments that are metered individually. The camera then compares the results to its database of about 100,000 photos and recommends or sets an appropriate exposure.

This light-metering method is the most suitable for beginners. It is useful for taking snapshots of rapidly moving objects or in situations where fast reaction is needed. On the downside, it will be more difficult to create the effect you want in your photos, as the camera matches the scene before it to a phantom database that you have no control over.

- Center-Weighted Metering: The camera measures the light in the central area of the photo. To use this method, move the camera around the photo area to measure the light reading at different parts. Then decide which part of the photo is most important and set the exposure accordingly.
- Spot Metering: This is the most accurate light-metering method. The camera measures the light at a spot in the center of the photo. Another way to shoot backlit photos is to use spot metering. Switch your camera to Spot Metering mode and point it at the subject. By doing so, you expose the subject correctly while overexposing the background.

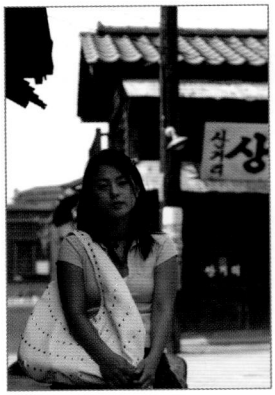

▲ Photo taken using matrix metering.

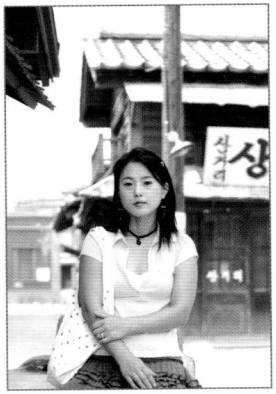

▲ Photo taken using spot metering.

tip Since you can't properly expose both foreground and background at the same time due to the wide tonal range in the scene, make sure that your subject's features are not left in the dark even if it means over-exposing the background.

tip If you can't meter light using your camera, use the Exposure Compensation menu on your camera to expose a back-lit photo and brighten it up.

Weather

Although you may assume that photos taken on cloudy days will not turn out well, cloudy days are actually better for taking photos of people and objects. On clear, bright days, you should attempt to take photos of your subject in the shade.

Cloudy days or a shady spot are better for taking photos because of the diffused lighting conditions. The clouds act as a filter for the strong sunlight and soften the photo.

However, you should avoid areas in deep shade and refrain from taking photos when the sun is at its brightest. If you must take a photo in the sun, avoid having the sunlight shine directly on your subject.

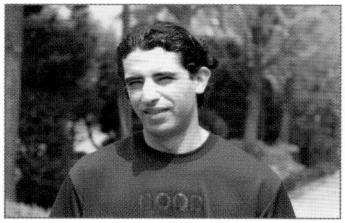

▲ Strong sunlight is harsh and it also makes your subject squint.

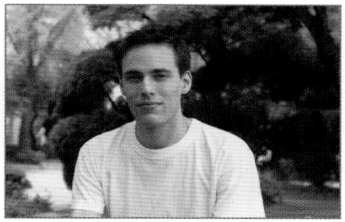

▲ Cloudy days, in general, are better for taking photos of people.

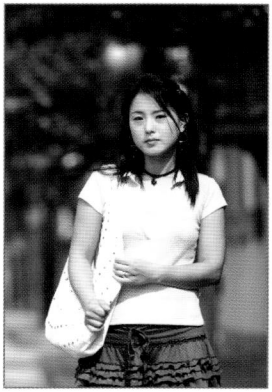

▲ Photo taken at noon (in direct sunlight) on a clear day. The contrast is too strong, making the photo look flat.

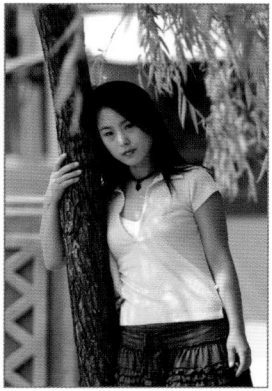

▲ On a clear and sunny day, take photos in the shade under a tree, for example, for good results.

Time of Day

Sunrise and sunset photos look very different, as the time of the shoot influences the colors that will appear in your photo. Photos taken before sunrise will have a bluish tint, but photos taken immediately after the sun rises will be reddish. The higher the sun is in the sky, the more accurate and clearer the colors will appear in your photo. This is especially true for shots taken at noon.

As the sun sets, the colors in your photo will appear warmer. Red and orange hues will appear in photos taken in the early evening, but as the sun sets, the sky will be filled with shades of purple, with hints of pink and green. The changing colors in natural light explain why your photos look different when taken at different times. The colors are warmest and softest approximately one to two hours before sunset. This is the time when most professional photographers take photos.

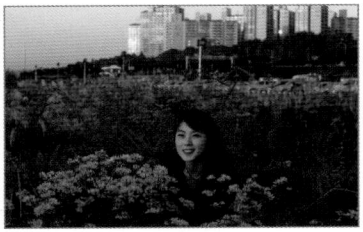

▲ Photo taken at early morning.

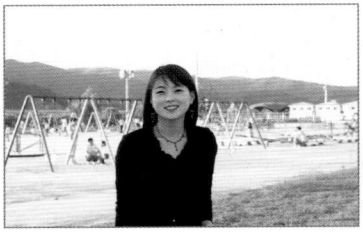

▲ Photo taken at noon.

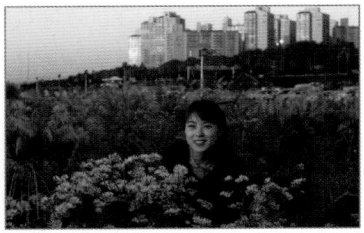

▲ Photo taken during sunset.

Fluorescent lights are commonly used in the home environment. As they have a higher color temperature (Kelvin temperature), they present a brighter and more active ambience to the picture. However, when shooting with AWB (Auto White Balance), they tend to produce pictures that have a bluish look. To prevent this, use a three wave light instead of a fluorescent one. As a three wave light has Kelvin temperature similar to that of sunlight, it can produce pictures with natural color.

When you cannot change your light settings, change your camera's white balance setting. In the "White Balance" menu look for the "fluorescent" setting. Once you set your white balance to fluorescent, you can take pictures that have an almost natural color. Alternately, you can custom-set your white balance. You can manually change your white balance setting using a grey card or white A4 paper, after you set your camera to custom white setting. Please refer to the camera's user manual. While it is definitely more time consuming, custom settings usually produce the best outcome.

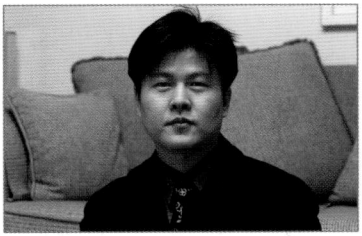

▲ A bluish picture of a person under a fluorescent light.

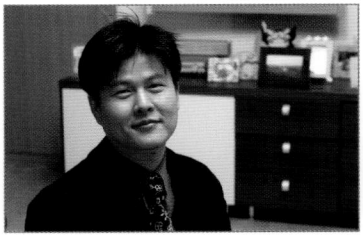

▲ A picture under a three wave light, free of bluish colors.

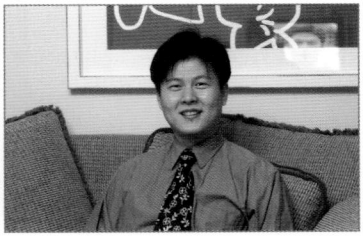

▲ A picture with a natural-looking color balance, taken with a custom white balance setting.

09 Using Flash

The flash, unlike other sources of light that provide continuous lighting, is a sudden burst of bright light. The flash is commonly used to light up backlit subjects, take night photos outdoors, or shoot in poorly lit indoor spaces. A built-in flash can usually light up to a maximum distance of 33 feet (10 meters). This is known as the flash depth. Check your camera specifications for the optimal distance to place your subject from the flash.

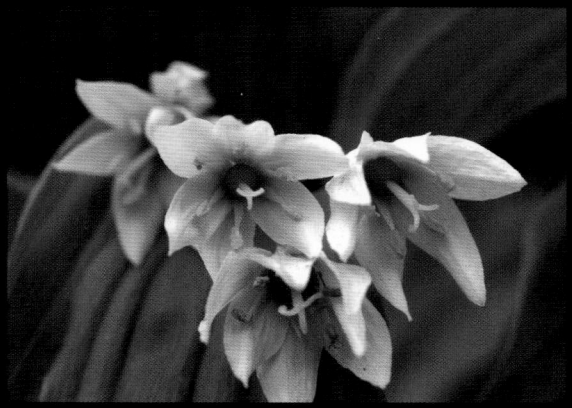

Internal Flash

Most digital cameras are equipped with a built-in flash that is either fixed or pops up when triggered. There is no other difference between these two types of built-in flash.

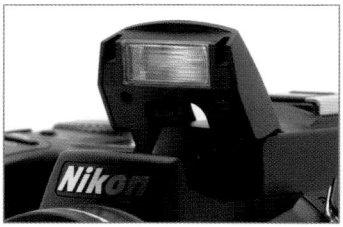

▲ Nikon Coolpix 8700 has a pop-up flash.

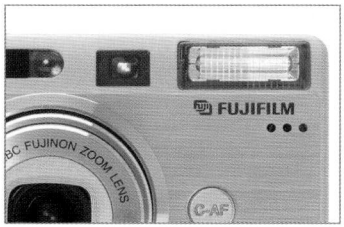

▲ Fujifilm Finepix F700 has a fixed flash.

External Flash

High-end cameras have a mount (usually on top) called a hot shoe to which you can attach an external flash. External flash units draw energy from their own battery source, so they have no effect on the battery life of the camera. On better camera models, you can tilt and swivel an attached flash unit to change the direction of light and create different lighting effects.

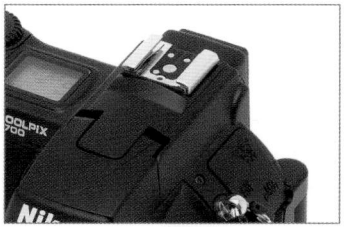

▲ Hot shoe.

As most digital cameras do not have a hot shoe, you can use a bracket to attach an external flash.

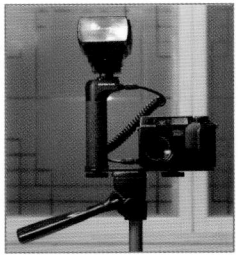

▶ Use a bracket on cameras without a hot shoe to attach an external flash.

Flash Modes

There are four basic Flash modes: Auto, Anytime (Fill Flash), Flash Cancel (Off), and Red-Eye Reduction. Depending on the model, some cameras also come with Slow Sync and Daylight Sync modes. Check your user manual to see which Flash modes your camera supports before continuing.

▶▶▶ Auto Mode

As the name suggests, the camera checks the intensity of the light in the surrounding area and automatically pops the flash if the lighting is poor. In most cases, the Auto mode is the easiest option for taking pictures. This mode is great for beginners because you don't have to think about lighting (the camera does the thinking for you), but this mode tends to light up your subject and leave the background in darkness.

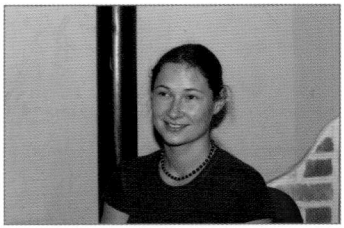

▲ The background in this Auto Flash shot did not turn out dark because the model was positioned near the wall, which reflected the light from the flash.

▶▶▶ Anytime Flash (Fill Flash) Mode

In this mode, the flash is set to go off whenever a photo is taken.

▶▶▶ Flash Cancel (Off) Mode

In this mode, the flash will not fire even when the lighting is poor. This mode is used when you want to take certain types of photos (silhouette, for example) or when taking photos at close range. If you fire the flash when you are very near your subject, the image will be overexposed.

▶▶▶ Red-Eye Reduction Mode

In poorly lit areas, our pupils will dilate to take in more light. So, when the flash is fired in low-light areas, the light from the flash enters the dilated pupils and bounces off the blood vessels at the back of the eyes, creating the red-eye syndrome we see in many photographs. In Red-Eye Reduction mode, a small, preliminary flash goes off to give the eyes time to adjust to brighter light, so that the pupils will constrict by the time the second flash is fired.

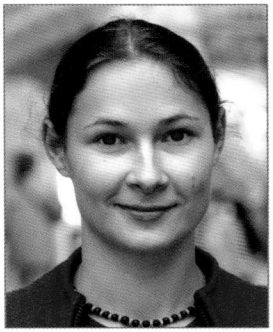

▲ Red eyes in a photo taken using the Auto mode.

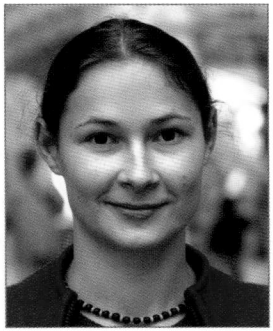

▲ Using the Red-Eye Reduction mode to prevent red-eyes.

tip Eliminating Red Eyes

One way to work around the red-eye problem is to take a profile shot of your subject so that her eyes are not staring directly into the camera. But the best way, of course, is to increase the ambient lighting, so that your subject's pupils won't expand as much.

▶▶▶ Slow Sync Mode or Night Flash

If you use the Auto mode to take a portrait shot at night, the subject gets most of the flash while the background remains dark. To prevent this from happening, use the Slow Sync mode. This activates the flash at the start of the exposure time and engages a slow shutter speed to let in more light and keep both subject and background illuminated.

In order to use this method, however, you must use a tripod, as even the slightest camera movement will blur your image as a result of the slow shutter speed. If you have a tripod and the time to set up the shot, this mode is recommended.

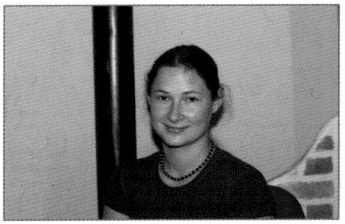

▲ Auto mode creates high-contrast images with harsh shadows.

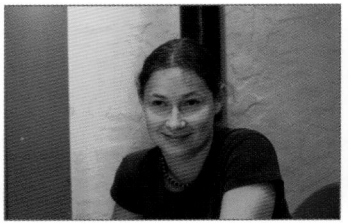

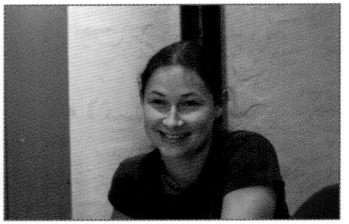

▲ Slow Sync mode captures more ambient light and creates better tonal range.

▶▶▶ Daylight Sync Mode

In this mode, the flash is set to fire even during the day to obtain an appropriate exposure. This mode is especially useful for taking more natural shots of backlit subjects. For example, let's say you want to take a photo of a subject who is standing in front of a window in daytime. The background is sufficiently bright, but shadows fall on your subject's face. Under such circumstances, use the Daylight Sync mode to illuminate both the subject and the background equally.

Softening the Flash

As the flash is a momentary burst of bright light, it is great for taking a freeze frame of moving subjects and for avoiding the motion blur caused by unsteady hands. When used under normal conditions, however, a strong flash can create harsh shadows and may produce washed-out photos. You can overcome this problem by lowering the flash output using the following accessories:

▶▶▶ Diffuser

If you have an external flash unit, attach a diffuser to lower the flash output and soften the light. Compare the photos on the right. The shot taken without a diffuser has harsh shadows, while the other looks softer and has captured more of the detail on the table.

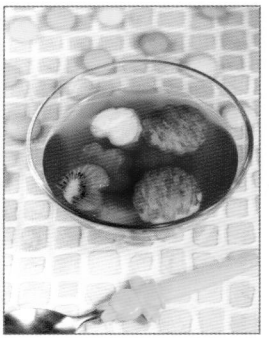

▲ Shot without a diffuser.

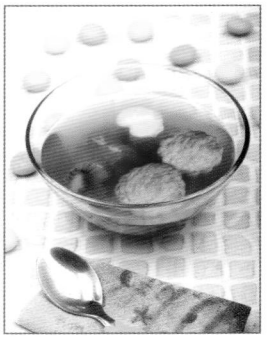

▲ Shot with a diffuser.

tip Although you cannot attach a diffuser to an internal flash, you can use semiopaque adhesive tape, plain white paper, or some other common household object to cover the flash and act as a diffuser.

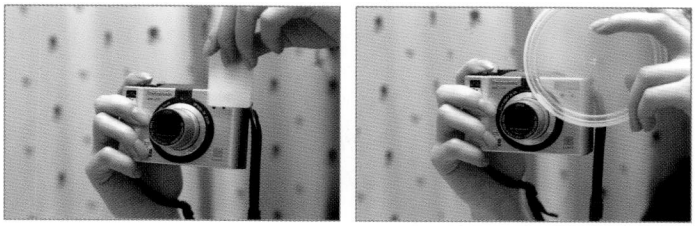

▲ Inexpensive way of diffusing the light from a built-in flash.

▶▶▶ Omni-Bounce

If you have an external flash, you can buy a semiopaque white cover called an omni-bounce to act as a diffuser.

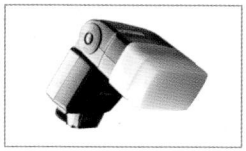

▶ An external flash fitted with an omni-bounce.

▶▶▶ Reflector

You can purchase a reflector or make one yourself. Any large piece of white board can be used as a reflector. By bouncing the flash off the reflector, you can diffuse the light and fill in the shadows.

Alternately, you can use a nearby wall or a low ceiling as a reflector, if you have an external flash. Whatever you use, pick something white so that there won't be an unwanted color cast over your picture.

If you are using a reflector, there is no need to use the Slow Sync Flash mode. Most cameras are set to a flash speed of 1/60 second, which is fast enough for shooting without a tripod. All you need to do is position the flash and take the photo.

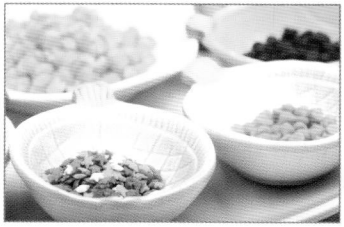

▲ To avoid under- or overexposing a photo, take a trial shot to estimate the flash intensity and exposure required.

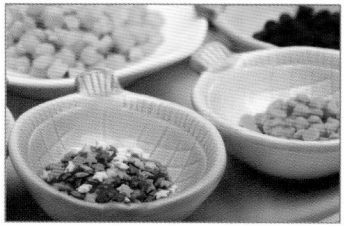

▲ Use the Exposure Compensation feature on the camera to get the right exposure.

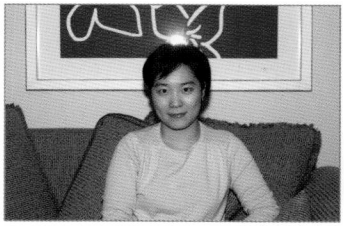

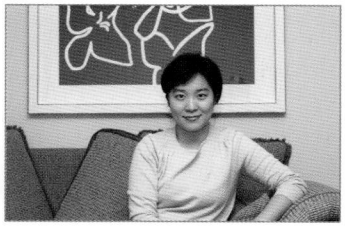

▲ Compare an image taken under direct flash (left) and one with flash bounced off the ceiling (right).

10 Creating Black-and-White and Sepia Images

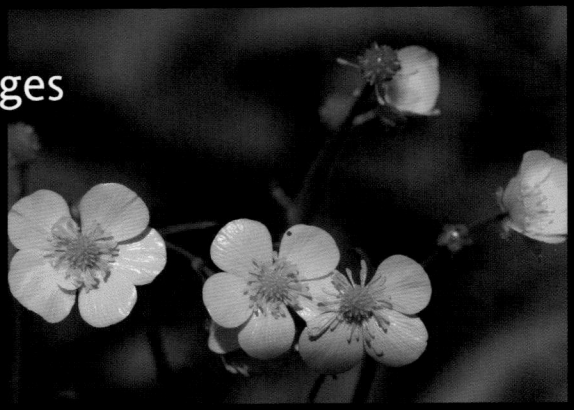

Before color film was sold commercially in the 1930s, most photographs were in monochrome. These monochrome photographs were normally in black and white, or toned to a certain color such as sepia. In photography, B&W is the common abbreviation for black and white. In this section, we will look at subjects and themes that are great for B&W and sepia photography.

About Black-and-White and Sepia Modes

With traditional film cameras, you have to use black-and-white film if you want to take black-and-white photos, or soak a black-and-white photograph in a toning solution to produce sepia images. With a digital camera, you only need to switch to the Black-and-White or Sepia modes.

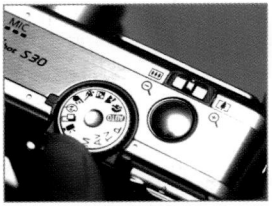

▲ Turn the camera mode dial to the Image Adjustment mode.

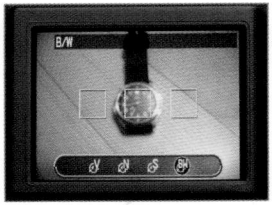

▲ Black-and-White.

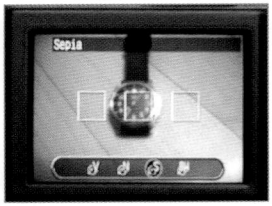

▲ Sepia.

Subjects and Themes

Photographers sometimes shoot in black and white or sepia to create a certain style or mood or to fix problems that will show up in color photos. Let's consider some situations where you might consider shooting in black and white.

▶▶▶ Photojournalistic Style

Photojournalistic style is a form of journalism that uses pictures as the primary medium to tell a story. This journalistic style, which uses text only as a supplement, is most frequently seen in newspapers or current affairs magazines.

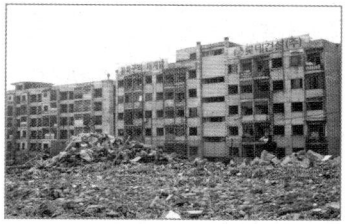

▲ Capturing this scene of a demolition site in black and white makes the scene look like a war photo.

▶▶▶ Antiquated Objects or Buildings

Antiquated objects, historical buildings, or old streets make great subjects for shooting in the Sepia or Black-and-White modes.

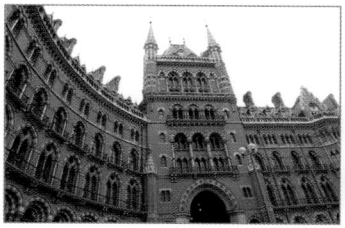

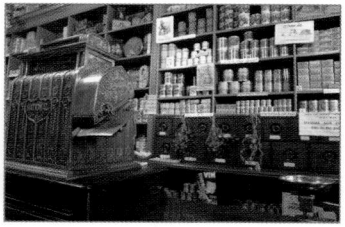

▲ You can make a recent shot look old by shooting in the Sepia mode.

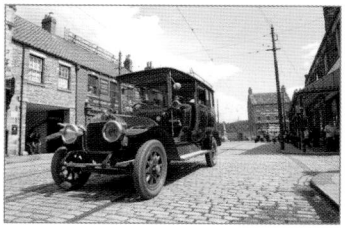

▲ You can also take a shot in black and white to convey a sense of history.

▶▶▶ Simplification

In color photography, the presence of different colors and different shades of colors can sometimes be distracting. When there is color in an image, you have to consider how the colors interact. For example, you will have to think about whether the colors contrast (for example, red and green) or form a continuous blend (for example, yellow and orange).

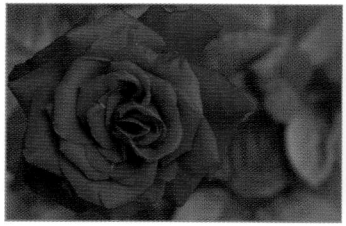

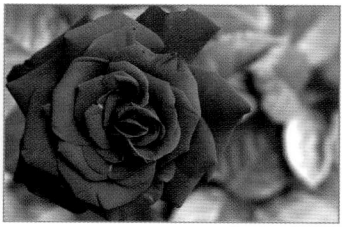

▲ After color is removed from the image, the texture on the rose petals becomes more obvious.

When you can't get the colors to look right in an image, consider shooting in black and white or sepia. This will remove the colors from the image, creating a simpler composition. With black-and-white or sepia images, the focus is on the shape, texture, lines, and the tonal range in the image. Tonal range refers to the range of brightness or darkness in the image. A high-contrast image will have a wide tonal range, while a low-contrast image will have a narrow tonal range.

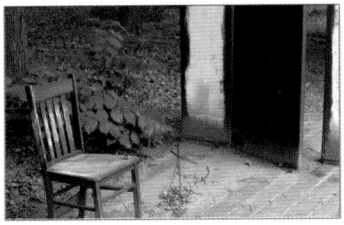

▲ Taking this shot in Sepia mode makes the leaves that interfere with the chair less distracting and keeps the focus on the chair.

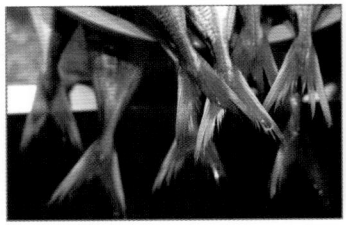

▲ Take black-and-white images of objects with strong outlines for an abstract study of shape and form.

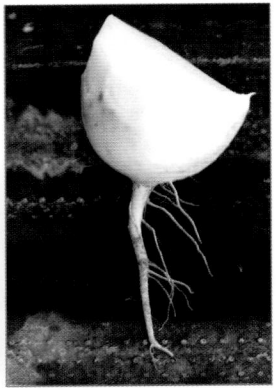

▶▶▶ People Photography

Taking sepia or black-and-white pictures of people or events can give the images a timeless quality. These tonal styles are especially popular for weddings and portraits.

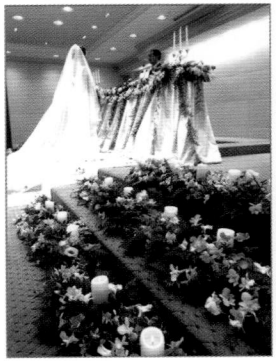

▲ You can create a photo journal for weddings.

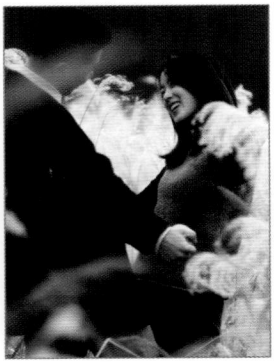

▲ Sepia and black-and-white images of people can create an impression of nostalgia.

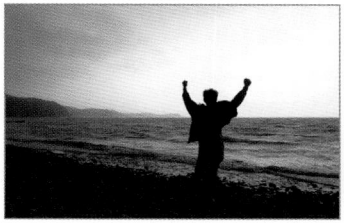

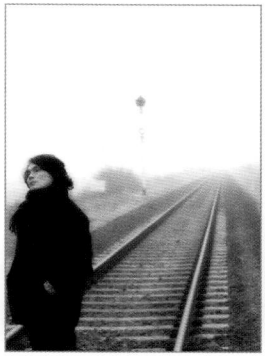

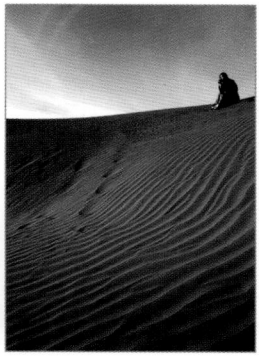

▲ High-contrast black-and-white or sepia images of people and landscapes can look very dramatic.

▶▶▶ Others Uses

There are two other less common situations for taking black-and-white images. First, if you need to take photos of documents or text, it is better to take the shot in black and white, as the high contrast makes the words easier to read. Second, you should note that black-and-white images take up less memory space, so if you do not have much memory left in your camera, you can consider taking black-and-white images.

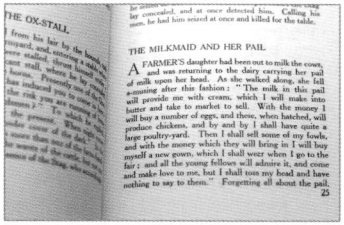

THE OX-STALL.

THE MILKMAID AND HER PAIL.

A FARMER'S daughter had been out to milk the cows, and was returning to the dairy carrying her pail of milk upon her head. As she walked along, she fell a-musing after this fashion: "The milk in this pail will provide me with cream, which I will make into butter and take to market to sell. With the money I will buy a number of eggs, and these, when hatched, will produce chickens, and by and by I shall have quite a large poultry-yard. Then I shall sell some of my fowls, and with the money which they will bring in I will buy myself a new gown, which I shall wear when I go to the fair; and all the young fellows will admire it, and come and make love to me, but I shall toss my head and have nothing to say to them." Forgetting all about the pail,

23

▲ The words in an image become easier to read if the image is in black and white.

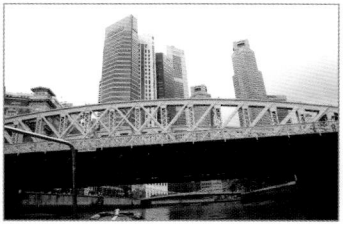

▲ The image size of this color photograph is 664KB.

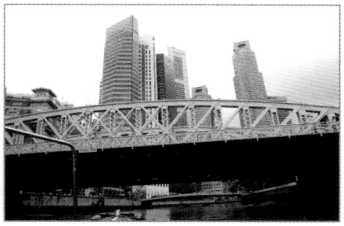

▲ The image size of the same photograph in black and white is 340KB.

11 Shooting Close-Ups of Small Objects

Another term for taking close-ups of small objects is macro photography. Macro photography can open up a whole new world by revealing amazing details of the things around you. Some possible subjects for close-up shots are flowers, insects, or water droplets. With a traditional film camera, you need a macro lens designed for taking close-up shots. Many digital cameras, though, have a Macro mode.

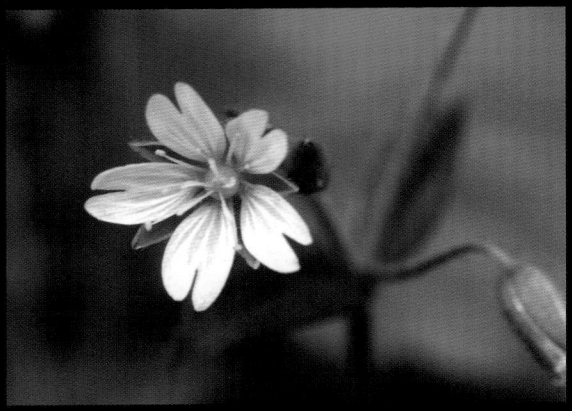

Definition

Strictly speaking, macro photography means that the subject is reproduced at a magnification of 1:1 or greater on the image. For example, if a petal is 1 cm long, its image will be 1 cm or larger. Macro photography is also used loosely to mean close-up photography.

Technical Requirements

▶▶▶ Focus

● Focal Length

The minimum focusing distance (focal length) of the lens determines how close you can get to the object. In order to get a good close-up, the focal length should ideally be 10 cm or less. Cameras with a good macro feature will allow you to get within 2 cm of the object. As the macro feature differs between cameras, you need to look up your camera's specifications in your user's manual.

tip Focal Length of Digital Cameras

Compared to traditional film cameras, most digital cameras have lenses with a shorter focal length, making them better for shooting close-ups.

- Focal Range

When shooting close-ups, the depth of field in your photos can drop greatly. This means that you have to work with a small focal range. For example, if you are taking a close-up of the dial pad on your cell phone, only some of the numbers on the dial pad will be in focus. This may or may not be the effect that you are looking for. Therefore, when using the Macro mode, you need to pay attention to the range where the object is in focus. You can, however, increase the focal range by closing up the aperture.

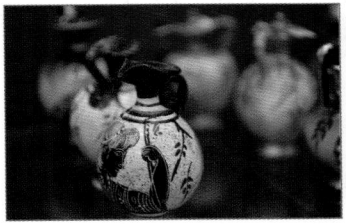

▲ Notice how this close-up looks fuzzy toward the edges.

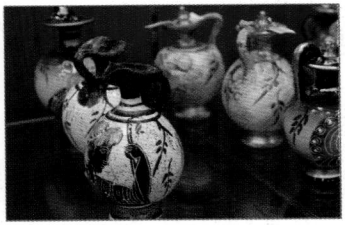

▲ Closing up the aperture increases the focal range and brings the edges back into focus.

▶▶▶ Lighting

Lighting conditions have a great impact on close-up shots taken indoors. Poor lighting conditions will make it difficult to focus on the object and your images will be underexposed. A single fluorescent lamp, for example, cannot light up a room sufficiently for a photo shoot.

- Built-In Flash

Using a digital camera's built-in flash for close-ups will overexpose the images, resulting in a loss of detail. You should use an external light source instead to get the right exposure and keep the detail in your photos.

- External Light Source

The most accessible type of external light source is a desk lamp. However, the regular incandescent (tungsten, for example) bulbs in these lamps will give a warm orange tone to your photos. In order to capture the natural color of your objects, use an inverter lamp, which emits light similar to daylight.

tip Intensity

When using an external light source, remember that brighter does not always mean better. You should adjust the light's intensity to enhance the object's texture and the mood of the photo. If necessary, use more than one lamp to get the desired effect.

● Angle

You must also consider the angle of the lighting. If the object is made of a reflective material, adjust the angle of the light so that the reflection is not apparent in the photo. Generally speaking, lighting the object from the side will highlight its texture and details.

▶▶▶ Background

A busy background detracts the focus from the main object. So, when shooting close-ups, you want to simplify the background as much as possible. One of the techniques is to use a background sheet. If the object is brightly colored, use a dark background sheet, but if the object is dark, use a light or brightly colored background sheet. When you use a backdrop, it is important to choose one that goes well with the objects you are shooting.

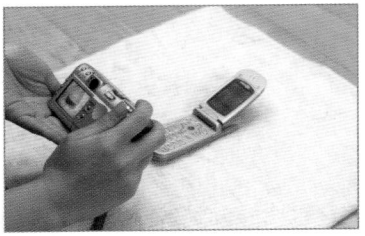

▲ Use a background sheet to simplify the background.

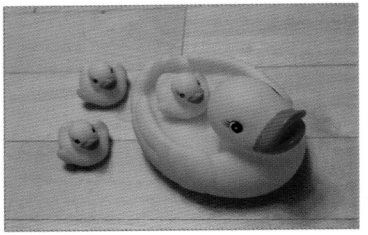

▲ Backdrop that does not go well with the object.

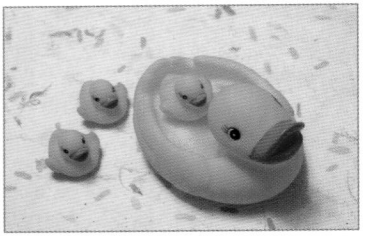

▲ Backdrop that works harmoniously with the object.

▶▶▶ Exposure

Taking an exposure reading on a small object can be tricky. You could end up with a reading of the background instead. To avoid this problem, use the more accurate Spot Metering mode when shooting close-ups.

▶▶▶ Using a Tripod

While shooting close-ups, the slightest movement or camera shake will give you a blurred photo. Therefore, you should always use a tripod whenever possible. A tabletop tripod is very useful for shooting close-up photos indoors.

Choosing a Theme

You have many options when it comes to choosing a subject for close-ups. You can take close-ups of flowers, insects, jewelry, or even documents and pictures. In this section, we will look at techniques for shooting some popular subjects for close-ups.

▶▶▶ Flowers

Flowers are a popular choice with most novice photographers. The main concern here is the wind factor. It can be hard to keep flowers or other objects that move in the wind in focus. If a flower doesn't stop swaying, use your hand or another object to hold it in place.

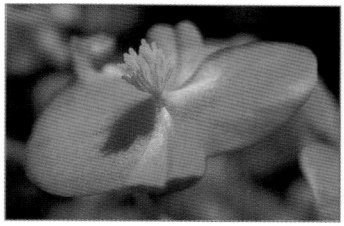

▲ Capturing the vivid colors of a flower using the Macro mode.

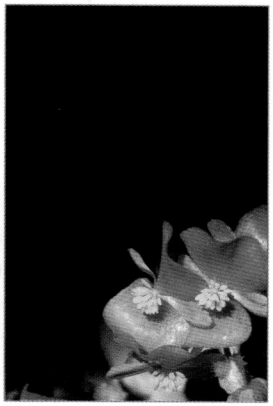

▲ A black background is used to keep the point of interest on the subject.

▶▶▶ Insects

Taking close-ups of insects is more difficult as they are usually small and mobile, making them challenging subjects. If you approach an insect slowly and quietly, you may be able to get a quick shot before it gets away.

An alternative method is to place your camera on a tripod and set it to focus on a spot likely to attract insects, such as a flower. Wait at a distance away from the camera. When the insect moves into place, use the camera's remote control to take the shot. You can take multiple shots with this setup and later choose the best photo from the lot.

You need good observation skills and some practice in order to take good close-ups of fast-moving insects. For beginners, it is best to practice photographing slower insects.

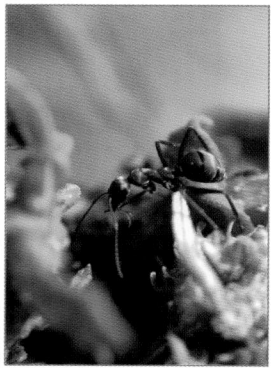

▲ Taking photos of ants requires super macro focal lengths of 5 cm or less.

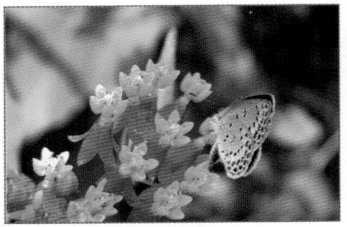
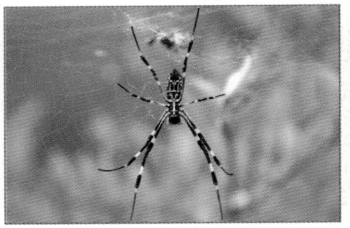
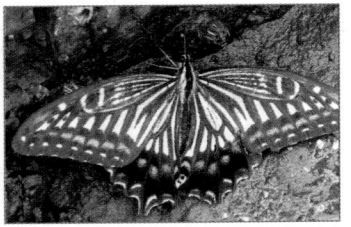

▲ Taking photos of butterflies or other insects requires patience and practice.

Documents

You can photograph documents of up to A4 size if you are using a digital camera with a high resolution. This feature is useful, for instance, when you find a good passage in a book and you need to make a copy for your own notes. But before you photograph documents, take note of any restrictions and copyright laws, and be wary of infringing upon any rights.

For good results, you should always use a tripod and illuminate the documents with an external light source. Dim surroundings will underexpose the photos and make the images fuzzy. Additionally, check that the page is properly secured and place the camera vertically over the page. You can photograph several pages at once or, if you want better-quality images, shoot a page in sections.

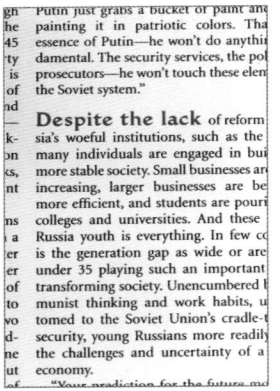

Putin just grabs a bucket of paint and
painting it in patriotic colors. Tha
essence of Putin—he won't do anythi
damental. The security services, the pol
prosecutors—he won't touch these elem
the Soviet system."

Despite the lack of reform
sia's woeful institutions, such as the
many individuals are engaged in bui
more stable society. Small businesses ar
increasing, larger businesses are be
more efficient, and students are pouri
colleges and universities. And these
Russia youth is everything. In few c
is the generation gap as wide or are
under 35 playing such an important
transforming society. Unencumbered b
munist thinking and work habits, u
tomed to the Soviet Union's cradle-t
security, young Russians more readily
the challenges and uncertainty of a
economy.

▲ Photo of a document.

Barrel Distortion

When you take a close-up of a shape with distinct outlines (documents, for example), you will sometimes see it bending or rounding at the edges in the photo. This phenomenon is known as barrel distortion and is an inevitable consequence of a camera's zoom lens.

Many photos taken with digital and compact film cameras that have zoom capabilities suffer from barrel distortion. For example, with a 35–105 mm zoom lens, barrel distortion is most pronounced when the lens is set at 35 mm. To reduce barrel distortion, you should set the lens at 70 mm or somewhere in the middle of the zoom range, or set the camera to Macro mode when you want to take close-ups of small objects.

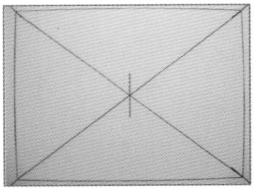

▲ Barrel distortion at a wide angle.

12 Taking Continuous Shots

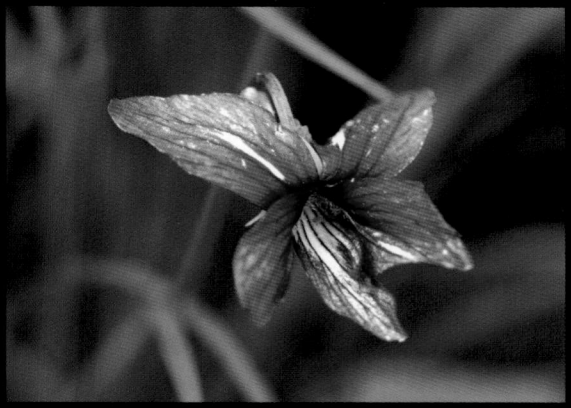

Many digital and film cameras have a Continuous Shot function, which allows you to take several photos in succession within a few seconds. Because you do not have to worry about wasting film in digital cameras, you can use this feature more often than you would with a film camera.

Understanding the Continuous Shot Feature

To shoot continuous photos, switch to the Continuous Shot mode and hold down the shutter-release button. After the shots are taken, the camera will take some time to record all the shots. During this time, the camera is in limbo and you cannot use it to take another shot. There are three factors to consider when evaluating or comparing the Continuous Shot function:

▶▶▶ Frames Per Second (FPS)

This is the number of photos that can be taken every second. Most digital cameras can take 2 or 3 photos per second, but high-end ones can take 10 to 15 per second.

▶▶▶ Maximum Number of Continuous Shots

This is the maximum number of continuous shots the camera can take while the shutter button is pressed. A maximum of "15 shots recorded at 3 fps," for example, means that the camera can take continuous shots for up to 5 seconds at the rate of 3 frames per second.

▶▶▶ Speed and Quality of Continuous Shots

Image resolution and quality are inversely related to the number of consecutive pictures that can be taken. For example, lowering the image resolution of a camera that takes a maximum of 15 pictures at 2 fps could increase the maximum number of pictures to 20 and improve the speed to 3 fps. Conversely, increasing the image resolution will result in fewer pictures taken and a slower fps rate. Check your user manual for your Continuous Shot function's speed and quality. It will read something like "2 fps at maximum resolution."

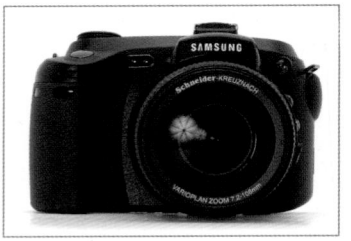

▲ The Samsung Pro 815 can shoot 10 fps in High Speed mode.

When to Use Continuous Shots

▶▶▶ Fast-Moving Subjects

The challenge of shooting fast-moving subjects is capturing them at the right moment. With the Continuous Shot feature, you can take successive shots of a single scene very quickly, select the ones you like best, and delete the rest. This increases your chances of getting a well-composed image of fast-moving objects or people, such as a train roaring past, a bird in flight, or an active child.

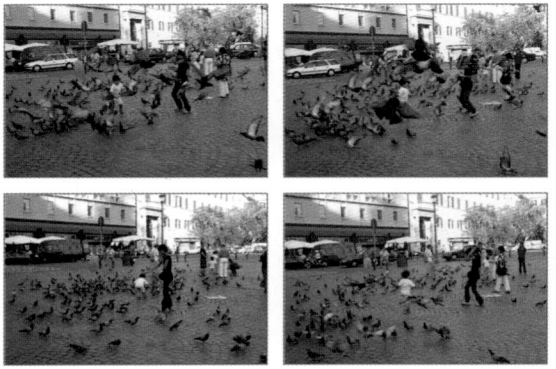

▲ Subjects moving randomly are hard to compose and keep in focus.

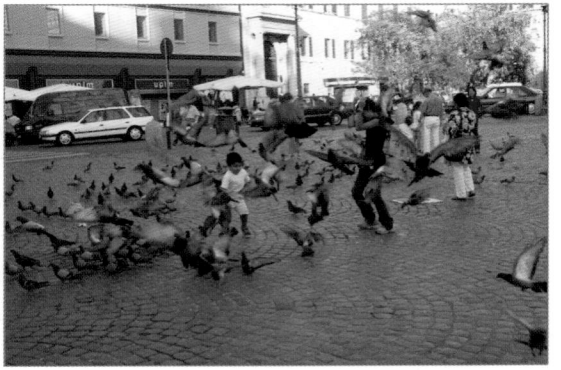

▲ Choose the best photo from the selection.

▶▶▶ Action Sequences

This feature is also useful for capturing the full sequence of a subject's motion. You may, for instance, want to record the fleeting expressions of a baby, or give a blow-by-blow account of a sports event in photos. You might ask a friend to take continuous shots of your golf swing so you can review and correct your posture.

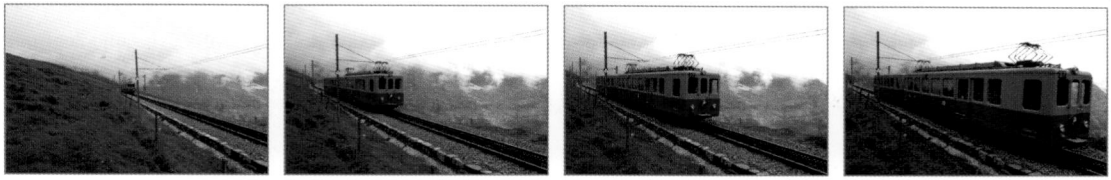

▲ Use the Continuous Shot feature to capture the train at the right distance.

Using the Continuous Shot Feature

▶▶▶ Lighting

Typically, the built-in flash is disabled during the Continuous Shot mode. If it is not, you should turn it off. This is because the flash cannot keep up with the speed of the continuous shots, so it will only be activated for the initial shot, leaving the rest underexposed.

With no flash, you have to make sure that the scene is sufficiently lit before shooting. If you are shooting indoors, use an external light source to improve the lighting conditions. If possible, you should also set the camera to a high ISO value for greater light sensitivity.

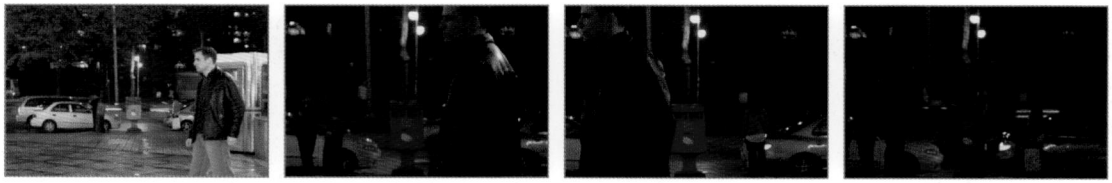

▲ The flash was activated in only the first of these four continuous shots.

▶▶▶ Shutter Speed

In most cameras, the shutter speed is automatically set to 1/30 second or faster to prevent motion blur. If you can adjust the shutter speed, set it to a minimum of 1/100 second when shooting fast-moving subjects.

▶▶▶ Auto Focus (AF) Mode

If you take continuous shots in the AF mode, the camera needs time to auto focus each shot and this can lower the speed at which your camera takes consecutive photos. If you know the direction your subject is traveling, pre-focus at a point in the frame and press the shutter when your subject comes into frame.

Other Types of Continuous Shots

Other than the Continuous Shot feature, some digital cameras have other modes—such as Auto Exposure Bracketing, Best Shot Selector, or Interval mode—that take continuous shots. These shots are different from those taken in the Continuous Shot mode in terms of quality, exposure, interval, or size, as they are meant to be used differently.

▶▶▶ Auto Exposure Bracketing (AEB)

The camera will shoot at three different exposures in three continuous shots when you use Auto Exposure Bracketing. For example, if the AEB is set to 1 stop, the camera will take the first shot at its recommended exposure, underexpose the second shot by 1 stop, and overexpose the third by 1 stop.

The AEB feature is good for situations where the light condition changes constantly, or when it is difficult to determine the exposure through the LCD.

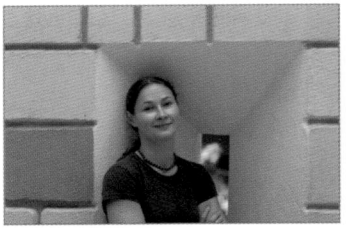

▲ Recommended exposure.

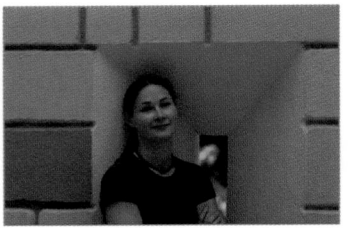

▲ 1 stop underexposure.

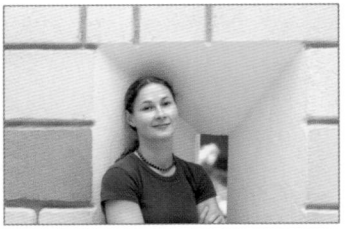

▲ 1 stop overexposure.

tip The AEB function, which is found in most digital cameras, sets the white balance, light sensitivity, and exposure automatically.

▶▶▶ Best Shot Selector

In the Continuous Shot mode, the camera will take consecutive shots up to the maximum number of shots supported by the camera as long as the shutter button is pressed down. If you use the Best Shot Selector, the camera will only save three or four of the sharper and better images to the memory card. This feature is recommended when you have difficulty getting the correct exposure and white balance for stationary subjects.

▶▶▶ Interval Mode

When using the Interval mode, you need to set the shutter-release interval. When the shutter-release button is pressed, the camera will take continuous shots according to the interval setting. The interval range can be between a few seconds to a few minutes. For best results, you should use a tripod.

Unlike the Continuous Shot mode, the Interval mode can only be found in high-end digital cameras. This mode is great for capturing the action sequence of slow-moving subjects like a snail moving along or a flower beginning to bloom. The feature is not designed to capture fast-moving subjects.

▶▶▶ Nikon's Multi-Shot 16 Feature

Nikon's digital cameras are programmed with a Continuous Shot feature called the Multi-Shot 16. In this mode, you shoot 16 consecutive thumbnail pictures by pressing the shutter button just once. Instead of saving them as separate, individual images, these thumbnails are combined on a single image like a collage.

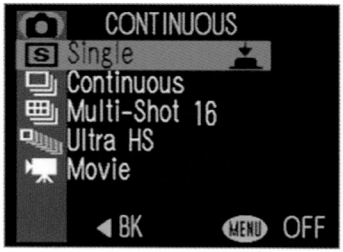

▲ Nikon's Multi-Shot 16 mode.

13 Taking Action Shots

In this section, you will learn to capture a freeze frame of a moving subject. For beginners, this can be challenging. In terms of equipment, you will need at least a semiautomatic camera to consistently make a moving subject look sharp and focused in action shots. With automatic cameras, it is often a hit-or-miss affair. Action shots are also challenging technically. This section will cover the essential techniques of action photography.

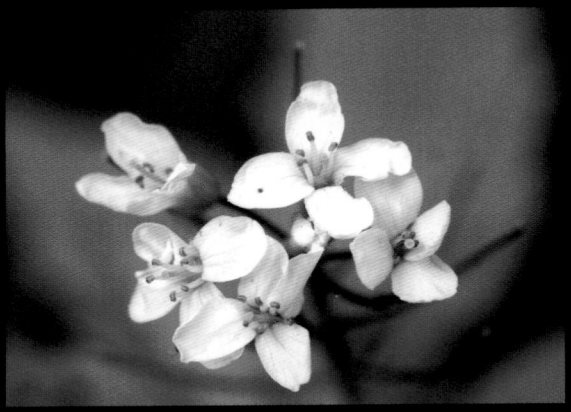

Stance

It is always important that you keep still while taking a shot, especially when you are shooting a moving subject, as the slightest movement will result in a blurred image. Adopt the positions we looked at in Technique 2, "Preventing Camera Shake and Blurring," or use a tripod.

Shutter Speed

For most moving subjects, you need to use a shutter speed of 1/250 second or faster. The shutter speed can be set using the Shutter Priority or Manual modes. Alternatively, you can set a large aperture using the Aperture Priority mode to force the camera to use a fast shutter speed to prevent overexposure. An aperture of *f*/2.8 or wider (i.e., smaller f-number) is usually large enough. With an automatic camera, you should switch to the Sports Scene mode ( ). You are more likely to take good action shots with the Sports Scene mode if the shot is taken in bright surroundings. The brightness will let the camera use a faster shutter speed.

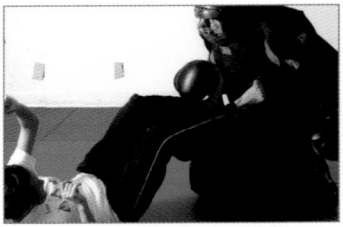

▲ To capture the right moment in sports photography, you need to keep your eyes behind the camera for the duration of the event. This shot was taken using a shutter speed of 1/250 second.

Sensitivity

If you can't get a fast enough shutter speed, you can try raising the camera's sensitivity to light so that the camera needs less light to be properly exposed, allowing a faster shutter speed. Because increasing the sensitivity introduces noise into your picture, this method should only be used as a last resort.

Panning and Tilting

To create a sense of movement in a picture, you can set a slow shutter speed and then move the camera using your hand or a tripod as a pivot to follow the subject's movement as you shoot. This will keep the subject in focus while blurring the background along the movement of your camera.

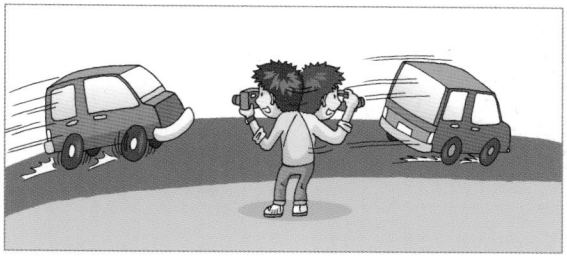

Moving the camera along the horizontal axis is called panning, while tilting moves the camera vertically. The key to keeping a moving subject sharp while blurring the background is to follow the subject at the same pace that it is moving.

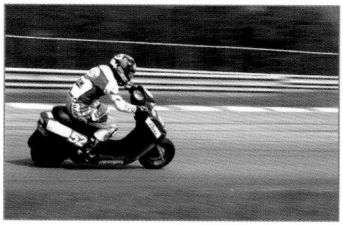

▲ Panning gives an image the sensation of movement.

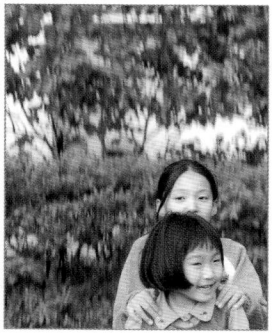

▲ Tilting is used here to take a picture of kids on a seesaw.

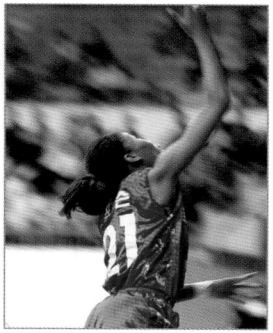

▲ This shot uses both panning and tilting.

When panning or tilting, you can adjust the amount of blur in the background by changing the focal length of the lens and the shutter speed. The amount of blur is also dependent on the subject's speed, the distance between the camera and the subject, and the distance between the subject and the background. A very blurry background gives the impression that subject is moving at a high speed.

▶▶▶ Focal Length

To create a more blurry background, you can use a telephoto lens or zoom in to fill your frame with the subject. When the view is magnified, moving the camera will blur the background even more. Conversely, zooming out will make the subject smaller in the frame and create a background with less blur.

▶▶▶ Shutter Speed

Another way of creating a more blurry background is to use a slow shutter speed while moving the camera. With slow shutter speeds, the subject would have moved a fair distance during the shutter release. This will allow you to pan more and create more blur in the background. With faster shutter speeds, the object wouldn't have moved much so the background will not be as blurred. When using slow shutter speeds, you want to be able to keep up with the subject. If you are unable to follow the subject with the camera, the subject will end up looking blurred too.

To photograph moving motor vehicles, a shutter speed of 1/60 second is usually long enough to blur out the background. To photograph a person walking, a shutter speed of 1/30 second (or greater, if you are able to keep up with the person without causing camera shake) is adequate.

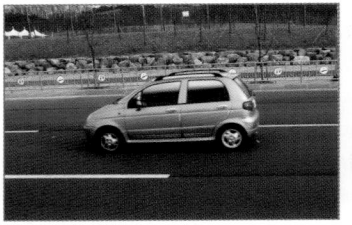

▲ Unsuccessful attempt at a panning effect due to shutter speed being too fast (1/500 sec).

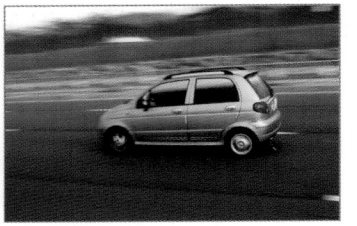

▲ Panning effect used successfully, thanks to an appropriate choice of shutter speed (1/60 sec).

▶▶▶ Object Speed

A fast-moving object requires you to move the camera quickly, and this in turns create more blur in the background.

▶▶▶ Distance

The distance between the subject and the background is another factor to consider. The greater this distance, the less blurry will be the background in the picture. Let's think about this for a minute. Say your camera is following the movement of a car and the background is a mountain in a distance. In this case, since the mountain is so far away, the relative position of the mountain hardly changes during the shutter release, resulting in less blur in the background. On the other hand, if you're taking a picture of a car whizzing through the city streets, the buildings in the background will show up in the picture as a complete blur.

14 Using White Balance

When professional photographers assess the lighting conditions of a location, the intensity of the light source is not the only factor they consider. This is because a shot of two equally lit scenes can look quite different with one looking warmer and the other cooler. This has to do with the color temperature of the light source. By using the White Balance feature on your digital camera, you can offset the color casts created by a light source's color temperature.

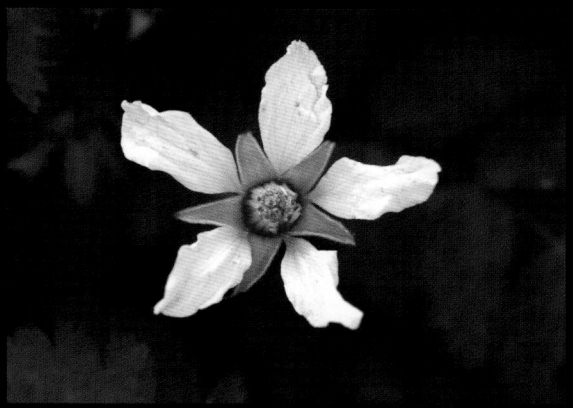

Properties of Light

▶▶▶ Natural and Artificial Light

Light from the sun is natural light. Examples of artificial light sources are incandescent light, fluorescent light, and flash from the camera. Light from the sun or from a light bulb may appear white or colorless to you. However, if you pass the light through a prism, you can see that it actually contains a range of colors, as in a rainbow. Light from different sources contains a mixture of these colors in varying proportions, with each light source having its own distinct color.

▶▶▶ Color Temperature

The color of a light source is best described by its color temperature, which is calibrated in degrees Kelvin (°K). Color temperature is a term borrowed from physics and is used to measure the quality of a light source. As the color temperature gets higher, the color moves from red toward blue.

In photography, the term daylight is used to describe the color temperature of sunlight between 10 a.m. and 2 p.m., which is about 5500°K. The color temperature of a tungsten light bulb is about 3000°K. Therefore, we say that daylight is much bluer than the light from a tungsten bulb, which has a reddish tint.

What Is White Balance?

Our eyes automatically adjust to different color temperatures so that a white piece of paper always looks white whether we view it by sunlight or incandescent light. Unlike the human eye, the image sensor in digital cameras records the color temperature of a light source, and this will appear in the photo as a color cast.

For example, if a scene is illuminated by a tungsten light bulb, the image will have an orange cast. The image sensor, therefore, has to be adjusted according to the color temperature of the light source in order to reproduce the colors in the scene accurately.

You can make this adjustment using the White Balance feature, which records the current lighting conditions or color temperature. The camera then adjusts the sensor's relative sensitivity to the colors so that the whites in the scene will also appear white in the image.

White Balance Modes

White is most accurately reproduced on clear days, which is why photos taken in sunlight preserve the natural color of objects. Under other lighting conditions, you need to select one of the White Balance modes for accurate results. Before you shoot, earmark a white piece of paper, area, or object in the scene as a reference point.
Next, select a White Balance mode and preview the results on the LCD monitor. Try a few modes until you get the result you want. Here's what the different modes are for:

▶▶▶ Auto

Adjusts the white balance automatically for lights with a color temperature between 4200°K and 7000°K. If the color temperature falls outside this range, the colors in the captured image may differ from the actual colors.

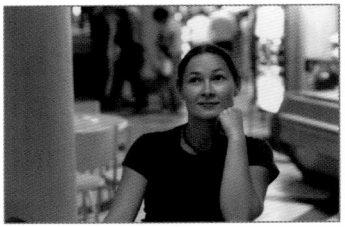

▲ Auto White Balance.

▶▶▶ Incandescent (Tungsten light)

Corrects the color of objects shot under incandescent lights. Color temperature is fixed at approximately 3000°K.

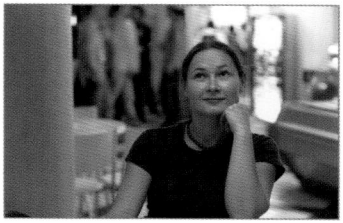

▲ Tungsten White Balance mode.

▶▶▶ Fluorescent

Corrects the color of objects shot under fluorescent lights. Color temperature is fixed at approximately 4500°K.

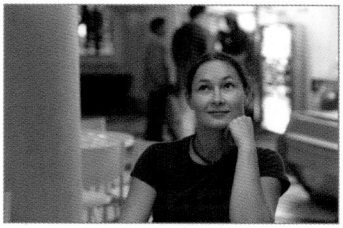

▲ Fluorescent White Balance mode.

▶▶▶ Daylight

This setting is programmed for taking pictures in direct sunlight on a clear day. Color temperature is fixed at approximately 6000°K. When taking photos outdoors on a clear day, both the Auto and Fine White Balance modes will preserve the natural skin tone.

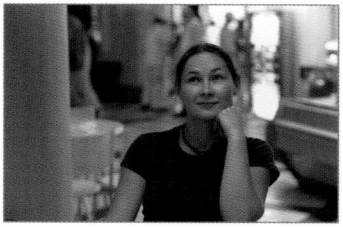

▲ Daylight White Balance mode.

▶▶▶ Cloudy

Programmed for shooting pictures under an overcast sky. Color temperature is fixed at approximately 7000° – 8000°K.

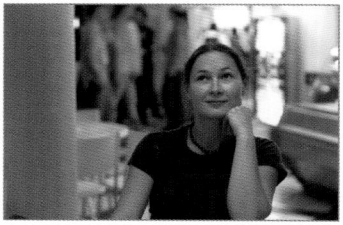

▲ Cloudy White Balance mode.

▶▶▶ Custom

Enables you to adjust the white balance manually to match the lighting conditions. If the weather is bad, or if you are taking photos indoors or under colored lights, the best way to reproduce accurate colors is to preset the Custom White Balance mode using a white piece of paper or any white objects.

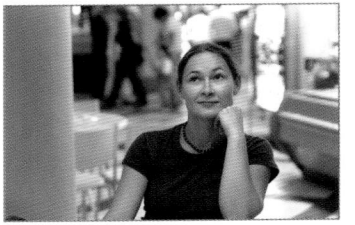

▲ Custom White Balance mode helps to maintain the natural skin tone.

tip Setting Optimal White Balance

Every color has a tonal value that tells us how bright or how dark a color is. On one end of the scale is pure white and on the other, pure black. The purpose of using a white piece of paper or any white object to set the Custom White Balance mode is to introduce a known color to the camera so that it can match what it sees on the paper to the actual color value. Before you customize the white balance, check that:

- The paper and the subject receive the same illumination.
- Your shadow is not cast over the paper.
- The paper shows through the entire frame.

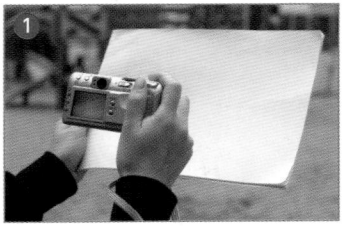

▲ Take a photo of a white piece of paper.

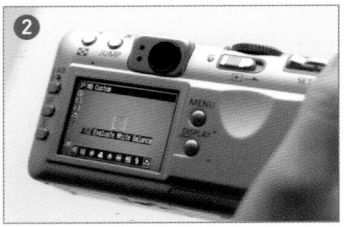

▲ Turn the dial to Custom White Balance or Manual White Balance mode, and load the photo of the white piece of paper to preset the white balance.

Choosing the Correct Mode

If you use the wrong White Balance mode, the colors in the photo will be different from the actual scene. For example, if you use the daylight mode, pictures taken under tungsten lights will appear reddish, while pictures taken on a cloudy day will appear bluish.

In order to preserve the natural color of objects, you need to choose the White Balance mode to match the color temperature of the light source.

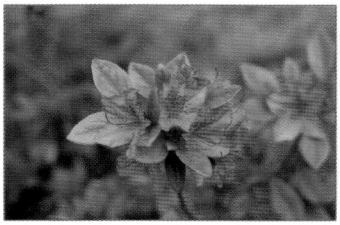

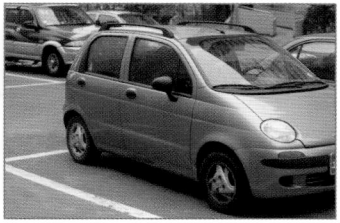

▲ White balance set for direct sunlight.

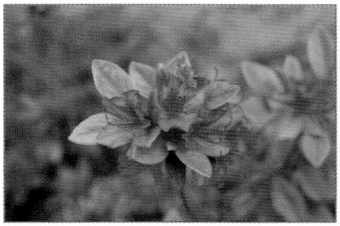

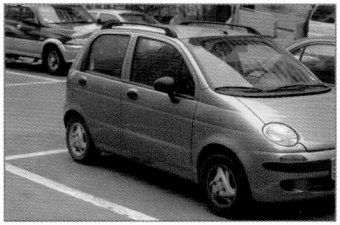

▲ White balance set for incandescent lighting.

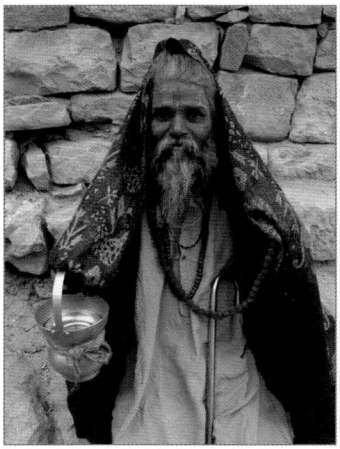

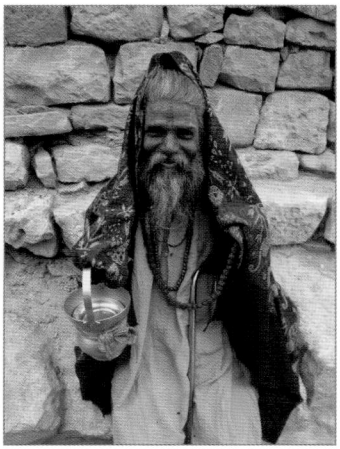

▲ You can take people photos with a variety of types of color balance, if you use white balance properly.

Using White Balance in Landscape Photography

By experimenting with the White Balance modes on your camera, you can change the colors of your landscape photos, giving them a different ambience and mood.

▶ The Incandescent mode adds a bluish tint to photos taken at dawn, giving them a cool look.

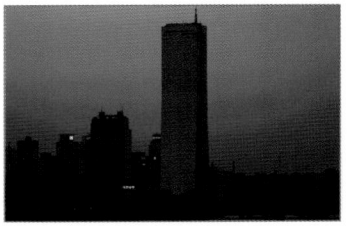

▶ The Flash mode adds a warm orange tone to a photo. It can be used to enhance the glow of the rising or setting sun.

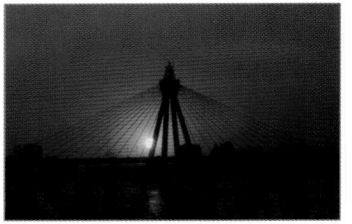

▶ By selecting the Custom mode and programming the camera to perceive a colored piece of paper as white, you can produce some unusual landscape photos. In this photo, the white balance was customized using a yellow piece of paper.

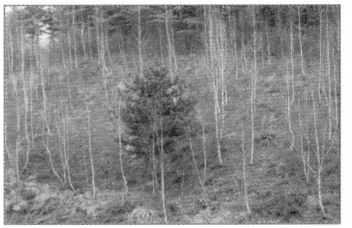

Chapter 2 | Advanced Features

- √ Use angled lighting for a more balanced, three-dimensional effect.
- √ Avoid direct light and backlighting.
- √ Try taking pictures of people and objects on cloudy days or in the shade.
- √ Note that the time of day will affect the colors in your shot.
- √ Turn off the flash if you don't need it.
- √ Take a profile shot if you are using a flash to shoot your subject in low light. This will prevent red-eye syndrome.
- √ Use a diffuser, omni-bounce, reflector, or everyday object, such as a piece of tissue, to soften the flash, if necessary.
- √ Consider using the Black-and-White and Sepia modes for a change of style.
- √ When shooting close-ups of small objects, remember not to get closer than your camera's minimum focusing distance.
- √ Try using the Continuous Shot function to capture fast-moving subjects and action sequences.
- √ Be sensitive to the light source's color temperature and adjust the white balance if necessary.

40 Digital Photography Techniques

Chapter 3

Photographing People

People are often the most fascinating and difficult subjects to capture in photography. Besides fussing over the usual things, such as focus, exposure, lighting, placement, and color, a good portrait photographer must be able to capture the character and personality of the person in the shot. For novice photographers, taking photos of family and friends is the easiest and most rewarding way to start photographing people. In this chapter, let's begin by learning to take photos of your loved ones and the people around you.

15 Taking Better People Photos

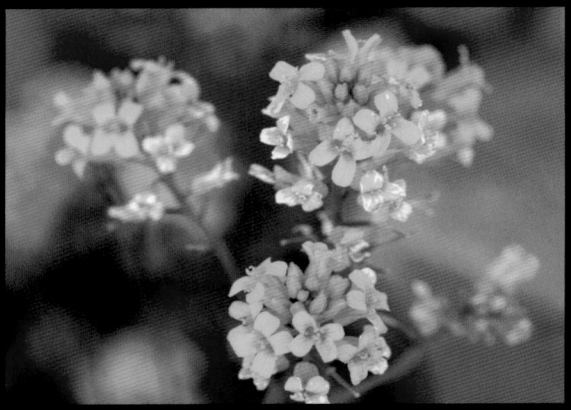

This section focuses on the essential skills and techniques that you will find useful for taking all kinds of people shots. It also explains the common mistakes made by beginners and shows you how to avoid them. We will cover such topics as background, pose, gaze, lighting, angle of view, and group photos.

Take Close-Ups

When taking photos of people, it is important to simplify the background so as to keep the focus on the subject. Taking close-ups of people will minimize a cluttered background and maintain the viewers' focus on the subject.

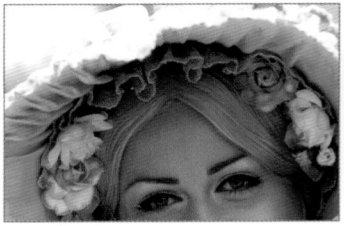

▲ Portrait shots need not include the entire face. You can study the subject's face and take a close-up of the most striking feature.

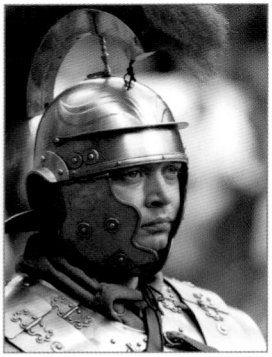

▲ Close-ups keep the person as the center of attention.

Make the Subject Feel Comfortable

People naturally tense up in front of the camera and start posing for the shoot. You should encourage your subjects to relax and adopt a pose that they feel comfortable with. It helps if you are friendly, sociable, and enthusiastic about taking their photos. This will produce more natural photos and make the photo shoot a lot more enjoyable for everyone involved.

Instead of shoving the camera in your subject's face, break the ice with an introduction and some lighthearted conversation. Because you can get great candid shots while your subject is chatting, laughing, or in the midst of doing something, you have to develop a discerning eye for candid moments, and learn to jump on photographic opportunities immediately.

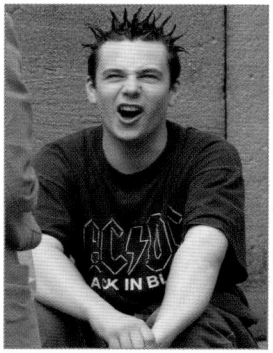

▲ You can only get natural shots if the subject feels comfortable around you.

Focus on the Eyes

The saying that the eyes are the windows to the soul may seem overworked and cliché, but it really applies to portraiture. A subject's gaze focuses our attention and is undoubtedly the most appealing element in a portrait. Perhaps it is because of this that many novices take photos with the subject looking straight at the camera. These front profile shots are common—perhaps too common—but they do not bring out the best in some subjects.

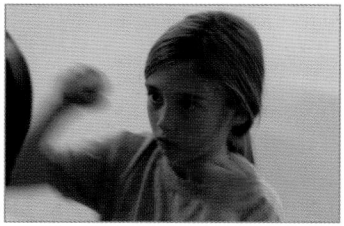

▲ Focus on your subject's eyes to capture her emotions and mental state.

Some people have more photogenic side profiles. Ask your subject to turn his head at a 45° angle, and capture his features in a better light. Remember to focus on the eye closest to the camera in order to draw your viewer's interest.

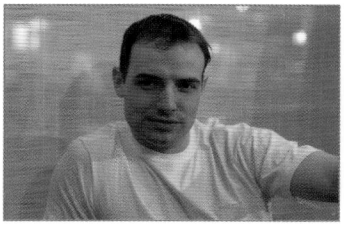

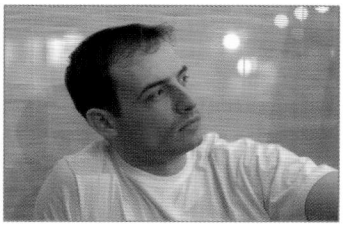

▲ Ask your subject to turn his head at a 45° angle if he has a good side profile.

There are many styles you can explore, but here are two to start with:

- Shoot at an angle of 45° from behind a subject who is looking at something else. The effect of this framing suggests a sense of longing and desire in the subject.
- When taking photos of two or more people, have each person look in a different direction. This has the effect of creating leading lines along their gazes, resulting in a dynamic photo.

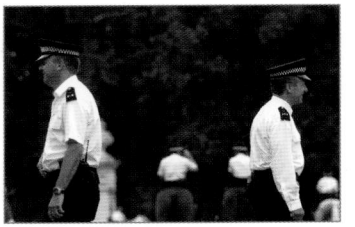

▲ Getting your subjects to look away from each other can produce an unusual composition.

Avoid Reflected Colors

If your subject is standing near a reflective, colored surface, the light hitting the surface may reflect a color cast onto the subject, creating unnatural skin tones. You should always check that your subjects are standing away from highly reflective surfaces like cars, mirrors, or metallic backgrounds.

Lighting

▶▶▶ Avoid Harsh Shadows

If the sunlight is casting shadows on the subject's face or if the lighting is making the subject look flat or two-dimensional, use a reflector to soften the light and prevent harsh shadows. Another method is to position the subject such that the subject's face is illuminated from the side. You can also use additional lighting such as a flash to fill in the shadows.

▶▶▶ Avoid Direct Light

Avoid light that shines directly on the subject. People with pronounced cheekbones, in particular, should avoid having their photos taken under the midday sun. The direct light will produce deep shadows under their eyes and cheeks. It will also make them squint. Photos taken on cloudy days or in the shade are most ideal because the light is softer and more flattering on the face. When taking photos in the shade, however, becareful to avoid having shadows cast over the subject's face.

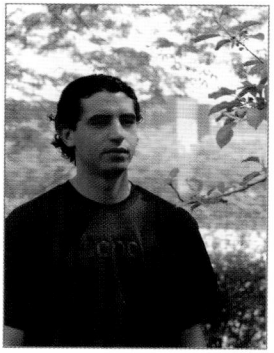

▲ A subject placed under the shade of a tree can end up with shadows on his face.

▶▶▶ Oblique or Side Lighting

Oblique or side lighting can add contours and depth to your subject's face. But overdoing it can produce harsh shadows and make the eyes appear sunken.

▶▶▶ Backlighting

Backlighting is a good way to emphasize the form and shape of your subject and separate him or her from the background. Backlighting is perfect for taking silhouettes of buildings, objects, and people.

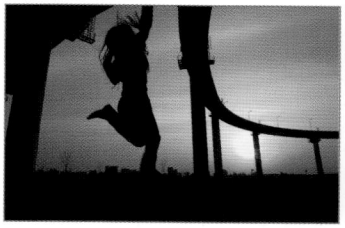

▲ Silhouettes taken at sunset.

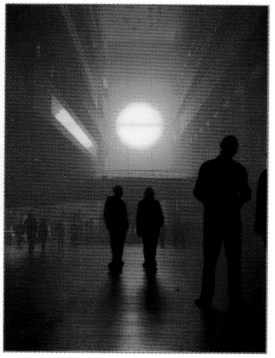

▶ An installation piece inside an art gallery provided a great opportunity for a silhouette shot. The sun that you see in the picture is the installation art.

Background

▶▶▶ Simplifying the Background

In situations where you have to include the background, try to keep it as simple as possible. Cluttered or messy backgrounds make for confusing photos, drawing attention away from the people in the photos. To further minimize the background, the light hitting the background should ideally be slightly dimmer than the light illuminating the subject.

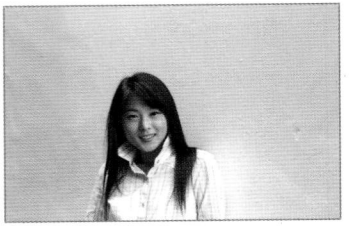

▲ Simplify the background to highlight your subject.

▶▶▶ Shooting Meaningful Backdrops

On the other hand, the background need not always be removed or kept simple. A setting that reflects the character and personality of the subject is more meaningful and will strengthen the appeal of the image. Try to take a shot with the subject assuming a natural expression and pose in her natural surroundings. But check that the surroundings do not overpower the subject visually.

The Focus Lock feature is great for shooting this sort of image. For instance, if you want the subject to be in focus, but not centered and blocking most of the background, press the shutter-release button lightly to focus on the subject first. Then move to the side to show more of the background.

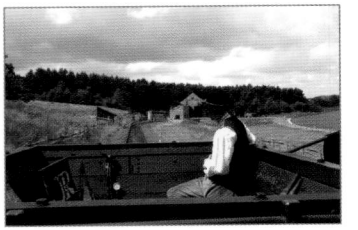

▲ A photo like this captures the character and personality of the subject.

Body Shape

Many people are dissatisfied with the way they look in photos. But the camera can minimize these flaws, in the hands of a skilled photographer. The popular refrain, "the camera doesn't lie," is really a lie. The camera lies all the time.

If you shoot your subjects from a flattering angle, you can change the appearance of their body. Taking photos of overweight people from the side, for example, will make them look slimmer. Other techniques include taking photos of underweight people from the front, tall people at eye level, and short people from below.

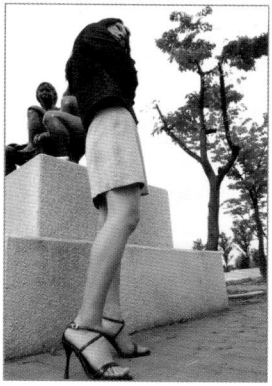

▲ Photo of a short person taken from below.

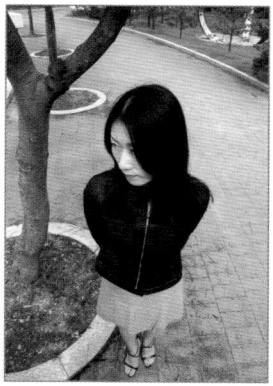

▲ Photo of a short person taken from above.

Group Photos

Sometimes you will have one or two people who close their eyes or look the other way in group photos. There are two things you could do to alleviate this problem. Instead of just taking one photo, take a few photos in succession and choose the best one. Alternately, instead of lining everyone up for a posed shot, try taking photos of the group while everyone's carrying on with their activities.

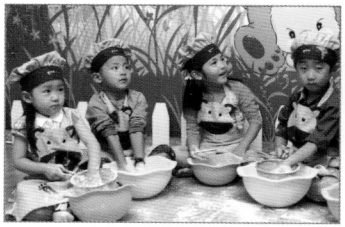

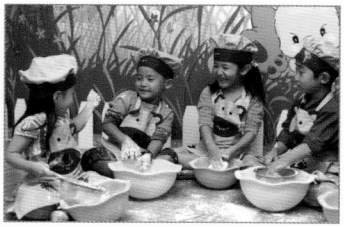

▲ Take a few shots in succession and choose the best one.

16 Changing the Camera Distance and Angle

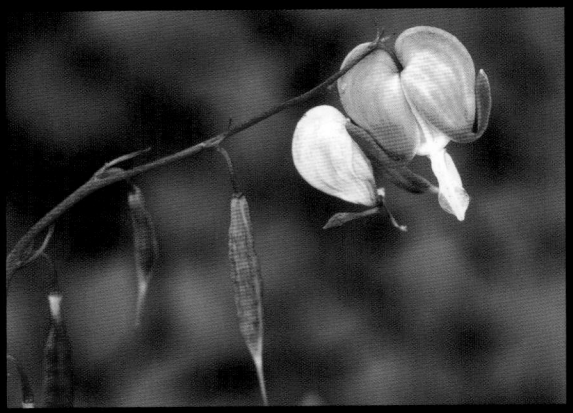

In this section, you will discover how the distance and angle of the camera can determine the photo's emphasis and the viewer's impression of the subject.

Camera-to-Subject Distance

Changing the camera-to-subject distance will change the perspective in an image. As the camera moves closer to the subject, the subject appears to increase in size relative to the background. As you move farther away from the subject, the subject becomes smaller relative to the background and the focus is shifted to the background or another part of the photo.

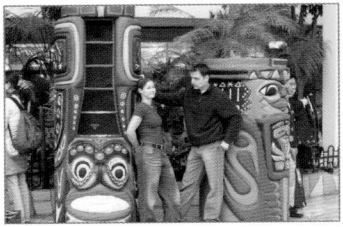

▲ A long shot emphasizes the background in the photo.

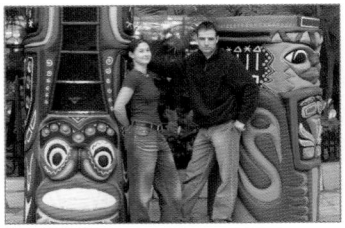

▲ A full body shot emphasizes both the subjects and the background.

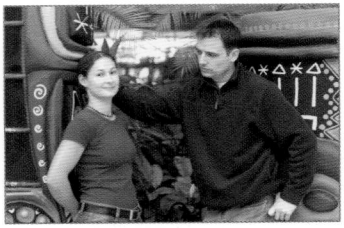

▲ A shot from the waist up gives more emphasis to the subjects.

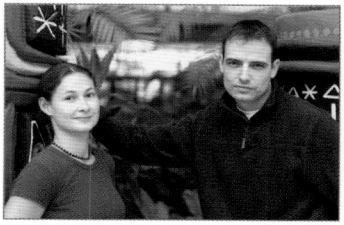

▲ A shot from the chest up removes most of the background.

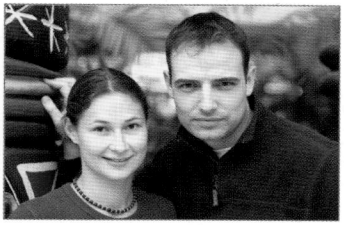

▲ A close-up gives the viewer a feeling of intimacy.

Camera Angle

The camera angle refers to the position at which the camera is aimed at the subject. The most common angle is at the eye level of the subject. You can also take the photo from above or below the subject's eye level. You should experiment and practice with different angles to find the angle that best enhances your subject.

In most photos of people, especially infants and children, the photographer takes the photo at the subject's eye level. This gives the viewer a sense of closeness and familiarity with the subject. Shooting from above or below the subject's eye level creates completely different effects. Shooting from above makes the subject appear small and diminutive, while shooting from below makes the subject look strong and powerful.

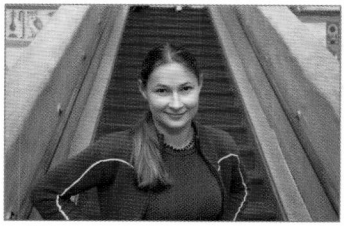

▲ Eye level shots create a sense of closeness and familiarity.

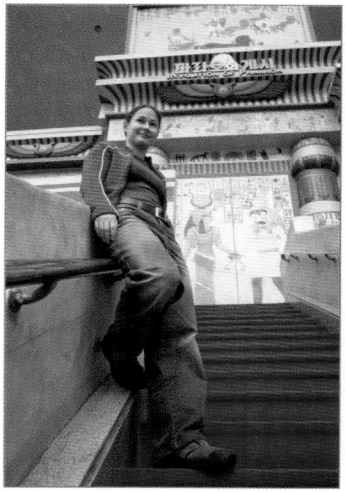

▲ Below eye level makes the subject appear strong and powerful.

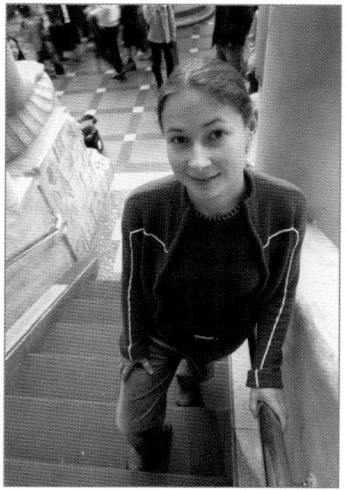

▲ Above eye level makes the subject appear diminutive and weak.

17 Using Selective Focus

When taking photos of people, you have to decide if the background is central to the theme of your photo. Is it a scenic spot or an important landmark? Does it say something about the subject? For portrait shots, many photographers choose to blur the background to keep the point of interest on the subject and create a soft, dreamy look. This technique is called selective focusing and there are a few ways of doing it.

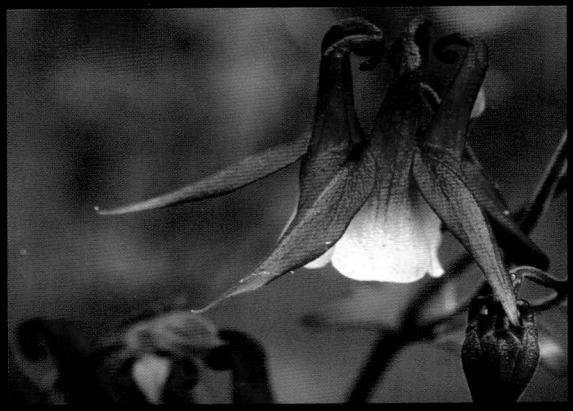

Adjusting the Aperture

Set your camera to the Aperture Priority mode if you have a manual or semiautomatic camera, and open up the aperture as much as possible in order to get a shallow depth of field and a blurred background. Once you have set the camera to the desired aperture value, the camera will automatically adjust the shutter speed for the appropriate exposure.

If your camera is fully automatic, you can activate the Character mode or Portrait mode to create the same effect.

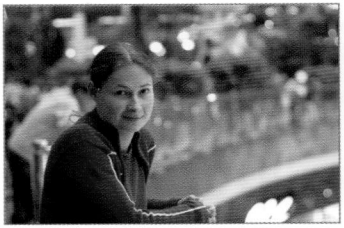

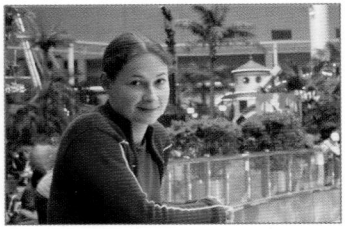

▲ Compare the range of focus between a shot taken with a big aperture (left image; *f*/2.0) and one shot with a small aperture (right image; *f*/8.0).

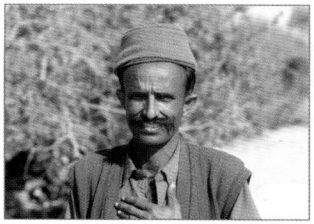

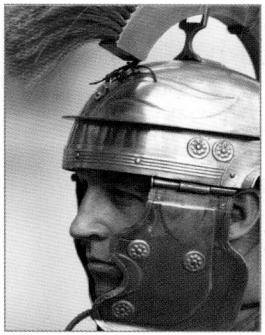

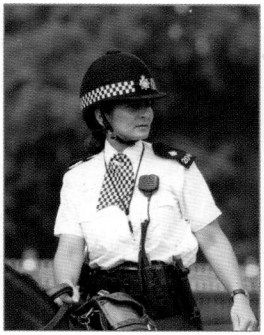

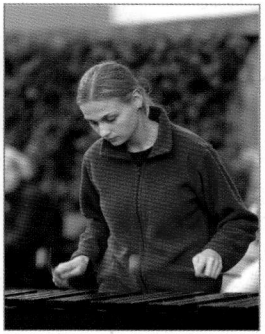

▲ ▶ Examples of selective-focus photography.

Using a Telephoto Lens

Another way of shooting selective-focused photos is to use a telephoto lens. Compared to wide-angle lenses, telephoto lenses have longer focal lengths and shallower depth of field. If you are using a zoom lens, zoom in to the telephoto range of the lens or set your camera to the Telephoto setting. For example, if you are using the ubiquitous 35–105 mm zoom lens, set the lens to 70 mm or above.

If you are using an automatic camera, you can selectively focus by setting the camera to the Close-Up Scene mode and zooming in to the Telephoto setting.

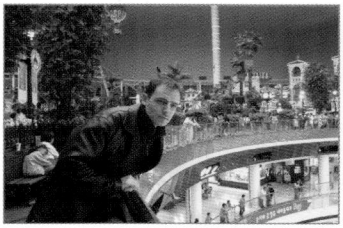

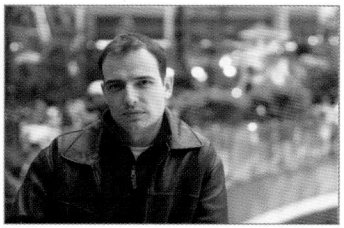

▲ A comparison of selective-focused photos taken using a wide-angle and a telephoto lens.

Using Selective Focus with Compact Digital Cameras

With a single-lens reflex (SLR) digital camera, you can preview the selective-focus effect directly through the viewfinder, which gives you a lot of creative control. This is not possible with compact digital cameras where everything appears in focus all the time, regardless of the settings you choose. To get the best selective-focus effects using compact digital cameras, follow these steps:

- If you are shooting macro close-ups, set your camera to the Macro mode or Close-Up mode and check that you do not go closer than the minimum focusing distance of the lens.
- Open up the aperture (small f-number) by selecting the Portrait mode.
- When using a zoom lens, zoom into the telephoto range of the lens or set the camera to Telephoto mode.
- When taking a photo, the distance between you and the subject should be closer than the distance between the subject and the background.

18 Photographing Children

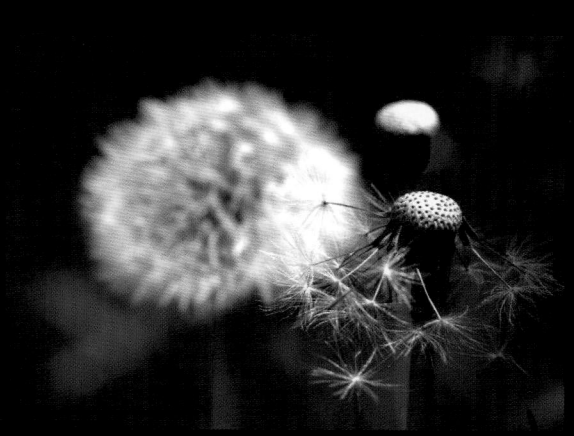

Children make great subjects for photos because they are active and lively and don't freeze up in front of the camera. At the same time, it is not easy to take their photos because they can be mischievous and restless. In this section, we will look at some time-tested techniques that will help you capture photos of children.

Use Fast Shutter Speeds

To prevent motion blur, you should always set your camera to the fastest shutter speed possible. On an automatic camera, you should set it to the Sports mode or Fast Action mode, which use a fast shutter speed to capture action shots.

If you can set the shutter speed on your camera, use a shutter speed between 1/250 and 1/1000 second when taking pictures of children. If you are at a sporting event, you should use shutter speeds of between 1/500 and to 1/2000 second.

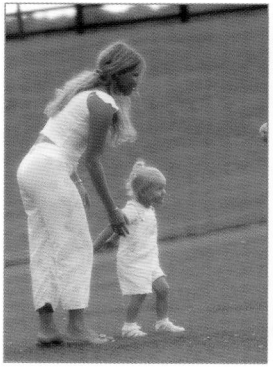

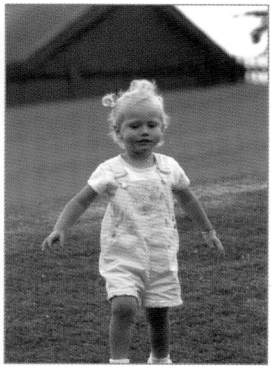

▲ Fast shutter speeds freeze the movement of fast-moving children.

Light Sensitivity (ISO) and Shutter Speeds

When the lighting is poor, fast shutter speeds are not feasible, as the image will be underexposed. To properly expose the image while using a fast shutter speed, the solution is to make the camera more sensitive to light (ISO). Most digital cameras support ISO ratings of 50, 100, 200, 400, 800, and 1600. The interval between these ratings (between ISO 50 and 100, for instance) is 1 stop—a term used to descibe intervals in aperture and shutter speed.

If you increase the ISO from 100 to 400, you are effectively increasing the sensitivity by 2 stops. If you keep the aperture and the exposure constant, you can increase the shutter speed by as much as 2 stops when taking a photo. For example, a picture taken at an ISO of 100 at *f*/2.0 and 1/60 second, and a photo take at an ISO of 400 (a difference of 2 stops) at *f*/2.0 and 1/250 second, have the same exposure. The downside of increasing the ISO is that your photos will have more electronic noise or graininess. Therefore, you have to strike a compromise between sharpness and graininess when you adjust the ISO.

Shoot at Their Level

If you take photos of children from above, their heads will look overly large while their legs will appear short and stubby. Another disadvantage is that you can't avoid a cluttered floor in your image. The trick is to shoot from the child's eye level, or be level with the part of the child's body you are photographing. Get down to the child's level for the best results.

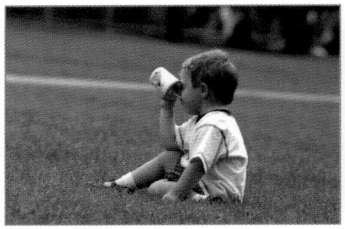

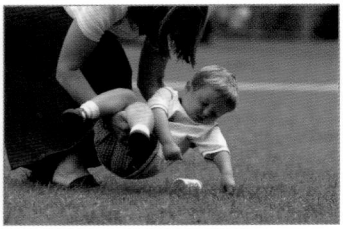

▲ Get down to the child's level.

Use the Continuous Shot Feature

The Continuous Shot feature on your camera allows you to capture a child's sequence of actions. Take three to five continuous shots and then select the ones you like. As usual, check that you are shooting with adequate lighting and the appropriate shutter speed or Scene mode.

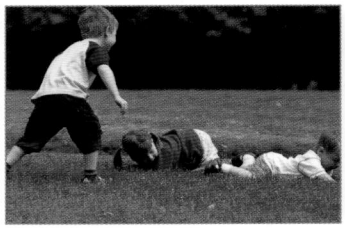

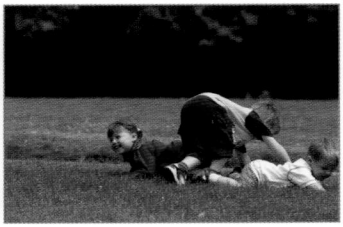

▲ Use Continuous Shot to capture the best moments.

Use Selective Focusing

Use selective focusing to keep the focus and attention on the child, especially if you are shooting in a crowded place. To get a good selective-focused photo using a semiautomatic camera, you should take the photo from a distance using the Telephoto mode or by setting the zoom lens to its telephoto range.

For example, if your camera has a 35–105 zoom, set the lens to between 80 mm and 100 mm. Next, open the aperture to its maximum to create a shallow depth of field and use a shutter speed of 1/250 second or faster. Finally, focus the camera on the child and press the shutter. If you are using an automatic camera, you can get the same effect by setting it to the Portrait mode.

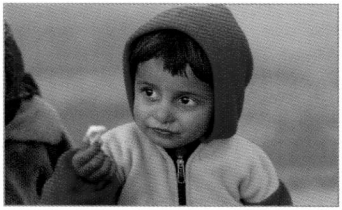

▲ Use a telephoto lens to focus the attention on the child.

Use Simple Props

Simple props, such as toys, will keep the child occupied and happy so that you can take natural shots of him playing and laughing. Movable props also help to make the photos livelier. For example, soap bubbles will engage the child and add an aesthetic quality to the picture.

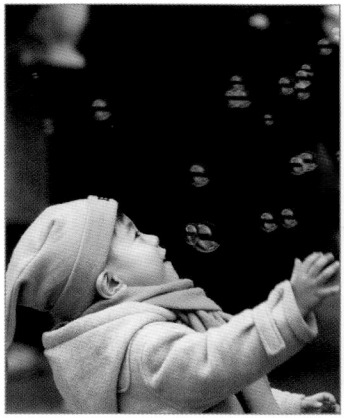

▲ A prop does not always have to be a toy. Soap bubbles work wonders!

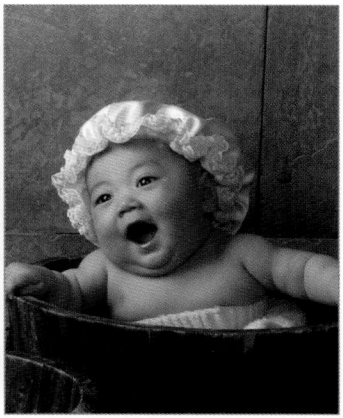

▲ In this photo, wooden tubs and a cute cap are used to create a country theme.

Compile a Photo Journal

One of the best ways to capture a child's growing years is to start a photo journal. Try to take more than just posed shots. Instead of focusing entirely on the child's activities, take some photos that illustrate the bond between family members and the child. Creative photographing will make the album more interesting. To take documentary photos, always have the camera on hand, and anticipate and position yourself for a shot even before it happens.

▶ Include family and friends in your shots, and try to capture a variety of themes.

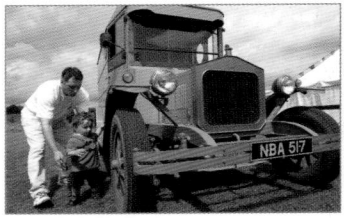

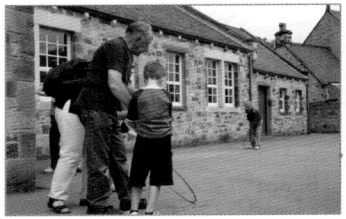

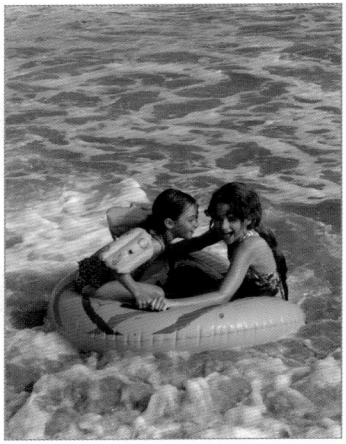

Ⓥ Close-Up Shots of Newborn Babies

Unaware of their surroundings, newborn babies are not afraid or self-conscious in front of the camera, making them great subjects for macro photography. Bear in mind that you don't have to photograph the baby's face all the time. Try taking close-up shots of its tiny nose, eyes, hands, or feet using the Macro mode. Don't activate the flash near a baby, though. Use a separate light source or move to a place with sufficient light instead.

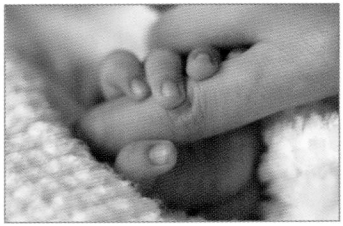

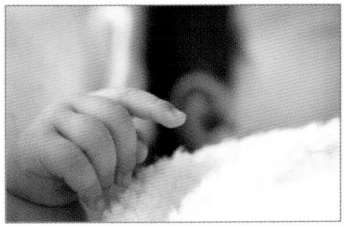

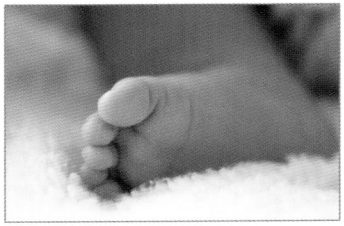

▲ Check the focusing distance of your macro lens before taking close-ups like these.

19 Shooting Self-Portraits

With film cameras, shooting self-portraits is a hit-or-miss affair. You point the camera at yourself, press the shutter-release button, and simply hope that the photos will turn out well.

With digital cameras, you can instantly review the self-portrait and adjust the camera position until you get it right. The odds of shooting a good self-portrait are better on a digital camera, and this is definitely a plus when you are traveling alone.

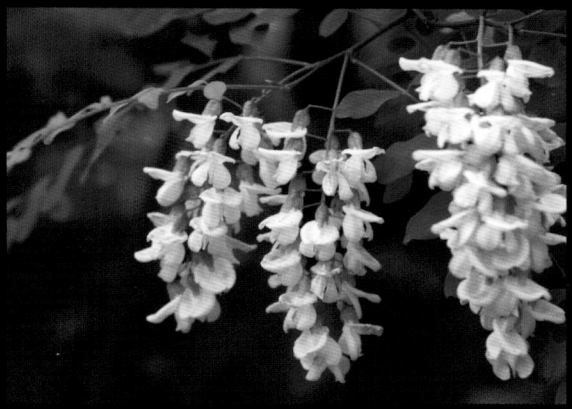

Handheld Self-Portraits

The fastest way to take a self-portrait is to hold the camera in both hands, stretch your arms way out with the camera directed toward you, and click the shutter-release button. The challenge is to keep the camera level and get your entire face in the picture. It will be easier if your camera has a rotating lens or LCD so that you can see yourself in the LCD as you compose the shot.

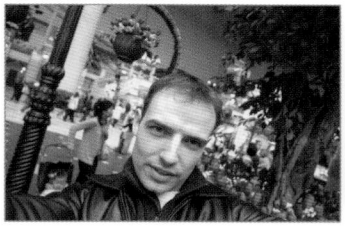

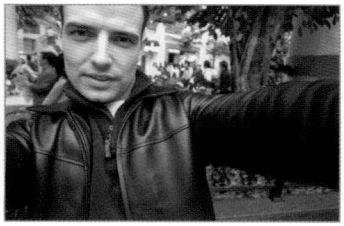

▲ Practice makes perfect.

▶▶▶ Camera Angle

Instead of always holding your camera straight out to shoot an eye-level photo, try holding it above or below for a completely different point of view.

If you are using a wide-angle lens, some distortion may be expected because of the design of wide-angle lenses. However, you can minimize distortion by zooming in slightly to a narrower angle. For example, if you are using a 35–105 mm zoom lens, you should set it to 50 mm.

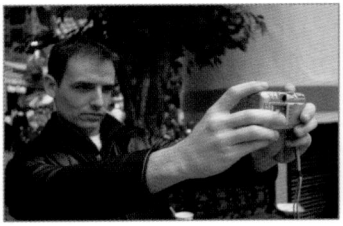

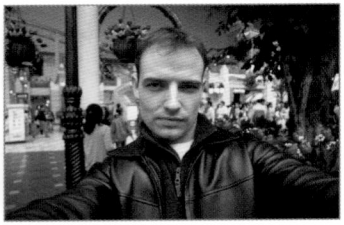

▲ Self-portraits are usually taken with the camera held straight out at eye-level.

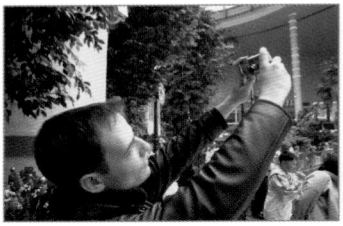

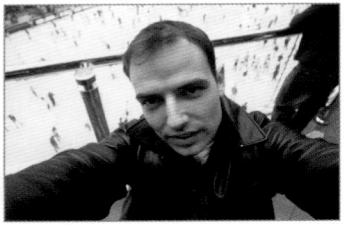

▲ Holding the camera above will capture the scene below, making the image appear small and enclosed.

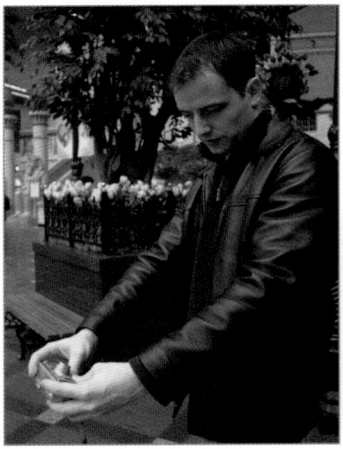

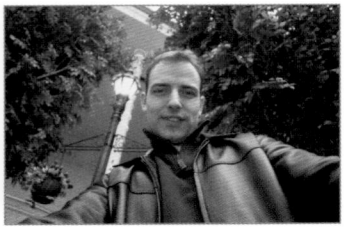

▲ Holding the camera straight below will capture the space above, making the image appear wide and open.

▶▶▶ Facial Expression

Most people stick to a single expression in all their photos. Some like to look cool and nonchalant, while others are always smiling in their photos. Practice taking your self-portraits with different expressions to convey different moods.

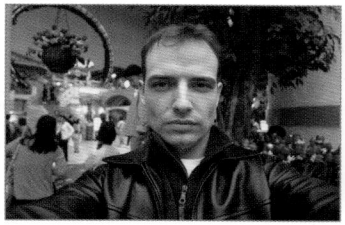

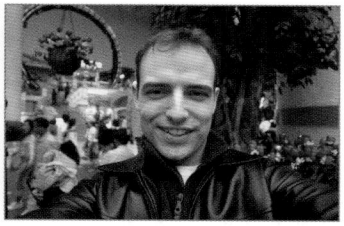

▲ Somber or happy? You decide.

Reflections as Self-Portraits

Try taking a picture of your reflection on a reflective surface like a mirror—a car mirror, a shiny glass, or a plate. You will capture a portrait of yourself as a photographer, a side that you don't get to see often.

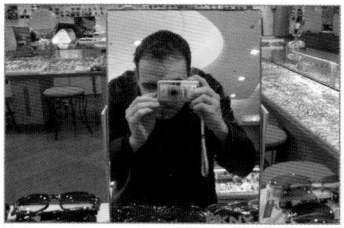

▲ Mirrors or car mirrors are commonly used when taking self-portraits.

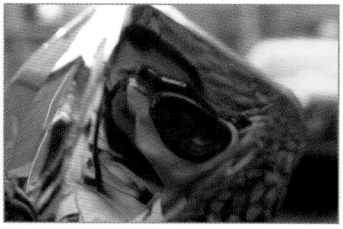

▲ Irregular reflections can produce artistic results.

Self-Portraits of a Group

Using a rotating lens or LCD, you can shoot group portraits easily. As you get better at shooting self-portraits, you may even be able to compose a shot that includes you, your companions, and the scene or landmark behind.

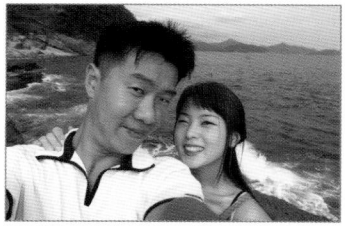

▲ A couple's self-portrait.

Using a Tripod

For outstanding self-portraits, you should use a tripod. A heavy tripod gives great support but is not easy to transport. Since most digital cameras are rather light, consider using a mini or tabletop tripod instead.

Using a tripod and the camera's Self-Timer mode, you can compose the photo to include the background. Set the timer to 10 seconds or longer to give yourself enough time to position yourself in the frame after pressing the shutter-release button. Try out different expressions and compositions for more experimental photos.

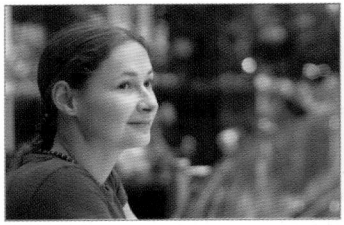

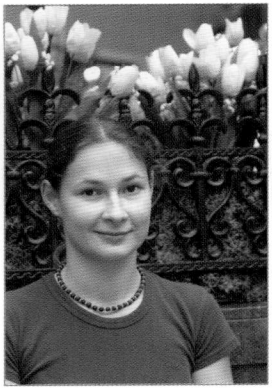

▲ ▶ Using a tripod allows you to look in different directions and include the background in the photo.

Self-portraits with good backgrounds

When shooting a self-portrait, keep in mind that often the photo can miss out on the background entirely and be over-dominated by your face. Better self-portraits show us a bit of background. Raise your arm a little further up to shoot from an upper diagonal side. You can get a more dynamic picture, with a slimmer and more attractive face, with the help of a good background.

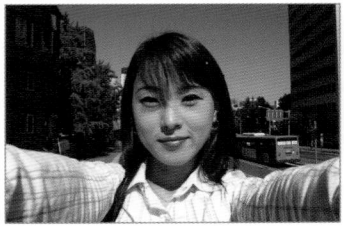

▲ This portrait dominates the frame.

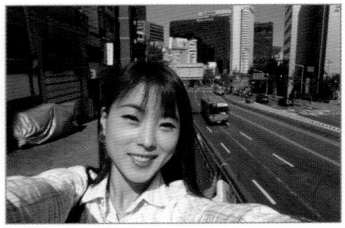

▲ A picture with good background and a slimmer face.

20 Using Light

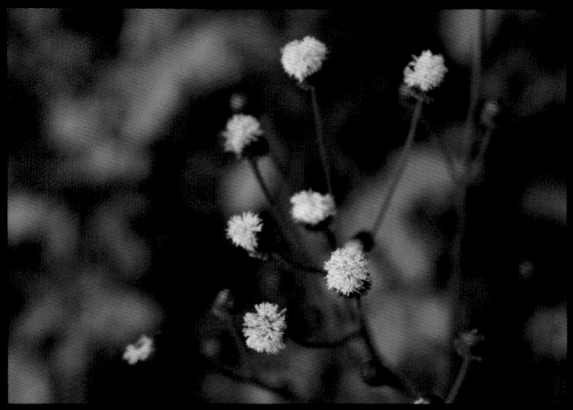

This section highlights a few common lighting techniques and mistakes associated with photographing people with a digital camera. You will learn when to use the Auto Flash mode or Slow Sync mode and how white balance affects skin tones. For more detailed instruction about lighting, refer to Technique 8.

Flash

If there is insufficient light, you can use the camera's built-in flash to light the scene. Flash can also be used indoors to freeze the actions of people who are moving.

▶▶▶ Auto Flash Mode

The Auto Flash mode is good for close-up photos or portraits that exclude the background. On the other hand, if you take a wide-angle shot in the Auto Flash mode, there is a high chance that you will overexpose the foreground subject while underexposing the background.

▶▶▶ Slow Sync Mode or Night Flash

To avoid a harsh, unnatural lighting effect, set the Flash mode to Slow Sync mode rather than Auto Flash mode. After the shutter-release button is pressed, the Slow Sync mode opens the shutter or activates the CCD long enough for the CCD to receive enough light to properly expose the image. This mode is wonderful for shooting stationary subjects, but you will need a tripod. If you want a more natural and softer look, bounce the light off a reflector or a low ceiling.

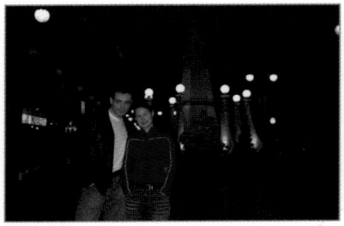

▲ You risk overexposing the foreground subject while underexposing the background in Auto Flash mode.

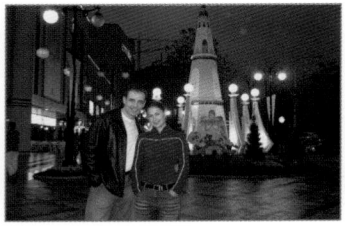

▲ Slow Sync mode lets in enough light to expose the background properly.

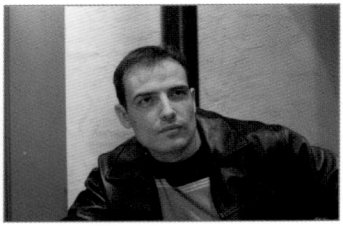

▲ Bouncing the flash off a low ceiling gives the room a soft lighting that is very forgiving of the subject' s skin blemishes and flaws.

Image Color and Skin Tone

In Chapter 2, we learned that different light sources affect the color balance of the photo differently. When it comes to shooting portraits, choosing the right lighting is particularly important, as a wrong skin tone is very obvious to the eye.

In general, you can use incandescent lights to create a warm and cozy feel, as they give the image an orange tint, while candles are good for creating a warm and romantic atmosphere. Halogen lamps, normally used in art galleries and exhibitions, will enhance the skin tone of your subject, but fluorescent lights will cast a bluish tint, making the subject look pale and the mood cold.

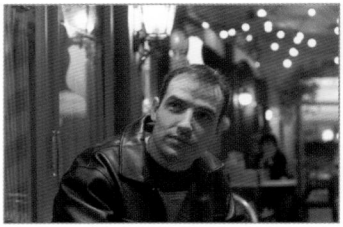

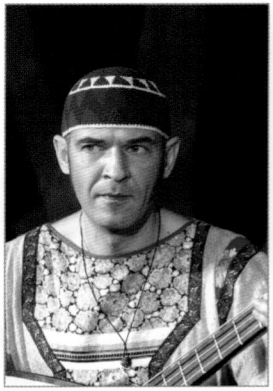

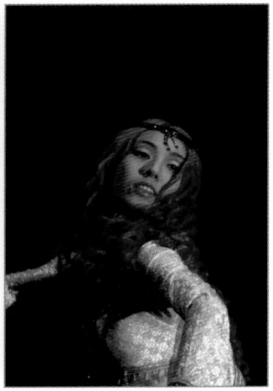

▲ Experiment with different types of indoor lighting to create different effects.

White Balance

The Custom White Balance mode is calibrated to compensate for the color temperature of a light source, so that a white piece of paper will always appear white in the image regardless of the color cast thrown by the light source. The Custom White Balance mode is useful if you want to ensure accurate color reproduction. But if you want to preserve the original tint of the light source and the atmosphere it creates, use the Auto White Balance mode instead.

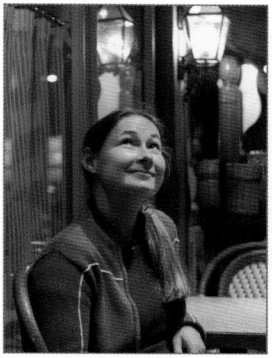

▲ Use the Auto White Balance mode to preserve the color of the lighting in your image.

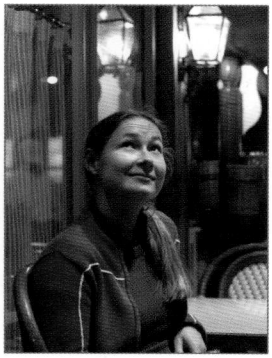

▲ Using the Custom White Balance mode to remove the color cast did not capture the ambience of the location.

Photos using a spotlight

"Portraits with a spotlight" refers to pictures that have the light concentrated on a specific spot, instead of on the overall figure. Strong light concentrated on one part creates a unique ambience, due to the stronger contrast. When shooting, try to find the various spotlights that naturally occur around you, and take photos that are like the ones taken in a studio.

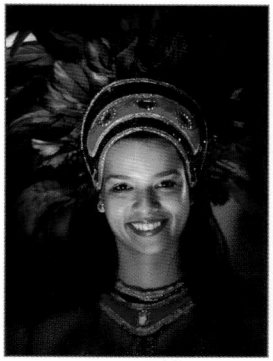

▲ A picture with a spotlight on the face.

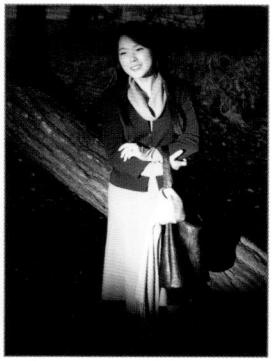

▲ A picture using a spotlight coming through the trees.

21 Manipulating Filters

Filters are placed in front of a lens to reduce glare, highlight certain hues, or create optical effects in images. There are also filters for protecting the lens. There are many filters on the market, but in this section, we will only look at those most suitable for use in people photography. You should note that you cannot attach filters to most automatic cameras. In other words, this feature is only available in mid- to high-end cameras.

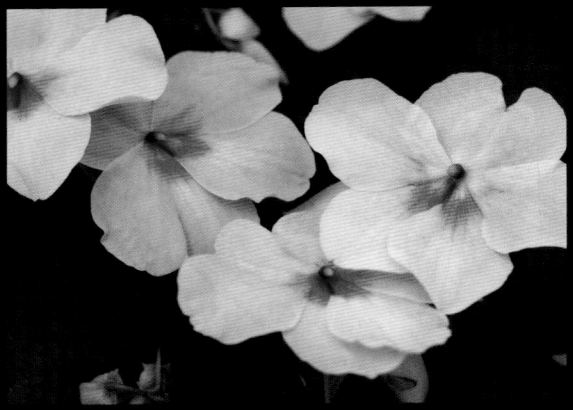

About Filters

In the past, filters were often used with traditional film cameras, but their importance has declined in the computer age. Now, any photo or image can be digitally altered to create similar filter effects (and many more) through image-editing software such as Photoshop.

However, filters remain popular with some photographers who want to see the effect in the viewfinder and create a composition in harmony with the scene. In addition, the effects created by such filters as the neutral density (ND) filter and cross star filters cannot be easily reproduced using image-editing software.

How to Use a Filter

If there are grooves on the lens housing, you can attach the filter by screwing it on. With most digital cameras, you will need to attach a lens adapter before you can attach the filter.

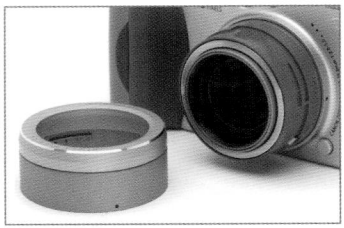

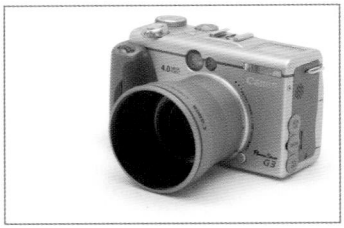

▲ Only a lens adapter made by the manufacturer of your digital camera will be compatible with your camera.

Filters for Shooting Portraits

▶▶▶ Polarizing (PL) Filter

This filter works in two ways. It reduces the glare or reflection from reflective surfaces like glass or water, enabling you to take sharper and clearer photos. It also gives your photos better contrast and color saturation when you are shooting color photos. The filter is great for capturing sharp, vivid photos of both people and landscape in the same frame.

To use a PL filter, rotate the filter on its mount until you get the desired effect. This is easy with a digital SLR camera where you can see the effect directly through the viewfinder.

With a compact digital camera, you can't preview the effect because the lens and the viewfinder are not connected. But you can work around this problem with some ingenuity. First, place the PL filter in front of the viewfinder and rotate it until you get the desired effect. Then, without rotating the filter any more, attach it to the lens. This method will give you some idea of the filter's effect on your image, but you need some practice to get it right.

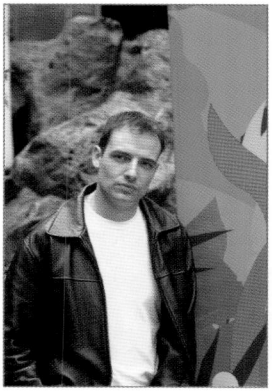

▲ Taken without the PL filter.

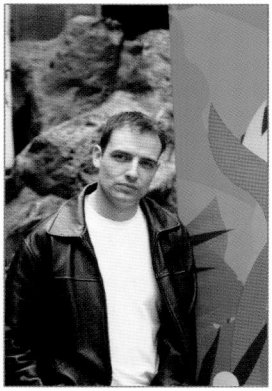

▲ Taken with the PL filter.

▶▶▶ Neutral Density (ND) Filter

The ND filter reduces the amount of light that enters the lens. In other words, it reduces the brightness of a scene. This filter is useful if you want to have a shallow depth of field when shooting in bright daylight.

As you know by now, you need to shoot with a large aperture in order to get a shallow depth of field. But this is impossible when you shoot in bright daylight, because no matter how fast you set the shutter speed, the aperture will remain small in order to compensate for the increased amount of light coming through.

With a small aperture, the depth of field will be too deep and you will be unable to take selective-focused shots. With this filter, you can reduce the scene's brightness without changing its color, thus allowing you to open up the aperture.

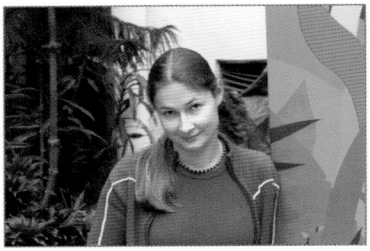

▲ Without the ND filter, the background will also be in focus.

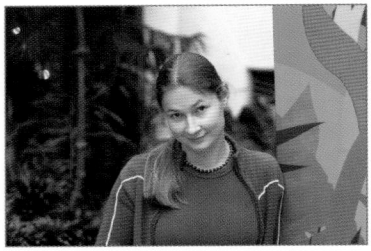

▲ With the ND filter, we can open up the aperture to take selective-focused photos.

▶▶▶ Soft Filter

This filter gives a soft, blurry look to your photos, similar to the blur effect in photo editing software. It is excellent for creating a dreamy, romantic mood, which is why this filter is commonly used in wedding photography.

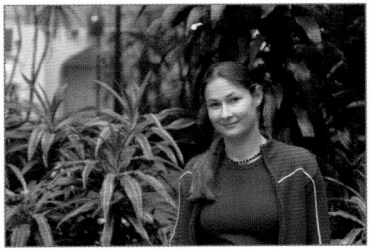

▲ Photo taken without the Soft filter.

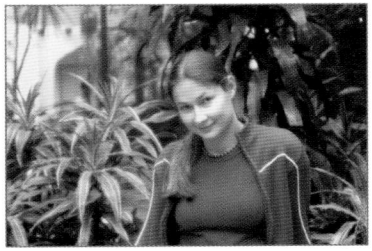

▲ Photo taken with the Soft filter.

▶▶▶ Cross Star or Starburst Filter

This filter has crosshatch marks on the surface that flare light rays coming through the lens into a given number of fixed lines away from the source point. The effect of this filter is most obvious when used in night scenes with street lamps or incandescent lights. As a rule, the smaller and more intense the light source, the more pronounced is the effect in the photo. This filter is great for creating a romantic ambience in photos.

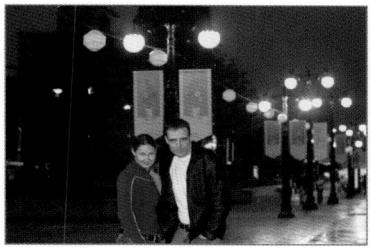

▲ Photo taken without the cross star filter.

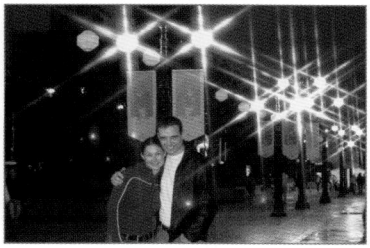

▲ Using the cross star filter gives a glamorous effect to the photo.

22 Photographing Weddings

A wedding is a joyous occasion and a great photo opportunity for photography enthusiasts. But it is not easy to take good wedding pictures and this is why professional wedding photographers are often paid handsomely. The main challenge in wedding photography is in capturing all the important moments and getting all the shots right the first time. In this section, you will learn to prevent or overcome the problems you may face in taking wedding shots.

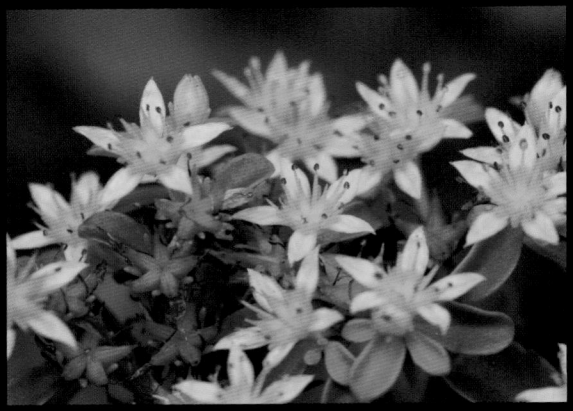

Memorize the Schedule

Weddings are a bustle of activity, and the bride and groom, together with their entourage, are constantly moving from one activity or location to another. To make sure that you capture all of the important moments, you have to memorize the wedding schedule in advance.

At the same time, you should consider the lighting conditions and general environment of the various locations and plan ahead. Once you know the schedule by heart, you can move on to the next location before the entourage and look for a good position to take the shot. On the wedding day itself, you should of course bring the schedule just in case you forget the time and location.

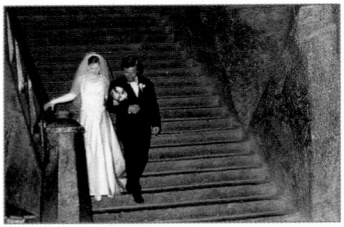

▲ If you know the wedding schedule, you can get to the next location before everyone else and find a good spot to take shots.

Be Well Equipped

Since a wedding is a once-in-a-lifetime event, you should be well equipped for the shoot. This is especially vital if you promised the bride or groom to be their backup photographer. The items that you must bring are an extra battery, perhaps even the battery charger if the event will take the whole day, memory cards, an external flash if you have one, and a tripod. As an added precaution, you should also test all of your camera equipment a day or two before the shoot.

Arrive Early

There are two reasons why you should arrive early. First of all, you will need time to set up your equipment, take some test shots to get the exposure right, and explore the location. Second, being early lets you capture pre-event activities that the couple may want to show their friends. Consult the couple about how early you should arrive.

Apply the Principles of Action Photography

All the rules for action photography, such as using a large aperture, fast shutter speed, and tripod apply. See Technique 13 on action photography. You should note that, unlike action shots of fast-moving objects which will require the use of a semiautomatic camera, people at weddings generally move more leisurely, giving you a fair chance of success at shooting weddings with automatic cameras.

Another useful technique for taking action shots, regardless of your camera type, is to pre-focus on a specific spot that you know the subject will go past. In wedding photography, this technique is most frequently used to take pictures of a wedding couple walking down the aisle.

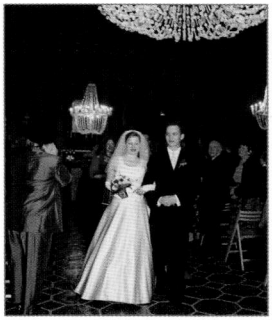

▲ Pre-focus on a spot by pressing down your shutter-release button halfway and releasing it only when the couple reaches the spot.

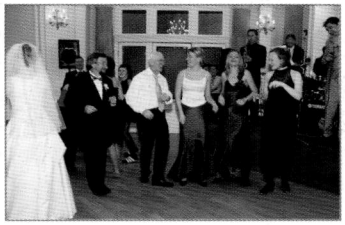

▲ Although this shot would look better if it excluded the bride, whose back is facing the camera, the photographer chose to take the shot anyway so as not to miss the moment. Another consideration is that the photo can be cropped later to exclude the bride and the singer.

Using Flash

At one point or another, the wedding festivities will probably take place indoors, and you will need to use a flash to take indoor action shots. If you take formal group shots indoors, you will find that you need to move farther away to include the entire group in the picture, and this could render your built-in flash ineffective because the distance is beyond the flash's range. The solution is to attach an external flash unit to your camera. If that's not possible, check the flash distance of your built-in flash and try to keep within the flash range.

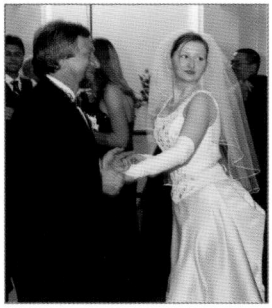

▲ Using the flash to freeze action.

Another important factor to remember when using the flash is to make sure that it doesn't fire when the professional photographer is taking a shot, as this will ruin his picture. It helps to remember that the wedding couple paid the professional photographer big bucks for the best possible pictures, and he should be given the consideration to do his job properly.

Posed Shots

If the schedule allows, you can take posed shots of the wedding party. When taking posed shots, there are some standard poses that you can try out. A popular pose is to have the bride or groom looking into the dressing mirror.

When taking posed shots of the bride, study her wedding gown, jewelry, and hairdo to look for the defining characteristics. With a low-back dress, you can take a shot of the bride's back view with or without her looking back over her shoulder. For very long trains, try arranging the train in a semicircle around the bride so that it flows and doesn't look like she's dragging it along. You may also want to use the soft filter to create the dreamy, fantastic look when taking posed shots.

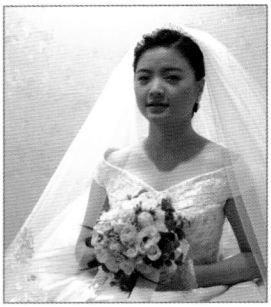

▲ A posed shot.

Photojournalistic Shots

On the other hand, if the wedding couple and almost everyone else are too busy to pose for you, you can take photojournalistic pictures. Photojournalism is a photography style much like the pictures you see in the newspapers. This style, often in black and white, is great for documenting a wedding to tell a story.

Taking photojournalistic pictures instead of formal shots at weddings may often be a better idea for photography hobbyists. This is because the couple and the entourage will not have time to work out their pose for you and you will end up taking pictures of the same pose as everyone else. While the couple and the official photographer are busy with the formal shots, take the opportunity to take alternative shots. For example, you can take pictures of the wedding invitation set against some decorative elements, the wedding couple figurine on the wedding cake, or the champagne glasses.

At times when you are unable to take good pictures of the wedding couple (for example, when you can't zoom in far enough when the couple is exchanging their vows), you should also explore alternative subject matter.

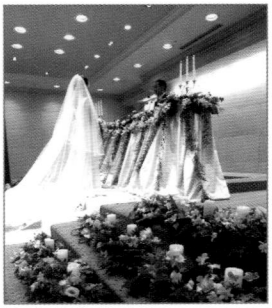

▲ A photojournalistic shot.

Chapter 3 | Photographing People

- √ Get closer to your subject.
- √ Make the subject feel comfortable.
- √ Focus on the subject's eyes.
- √ Consider the lighting's effect on the subject's features.
- √ Decide if you should simplify the background or include meaningful backdrops.
- √ Consider the effect the camera position will have on your subject's body shape.
- √ Take more than one shot for group photos to ensure that everyone is looking at the camera.
- √ Use the Portrait Scene mode, open up the aperture, or zoom in to blur the background.
- √ When taking photos of children, use a fast shutter speed, go down to their level, use the Continuous Shot function, and experiment with simple props.
- √ Try taking self-portraits from different angles.
- √ Use the flash to freeze action.
- √ Use the Slow Sync mode or Night Flash to keep both your subject and background illuminated when taking a shot at night.
- √ Adjust the white balance if you do not like the color cast on your subject's skin.
- √ Use a polarizing (PL) filter to reduce glare or reflection.
- √ To blur out the background when taking a shot in bright daylight, use the neutral density (ND) filter to reduce the amount of light entering the camera.
- √ Use the soft filter for a dreamy look.
- √ Try using the cross star or starburst filter when shooting on the streets at night to create starbursts for a romantic ambience.
- √ For wedding events, use fast shutter speeds and try to anticipate good picture opportunities.

40 Digital Photography Techniques

Shooting Landscapes

Chapter 4

While people photography is about reacting fast enough to capture the right moment, landscape photography is mostly about waiting for the right moment. Generally, unless you are on the trail of a twister or some other exceptional weather phenomenon, most landscape shots are fairly static shots of nature and cityscapes.

With landscape photography, there is no hurry. Take time to try the different lenses, experiment with different compositions, and wait for the right light or time to shoot your photo.

23 Landscape Photography Essentials

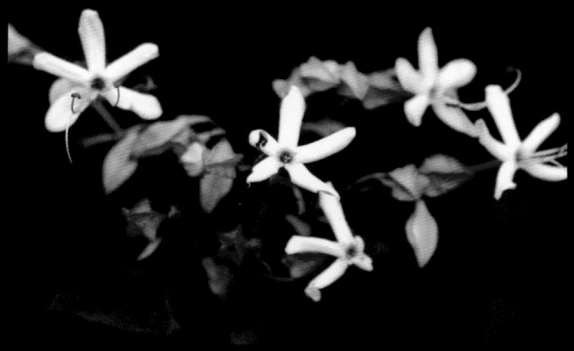

In order to take outstanding photos, you need to develop an eye for the beauty around you. The next time you come across a good photo, make a point to study it carefully and think about how it was shot. For landscape photography, you need to be sensitive to the light conditions, and how sunlight changes the mood of the landscape. You also need to learn how to compose well-balanced landscape shots.

Choosing a Scene

Apart from dangerous situations such as a safari photography outing, you should always get out of your car and explore your surroundings on foot in order to find the perfect scene. When a view strikes an emotional chord, you will know instinctively that you have found your subject matter. Then you should wait patiently for the perfect time, light, and weather conditions to take the photo.

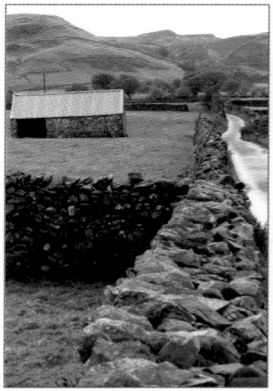

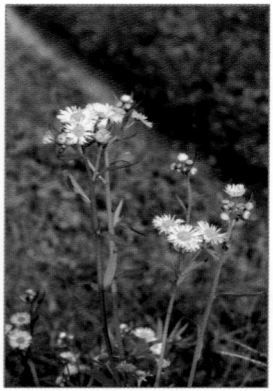

▲ You must actively go in search of a good scene for your photos.

Composition Is Everything

▶▶▶ Horizontal or Vertical?

Composition is the most critical factor in landscape photography, so you should spend more time composing or trying out different compositions. Horizontal photos exude a sense of stability and emphasize the breadth of a scene, whereas vertical photos emphasize height and depth.

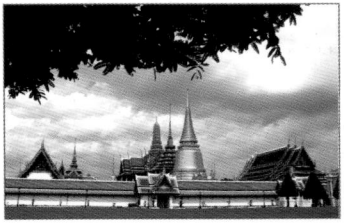

▲ A horizontal photo is used to capture the expansiveness of a scene.

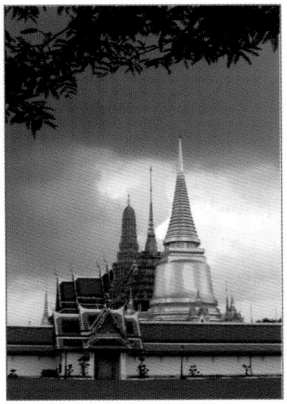

▲ A vertical photo emphasizes height.

▶▶▶ Camera Angle

You should also consider the effect of the camera angle on your photo. A low angle adds vitality and dimension to the scenery, whereas a high angle gives a down-to-earth feel. With practice, you can develop a visual sense of the angles and compositions that work best with certain situations.

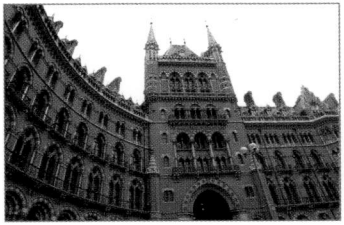

▲ A low-angle landscape photo appears majestic and full of life.

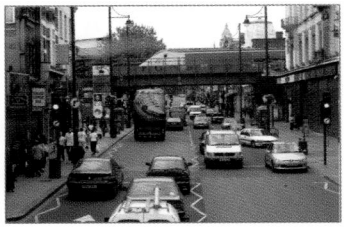

▲ A high angle landscape photo gives an enclosed, down-to-earth feel.

▶▶▶ Balance

If the composition is unbalanced, the photo will look unattractive even if the scene is fantastic.

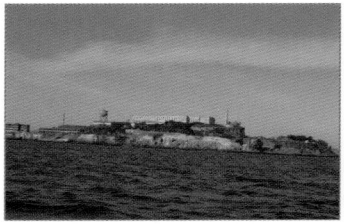

▲ The horizon is slanted, making the photo look unbalanced.

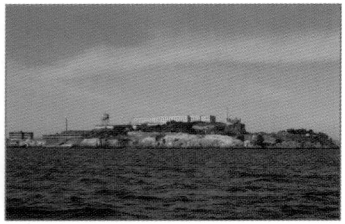

▲ The re-composed photo looks much better.

▶▶▶ Break Away from Convention

Conventional landscape photos place the main point of interest at the center of the frame. This sort of composition is fine, but it can be boring after a while. Try placing the subject off-center for bold and interesting effects.

▲ Think of a few different subject placements and experiment with them.

▶▶▶ Simplify the Background

A good landscape photo harmonizes the subject with its surroundings. One way of doing this is to keep the focus on the subject by simplifying the background and eliminating unnecessary elements. This is why landscape photography is an exercise in the beauty of subtraction.

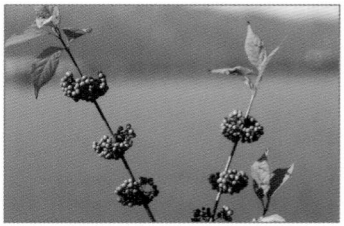

▶ Remove unnecessary elements from the background to emphasize the subject.

Pan Focusing and Selective Focusing

▶▶▶ Pan Focusing

Pan focusing is a technique used frequently in landscape photography to keep the entire photo sharp and clear. The effect is achieved by using a wide-angle lens and a small aperture (*f*/8 or higher), if you are using a semiautomatic camera, to keep both the foreground and background in focus. On an automatic camera, zoom out to the wide-angle setting and select the Landscape Scene mode, which sets the focus at infinity. Pan focusing is another way of saying that the image has a deep depth of field.

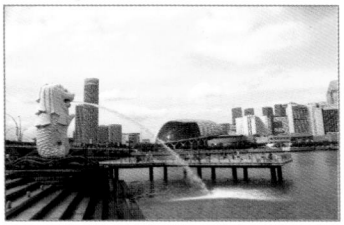

▲ Use pan focusing to keep everything in sharp focus.

▶▶▶ Selective Focusing

Use the selective-focusing technique with a large aperture (*f*/2.8–*f*/4) if you want to limit the focus on a particular object. You can do this by setting your camera to Telephoto mode or, if you are using a zoom lens, setting it to 70 mm or above.

Depending on the camera distance, you can also use the Portrait or Close-Up Scene modes and zoom in to the Telephoto setting to shoot a selective-focused photo.

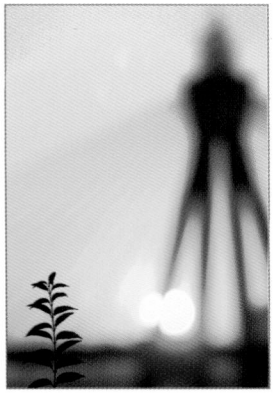

▲ Use selective focusing to emphasize a particular object.

The Changing Light

Besides composition, light is the other key element in landscape photography. Natural light changes continuously throughout the day, which is why photos of the same scene taken at different times of day will appear drastically different.

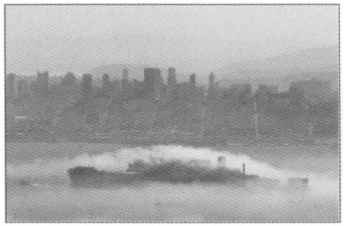

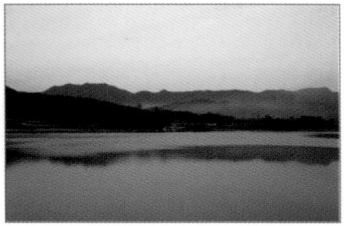

▲ Two images shot at dawn.

You have to be sensitive to the changing light conditions in order to capture a scene with the appropriate mood. Take note of the direction of the light. In general, backlighting emphasizes the shapes and forms in the landscape, whereas oblique or side lighting tends to enhance the contours and textures of the landscape.

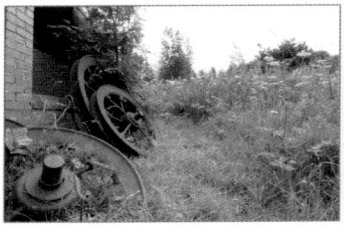

▲ Image shot during the day.

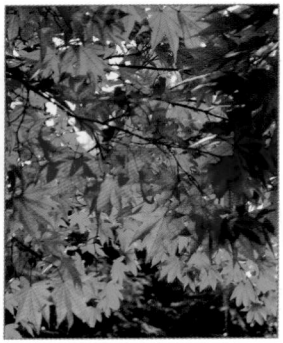

▶ Backlighting emphasizes the shape and form of the leaves.

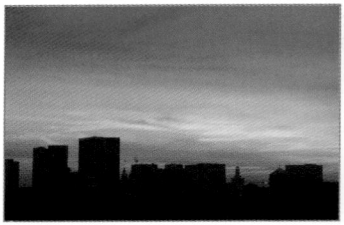

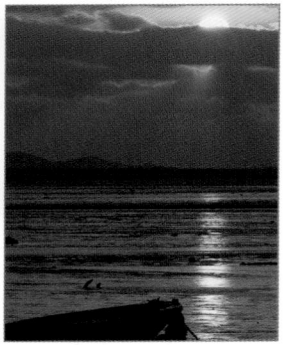

▲ ▶ Image shot at sunset.

Using Fill Flash

Although the flash is normally used for poorly lit areas, using it to shoot objects in nature can create wonderful results. Set the Flash mode to Fill Flash mode, focus on a nearby object in the foreground, and then trigger the flash. Because the light from the flash does not spread over a wide area, this will make the object in the foreground look sharp and stand out from the background.

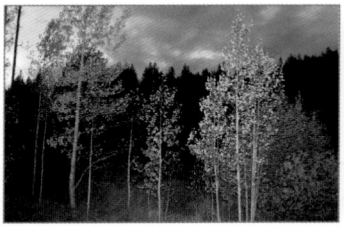

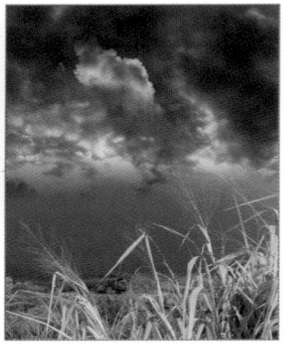

▲ ▶ Use the Fill Flash to give more depth to the scene.

24 Vacation Photos

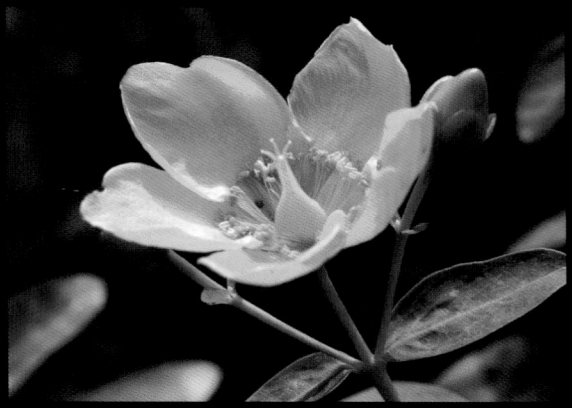

Since the camera is an essential companion for travelers in the 21st century, this section is tailored to photography situations commonly encountered by travelers. These practical skills and techniques will help you maximize the photo opportunities that arise in your travels.

Tourist Attractions

To get a good photo of a tourist attraction, find a spot where you can get a nice angle and check that neither people nor buildings block your view. In summer months or during extended holidays, this can be difficult as you have to fight with hordes of tourists, all armed with a camera just like you. In winter months, it is much easier to get a clear shot with few or no tourists in them, and this will improve the ambience of your photos dramatically.

▶▶▶ Be Original!

Many people recognize famous tourist attractions through postcards and travel books without even visiting the actual location. This is because many of us take our photos from the same designated scenic spot. Try to shoot from a different view or incorporate the less-photographed elements in your photos to set your vacation photos apart from everyone else's.

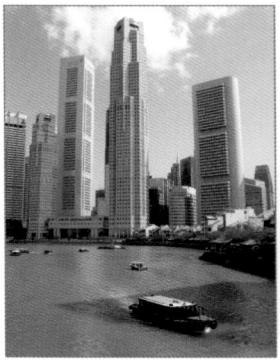

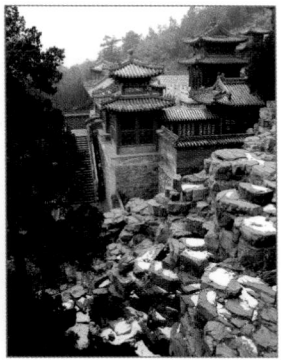

▶ Look for a unique scene.

▶▶▶ Include Variety

Make it a point to vary the angle and composition of your photos. You should also think about giving your photos a personal style. If you have the time, visit the same sites at night to take photos with a different mood. Some scenes or landmarks, which look plain or dull in the day due to air pollution, will look much better as night shots.

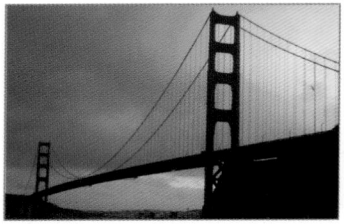

▲ Photos of world-famous sites are the highlight of travel photos.

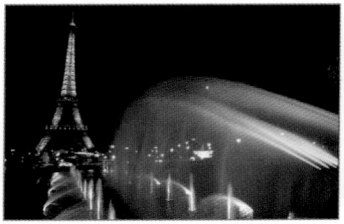

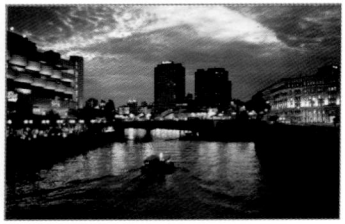

▲ Try to take some night shots as well.

▶▶▶ Special Events

Special events are sometimes held at tourist spots or concert halls. To avoid jostling with the crowd and taking pictures of the back of people's heads, go early and find a good spot.

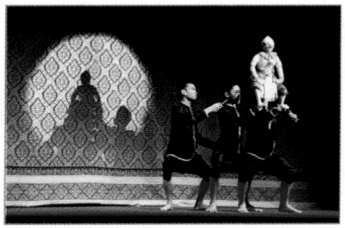

▲ You may need to leave your seat and get close to the performers when taking pictures at concerts.

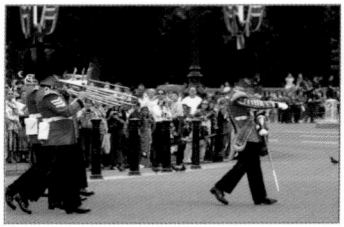

▲ Scout the area for a good location to view the event.

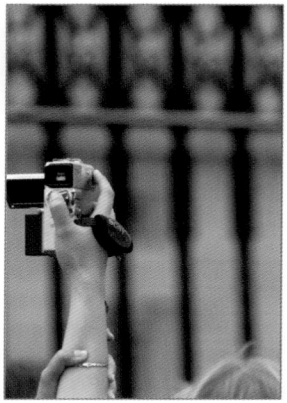

People, Objects, and Locations

Although most of the photos you will take while on vacation will probably be landscape photos, remember to get a good mix of photos of yourself and your travel companions, in order to capture the memories you share together.

▶▶▶ Facial Expressions

Be attentive and capture a range of expressions to document the highs and lows of your voyage.

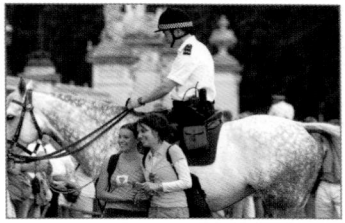

▲ Smile for the camera.

▶▶▶ Memorable Objects or Souvenirs

Try to include street signs or other objects unique to the areas you visit in your photos. Street signs can help you remember where you have been, especially if you take a whirlwind tour, while interesting objects make great conversation topics for your friends and family back home.

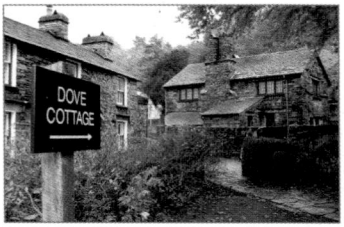

▲ Signposts help you remember where you've been.

▶▶▶ Shooting from Inside a Moving Vehicle

You will sometimes see a great view while you are inside a moving vehicle. Increase the sensitivity (ISO) of your camera to produce sharper images.

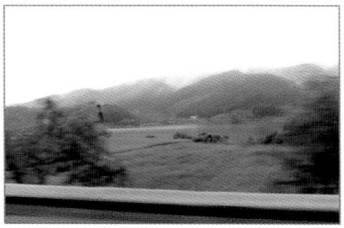

▲ Landscapes shot from moving vehicles often contain blurry motion lines.

Taking Photos through a Window

- Place the camera at an angle and as close as possible to the window to cut down on reflections.
- Select the Landscape Scene mode to set the focus to infinity. If your camera is set to autofocus, it may end up focusing on the windowpane, leaving the scene a blur.

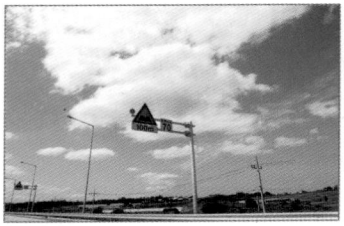

▲ Take the photo at an angle to avoid capturing the reflections on the window.

▲ In this shot, the Landscape Scene mode was not used, to capture the ice crystals on the plane window.

- Buses and planes do not use flat glass, but the thick, bending glass that is used for windows. That is why the view through the center of the window is relatively vivid, while the view through the edges is distorted and duller. When shooting through this type of window it is better to shoot with a zoom through the central area of the window.

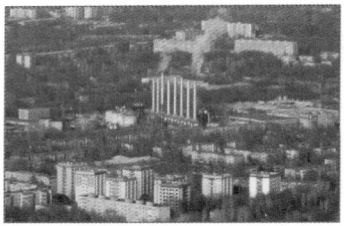

▲ Views from the edges are not vivid.

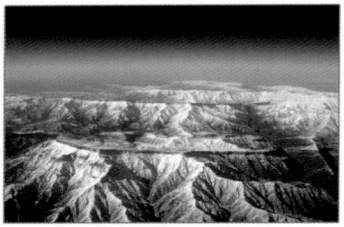

▲ Take your picture through the central part of the window.

▶▶▶ Combining Subject and Background

If you stand too close to the subject, you will neglect the background, but if you stand too far away, the subject becomes indistinguishable from the background. To give equal importance to the subject and the background, shoot at a distance and angle that will give a sense of balance between the two.

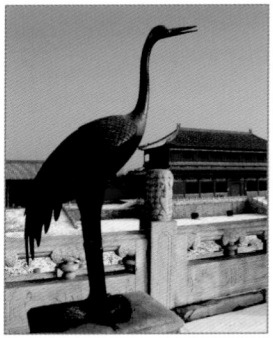

▶ In this shot, the foreground subject leads the viewer's gaze into the building in the background. This technique of using a foreground interest to lead into the background is often used to create depth in a picture and to avoid having a flat, boring composition.

25 Rainy Day Photos

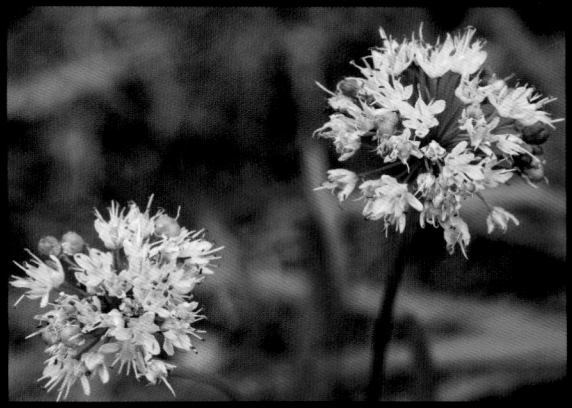

Rainy days are great for taking landscape photos because the falling rain cloaks the landscape in a shroud of mist and water, and the resulting low-contrast scene with muted colors can give a painterly quality to your photos.
In this section, you will learn how to protect your camera from the rain and how to take good photos on a rainy day.

Protecting the Camera

Digital cameras, like all electronic products, are very sensitive to moisture and humidity. You need to take extra care to protect your camera from the rain. Most people would take a shot holding the camera in one hand and an umbrella in the other. This is ineffective because strong winds can get rain on the camera. Here are a few ways to protect your camera from the rain:

▶▶▶ Waterproof Case

The most secure method is to use a waterproof case, which is designed for underwater photography. As such cases are very expensive, it may not be most practical solution.

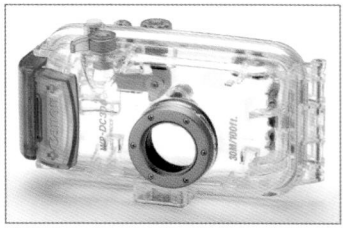

▲ Your best bet is to use a waterproof camera case, but these cases are very expensive.

▶▶▶ Plastic Wrap

Take a common household plastic bag, wrap it around your camera, and make a hole in the plastic for the lens. This is an inexpensive option for amateurs.

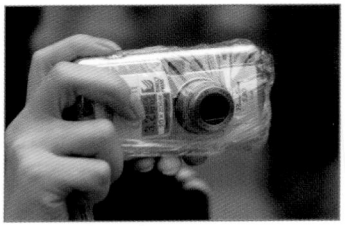

▲ Wrapping the camera in a plastic bag provides inexpensive protection.

▶▶▶ Waterproof Camera Bag

Waterproof camera bags have great water-resistant capabilities and are cheap, making them effective as well as practical.

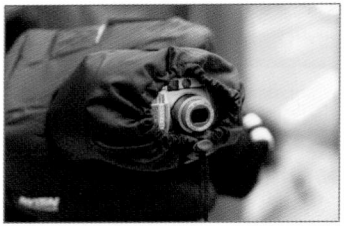

▲ Waterproof camera bags are not only great for rainy days but also for winter outings.

tip If All Else Fails...

If you cannot effectively shield your camera from the rain, take photos from inside instead.

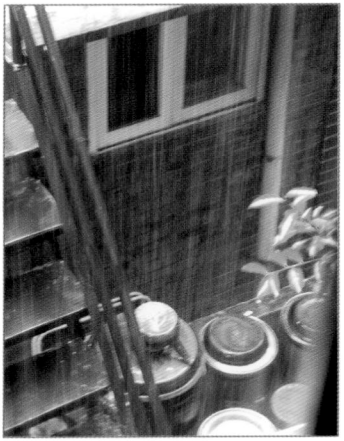

▲ A rainy-day photo shot from inside.

Tips

- Camera Shake

On rainy days, you may need to use a slow shutter speed due to the poor lighting condition. On an automatic camera, you can try shooting in the Party/Indoor Scene mode. As this increases the risk of motion blur, use a tripod.

- Artificial Rain

If you don't like getting wet, an alternative is to use a garden hose and create artificial rain. This lets you control the rain and use it to mimic the effects of a summer downpour.

- Adding Accents

If the scene is universally dark and gloomy, try to compose the shot with a brighter object in the foreground to add accents to the photo.

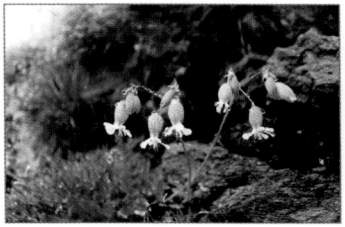

▲ Use flowers as accents.

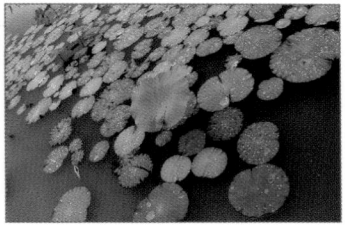

▲ Use lotus leaves as accents.

Taking Photos of Raindrops

If you want to capture the falling rain, set the scene against a dark background. Set the shutter speed between 1/250 and 1/1000 second or use the Sports Scene mode.

You can also create a rainy-day mood by taking photos of raindrops on leaves, raindrops hitting the windowpanes, or people holding umbrellas. Using selective focusing (Portrait Scene mode or Close-Up mode) and a telephoto lens, you can create a dreamy, misty effect.

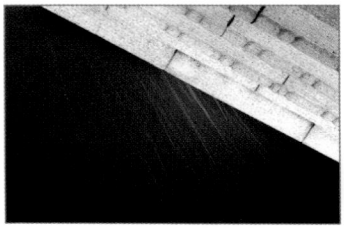

▲ A picture of raindrops taken with a slow shutter speed (1/10 sec).

▲ A picture of raindrops with a fast shutter speed (1/250 sec).

26 Snowy Day Photos

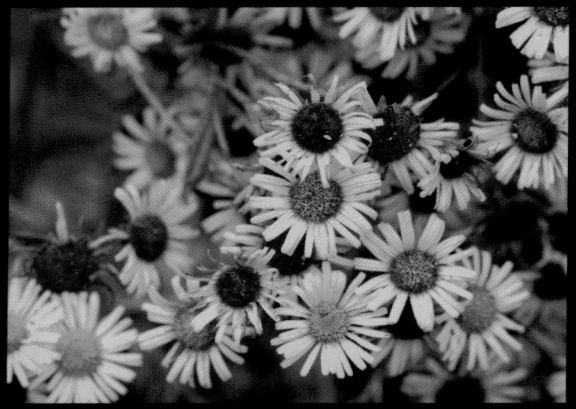

For the most part, you should take the same precautions when photographing on snowy days as you would on rainy days. There are, however, additional factors to keep in mind to protect the camera from the snow.

Battery

Apart from waterproofing your camera, you should always have an extra battery on hand. The battery will drain rapidly when out in the cold, so try to keep it warm by carrying it in your pocket.

Shutter Speed

Set a shutter speed faster than 1/100 second or use the Sports Scene mode to capture the falling snowflakes. Press the shutter-release button as soon as you find the perfect balance between the subject and the falling snow.

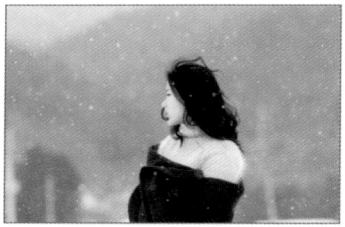

▲ Capture the right moment with a fast shutter speed.

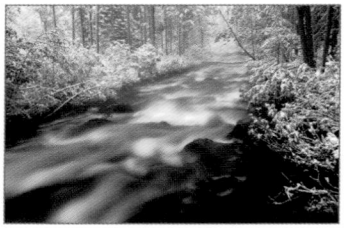

▲ A slow shutter speed gives a silky texture to this river, enhancing the dreamlike quality of the image.

Polarizing (PL) Filter

A clear morning or night is best for taking photos of snowy landscapes. If you have a polarizing (PL) filter, use it to enhance the contrast and saturate the colors.

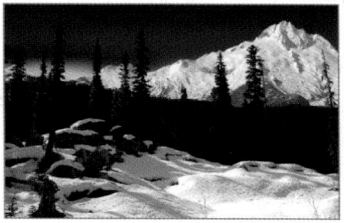

▲ Use a PL filter to enhance the contrast.

Exposure

One of the most crucial factors in snow-covered landscape photography is the exposure. Because the snow is white and your camera's exposure meter is calibrated to 18 percent gray, you will get an inaccurate exposure reading if you take the reading off of the snow. If you follow this reading without adjustment, your photos will be underexposed and the snow will look gray instead of white.

This can be corrected by increasing the exposure. Although it may vary depending on the weather and the amount of snow, raising the exposure by 1/2 stop or 1 stop can usually correct the underexposure. If your camera has AEB, or Auto Exposure Bracketing mode, use it to get the best results.

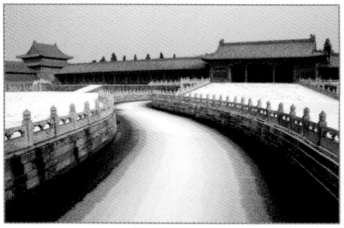

▲ Exposure increased by 1 stop.

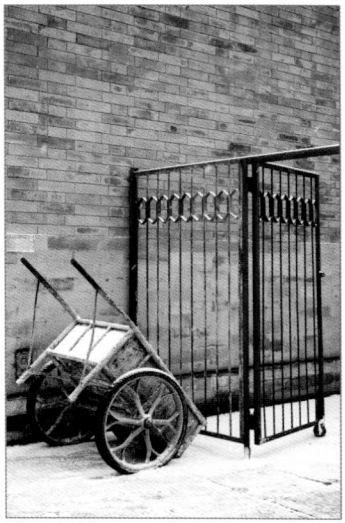

▶ For gray, urban landscapes, it may be advisable to shoot when the city is covered in snow, as the highlights from the snow will give the scene a pure, refreshing appeal.

27 Night Photography

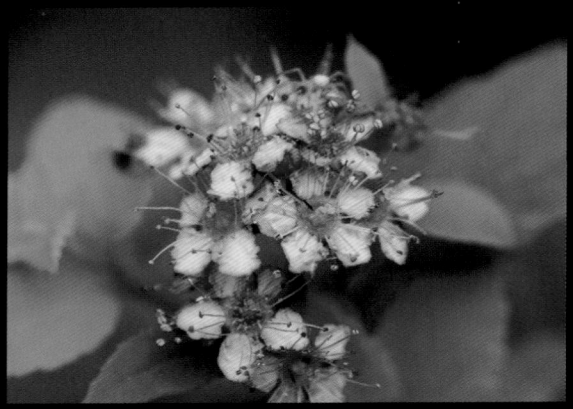

Novice photographers often hesitate to take outdoor photos at night, because such photos require the use of a tripod or other accessories and it is quite difficult to get the exposure right. In this section, you will learn that it is not difficult to take stunning photos at night, capturing city lights, creating traffic light trails, and shooting photos of fireworks.

Capturing City Lights

Light sources like streetlights, automobile lights, neon signs, and brightly lit buildings or areas offer many opportunities to take photos of the city at night. With good planning, you can take captivating shots of brightly lit areas that stand out against the dark.

▶▶▶ Camera Shake

A tripod or some other on-location support is essential for night photography because it will keep your camera steady during long exposures. Professional photographers will also use a cable release or the Remote Control function on their cameras to trigger the shutter-release button. This is to prevent camera shake, which becomes more obvious on the image during long exposures. For beginners, neither the cable release nor the Remote Control function are really necessary. Just a firm but gentle press on the shutter-release button will do.

▶▶▶ Shutter Speed

You need a digital camera that supports shutter speeds of 1 second or longer.

▶▶▶ Adjusting the Exposure

Using the Automatic mode to take a photo of the city at night will produce a photo with a dark background. You can try to compensate for this by increasing the exposure using exposure compensation. Although this will make your photos brighter, you will not be able to capture the actual mood of the scene. To reproduce the brightness of the scene more accurately, set your camera to Spot Metering mode and reduce the exposure by 1/2 stop.

If you can't adjust the exposure, use the Night Landscape mode, which turns off the flash and uses a slow shutter speed to take in the city lights.

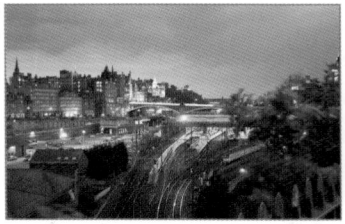

▲ Increasing the exposure under Automatic mode will make your photos too bright.

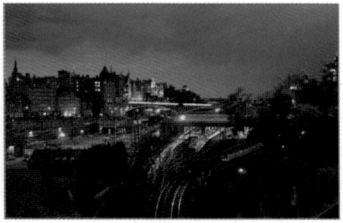

▲ Use Spot Metering mode and reduce the exposure by 1/2 stop to more accurately reproduce the scene.

▶▶▶ Time of Night

Night photography refers to photos taken from the moment the sun goes down to the moment the sun begins to rise. Photos taken at dawn and at dusk have a bluish tint because there is still some light in the sky. This light has a high color temperature, giving your image a bluish color cast.

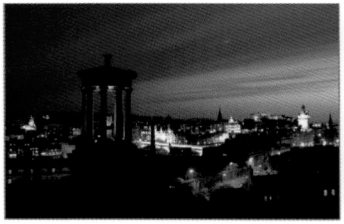

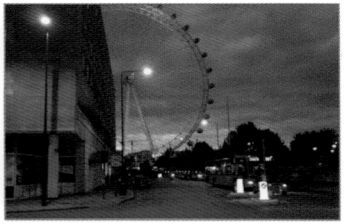

▲ Photos taken right after the sun goes down appear bluish in tone.

For photos taken in the middle of the night, the sky appears completely black because there is no longer any light in the sky. Experiment with taking photos of the city at different times of the night.

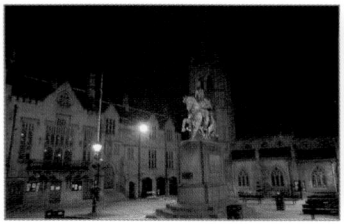

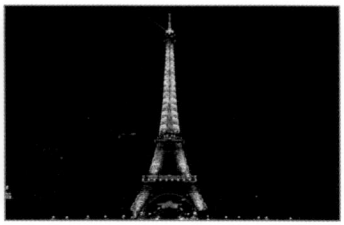

▲ In photos taken in the middle of the night, the sky appears black.

Creating Traffic Light Trails

Setting the shutter speed to 2 seconds or longer in the Shutter Priority or Manual mode will allow you to capture the light streaks or trace the movement of lights from moving vehicles. This method captures the movement of light sources in a way that is not normally visible to the human eye. When photographing light trails, you should check that the scene is dim enough. If is too bright, it will cancel out the light trails in the photo.

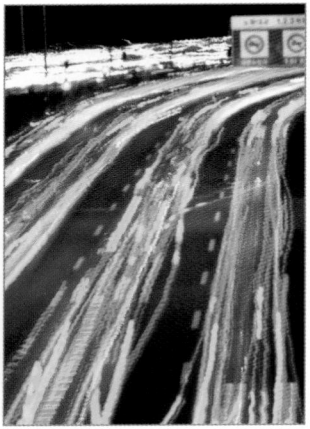

Even if you can't set the shutter speed on your camera, you can still create this effect by using the Night Landscape Scene mode. Your camera must support shutter speeds of 2 seconds or longer, though.

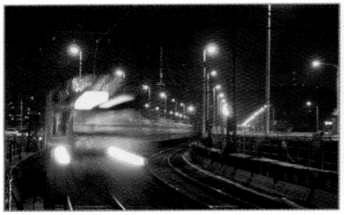

▲ The light streaks brighten up the image considerably.

Cut out the Noise

Slow shutter speeds have a tendency to add electronic noise to your photos. This can be reduced somewhat by using a low sensitivity setting, for example ISO 50 or ISO 100. On some entry-level cameras you can activate the Noise Reduction mode to cut down the noise, while on others the camera automatically processes photos taken in the Night Landscape mode to reduce noise before saving them to the memory card.

To photograph traffic light trails, position your camera where there are a lot of cars. Remember to keep a safe distance. Since you need a slow shutter speed of 2 seconds or longer, you should use a tripod or place your camera on a flat surface when taking the photo. You should also bracket your exposures for the same shot.

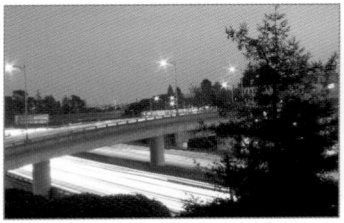

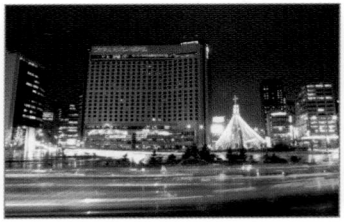

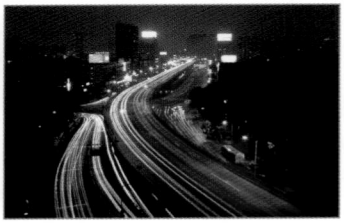

▲ Shot at a shutter speed of 30 seconds.

Shooting Photos of Fireworks

To take photos of fireworks, you will need to bring a tripod. Once you reach the scene, check the wind direction. Because the smoke from the fireworks can get in the way of your photos, your back should always be to the oncoming wind.

To get a good composition, include people, buildings, or water in the foreground to give the viewer a sense of the location and the magnitude of the fireworks display.

On an automatic camera, you can set it to the Fireworks Show mode, which uses a slow shutter speed, responds more rapidly to the shutter-release button, fixes the focus at infinity, and turns off the flash to capture the display. Not all automatic cameras come with this mode so you should check your camera's specifications.

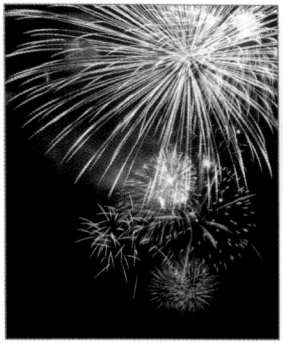

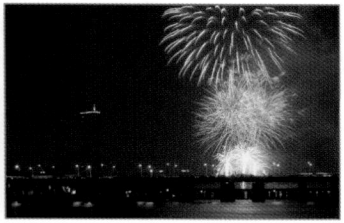

◀▲ A shutter speed of 8 seconds was used to capture several fireworks in one photo.

If you have a semiautomatic camera, you should set the shutter speed to 3 seconds or longer at most fireworks displays. Since you will never know when the climax of the display is coming, always make sure you have ample memory space and keep your attention on the fireworks right up to the end.

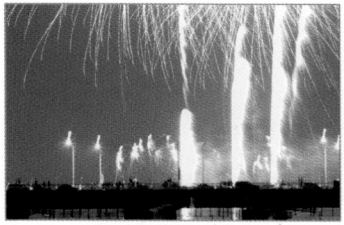

▲ Use a telephoto lens to fill the frame with an electrifying and impressive view of the fireworks.

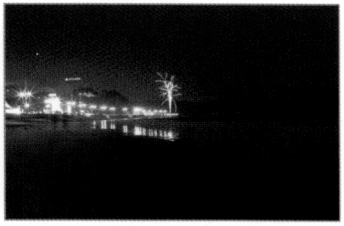

▲ Focusing on the foreground has the effect of diminishing the size of the fireworks. Be careful to avoid this.

28 Capturing Sunrises and Sunsets

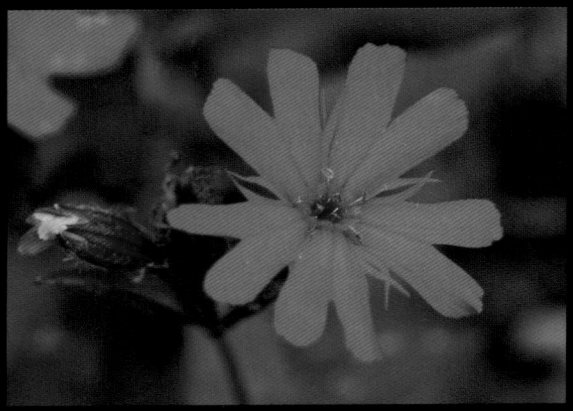

It is relatively easy to take good photos of sunrises and sunsets, because errors in exposure will not drastically affect the final image. This is one reason why sunrises and sunsets are among the most rewarding subjects for novice photographers. In addition, the dramatic display in the sky is there for all to see, so you may not need to venture far to take the shots.

Planning

Since you only have a short time to capture the rising or setting sun, you should plan your shot beforehand and look for a location with a clear view of the sky. The best time to shoot is about half an hour before or after the sun rises or sets. This is the time when the sky and the landscape are bathed in a warm, golden hue.

Use a Telephoto Lens

A telephoto lens is essential. With 3× zoom lenses like the 35–105 mm lens, you can get a nice shot of the landscape with the sun in the background if you set the lens to its maximum telephoto capability.

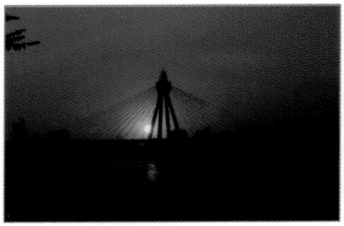

▲ Sunset taken with a 50 mm lens.

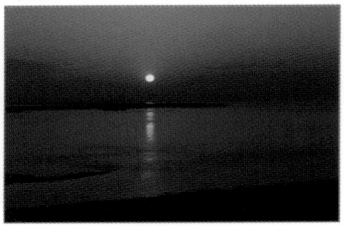

▲ Sunrise taken with a 50 mm lens.

However if you want the sun to dominate the frame, you will need a digital camera with a higher telephoto capability. Alternately, you can use your camera's digital zoom feature and include nearby buildings or objects in your photo to make the sun look larger in comparison.

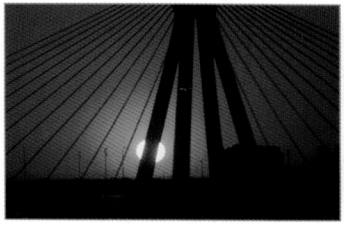

▲ Using a 200 mm lens to fill the frame with the sun's orange hue.

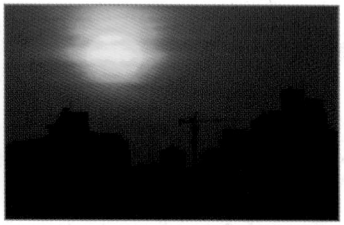

▲ This sunset was photographed using a 400 mm lens. The photo includes the nearby buildings to show the sun setting on the city.

Rule of Thirds

In general, photos with the subject directly in the center look less interesting than photos with the subject off center. For example, if you are taking photos of a sunrise or sunset, divide the frame into thirds and place the sun or horizon on the lower 1/3 of the frame to emphasize the sky, or the upper 1/3 of the frame to emphasize the water or land mass.

For a more detailed discussion of the Rule of Thirds, refer to Technique 7, "Composing a Shot." The Rule of Thirds is only a guide, and in some instances, it may make sense to center your subject.

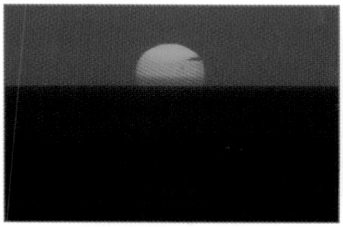

▲ Emphasis is placed on the ocean.

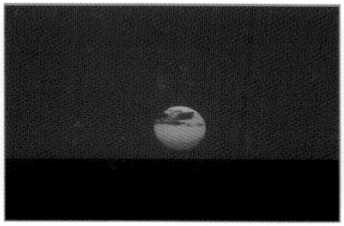

▲ Emphasis is placed on the sky.

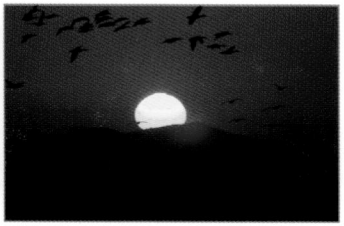

▲ Capturing birds in flight adds movement and accents to the image.

Capturing the Changing Hues of the Sky

The sky is at its most beautiful when the sun is on the horizon. However, you can get a better range of colors in the sky when the sun has dipped below the horizon or when it is about to rise. Since the sun is not in the scene, it is also easier to get the correct exposure.

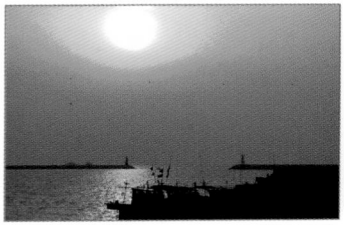

▲ At sunset, the ocean looks golden.

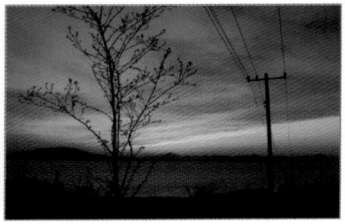

▲ Vibrant hues fill the sky at sunset.

Be sensitive to the changing light. At sunrise and sunset, the sky can put on a show of reflected light that dramatically lights up clouds or bathes the landscape in a warm, soft glow. The best thing about shots of sunrises and sunsets is that they are always unique. You can't take another shot with the exact same combination of cloud cover, lighting, and hue.

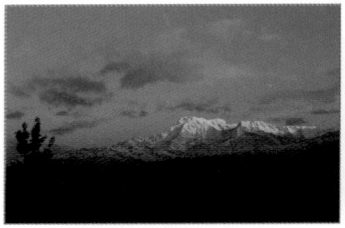

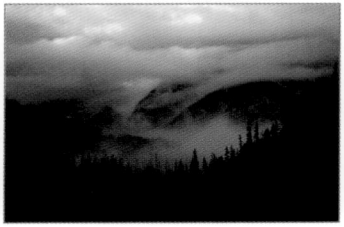

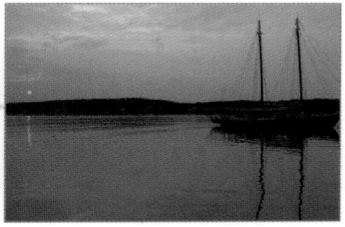

▲ Capturing the beauty of sunrise.

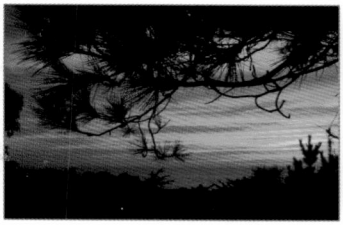
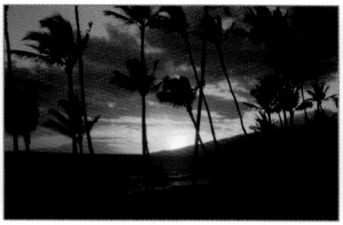
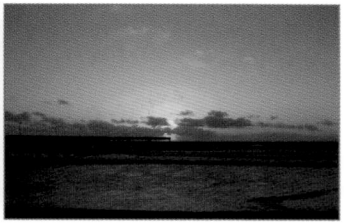

▲ Capturing the beauty of sunset.

It is easy to shoot silhouette pictures during sunrise and sunset. Silhouette photos emphasize the shape of the subject by shooting it dark with the extreme contrast provided by backlight or a sunset. You have to set your exposure manually or adjust the exposure to (−) to take silhouette photos. If you set your exposure to automatic, it will take bright pictures, not silhouette ones.

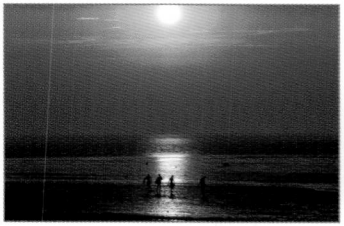
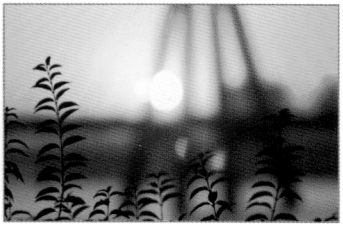

▲ Try shooting various silhouettes during sunset.

29 Creating Panoramas

In the past, panoramic photographs could only be taken with special panoramic film cameras. Today, you can take panoramic photos with any digital camera that has a Panorama mode. This function is particularly useful for conveying the scale and sense of openness of an expansive landscape. In this section, you will learn how to take panoramic shots and use photo editing software to stitch a panoramic photo on the computer.

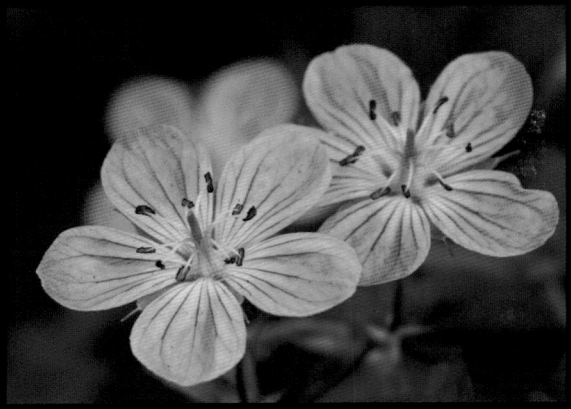

Use the Panorama Mode

To create a seamless panorama, you should take a series of shots around a single point of rotation. In other words, you should rotate your camera around the same point when shooting left-to-right or right-to-left portions of the scenery. You can also shoot from top to bottom or bottom to top for a vertical panorama.

The LCD displays the previous shot so that you can keep your photos straight and level with the ground. The series of shots will later be stitched together to form one panoramic shot using either the proprietary stitching tool bundled with your camera or independent computer software.

Although panoramas are mostly shot to emphasize the grandeur of a landscape, they can also be used to bring out other elements such as people and objects.

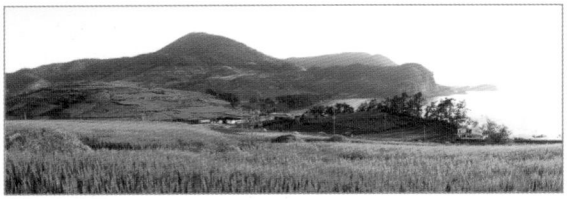

◀ A single photograph would have had to sacrifice either the mountain or the sea if not using the panoramic format.

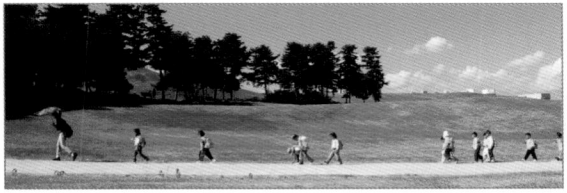

◀ In this photo, the panoramic format is used to highlight the journey of the people; the landscape, in contrast, is not the main focus. Be on the lookout for opportunities to shoot such offbeat compositions!

Use a Tripod

You need a sturdy tripod in order to keep all the shots level with the ground. Depending on whether it is a horizontal or vertical sequence, always keep the camera parallel with the horizontal or vertical axis. In order to create a seamless panorama, do not move from your position while photographing. Do rotate your camera a little at a time to make sure that the shots overlap. In addition, you should not readjust the height of your tripod once you start shooting.

It is possible to shoot panoramas without a tripod, but you will need to keep your body still, your hands steady, and your movement controlled. As is to be expected, these photos will not align as well as those shot with a tripod, so you will need to rotate and crop the shots in an image-editing program.

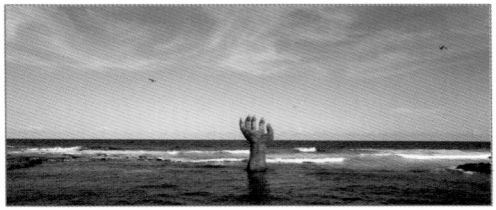

▲ Keep your photos aligned.

Maintain the Same Exposure

When taking panoramic photos, you will be taking several photos across a wide area. Each area will have a different amount of light and shade, resulting in a slightly different exposure for each of the shots. When this happens, your panorama will appear patchy and uneven when you combine the photos.

To avoid this problem, set a fixed exposure for all the shots if your digital camera allows for manual exposure adjustment. Alternatively, set the camera to AE-Lock (Auto Exposure Lock) to ensure that exposure and white balance setting is consistent throughout. The settings are locked to that of the first image in the series after turning on the Panorama mode.

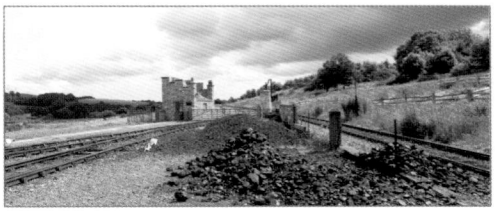

▲ Fix the exposure before taking a series of shots.

Beware of Distortion

A wide-angle lens will create slight distortions at the edges of individual shots. These subtle distortions will become noticeable when you stitch your photos together. To minimize distortion, you should zoom to the telephoto range or set your camera to the Telephoto mode.

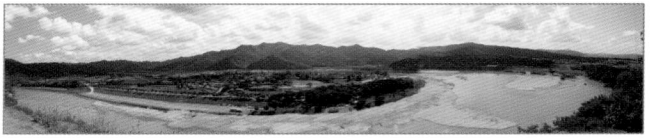

▲ A wide-angle lens will warp the edges of the photo.

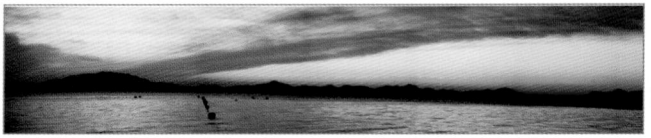

▲ Use a telephoto lens to eliminate distortion.

Overlap Photos As You Take Them

Make sure that the photos in the series overlap at the edges. The Panorama mode uses the overlapping areas to match the photos seamlessly. It is recommended that each of your photos should overlap by about 20 percent.

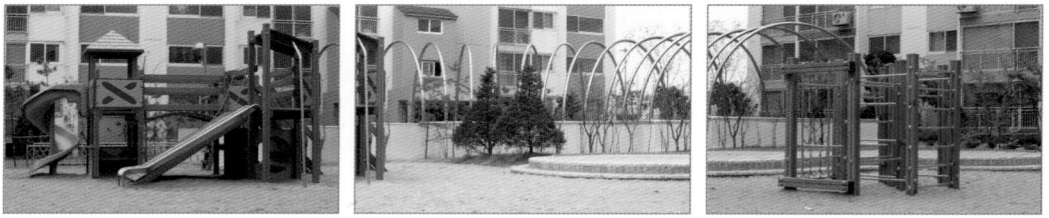

▲ Photos with overlapping sections.

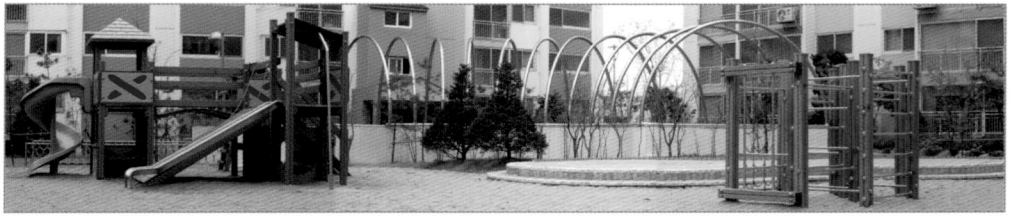

▲ Using these overlaps you can create a smooth panorama.

Combining Panoramas on the Computer

In this step-by-step example, we will show you how to create a panorama using PhotoStitch—Canon's easy-to-use software for stitching panoramas. PhotoStitch is bundled with many of Canon's digital cameras, but you can also buy it separately.

① Start the program. Click on the Open icon and select the photos you want to combine as a panorama.

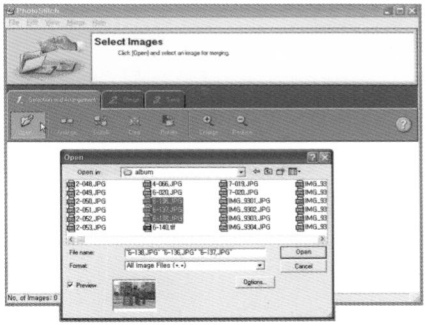

② Open the selected photos. After placing your photos in their proper order, click the Merge tab and then click the Start icon to combine the photos into a panorama.

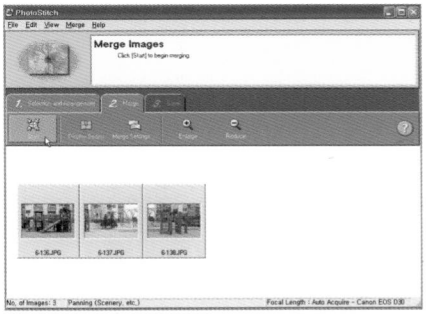

③ Click the Save tab. You will see a green line appear. This line is used to de-clutter your panorama.

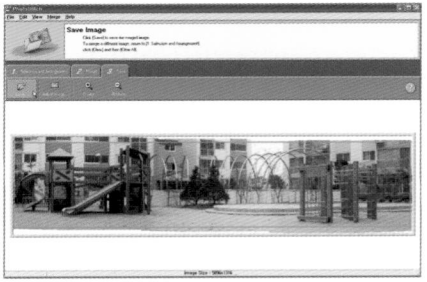

④ Click the Adjust Image icon so as not to save the areas outside the green line.

⑤ Check the Crop option and then click Save to save your panorama.

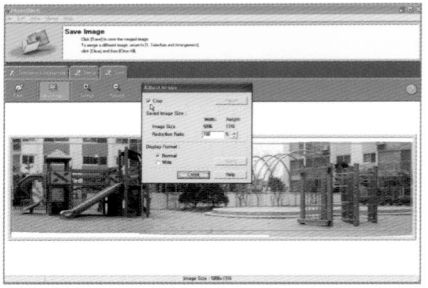

⑥ The panorama is now complete.

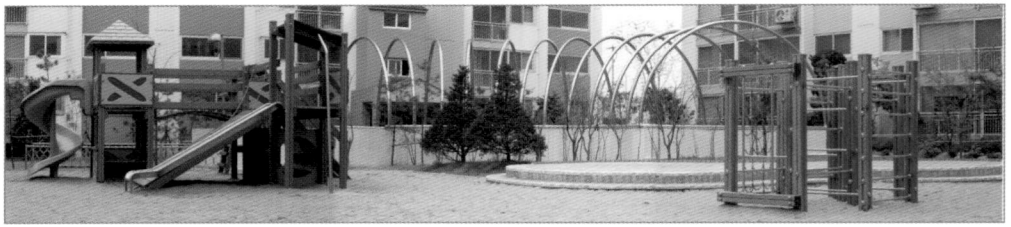

Chapter 4 | Shooting Landscapes

- √ Explore your surroundings.
- √ Try out different camera angles, orientations, and styles.
- √ Check to see whether the composition is balanced.
- √ Simplify the background.
- √ Choose to either blur out the background or keep everything in focus.
- √ If a scene or landmark looks dull because of air pollution, try taking the shot when it is lit up at night.
- √ Go early and get a good spot when shooting events.
- √ When taking photos through glass, shoot at an angle and select the Landscape Scene mode.
- √ Use plastic wrap, a waterproof camera bag, or a waterproof case when shooting in the rain.
- √ In winter, bring an extra battery and keep the camera warm by carrying it in your pocket.
- √ Use a polarizing filter to enhance the contrast and saturate the colors.
- √ Try using a slow shutter speed when taking pictures of rivers and streams to create motion streaks.
- √ Raise the exposure by 1/2 or 1 stop or use the Auto Exposure Bracketing mode when shooting snow scenes.
- √ When shooting at night, use a tripod or some other on-location support, and set a shutter speed of 1 second or longer.
- √ Set the shutter speed to 2 seconds or longer to capture traffic streaks.
- √ If you can't adjust the shutter speed, try using the Night Landscape Scene mode.
- √ Zoom in to the sun when taking pictures of sunrises and sunsets.
- √ Take pictures half an hour before or after the sun rises or sets to get a better range of colors in the sky.

40 Digital Photography Techniques

Experimenting with Common Themes

Chapter 5

It is important to realize that there are no hard and fast rules to follow in photography. After you have mastered the basic skills, you will need to explore different themes and experiment with various scenarios in order to shoot better photos. Of course, the more practice you put into taking different kinds of photos, the better you will be at creating and handling different scenarios. This chapter will explore some common photographic themes such as food, products, cars, and architecture.

30 Photographing Food

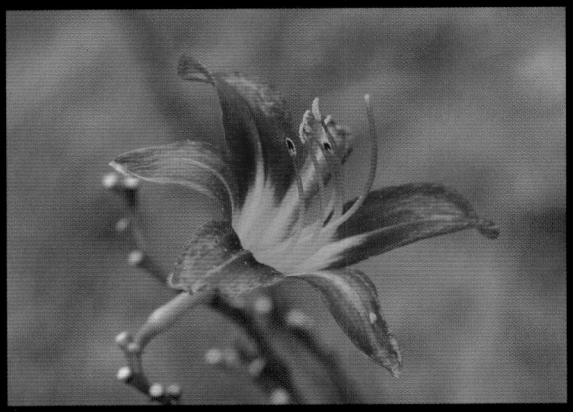

Food photography is a specialized field of photography. Commercial photos of food are usually taken in a studio with a food stylist, an art director, and a professional photographer.
It is, however, possible for photography hobbyists to shoot photos of food outside the studio.

Capturing the Essence

The secret to food photography is in capturing the defining characteristic of a food and making it look as delicious as possible. For instance, photos of pizza could focus on the soft, melting cheese, while photos of coffee could have a close-up shot of the steam slowly rising from the cup. The idea behind food photography is to convey the taste and scent of the food to the viewer.

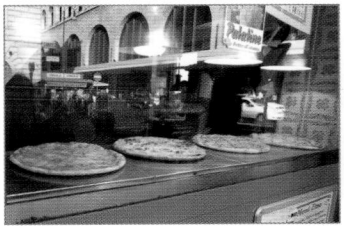

▲ A general shot of pizzas through the window fails to excite taste buds.

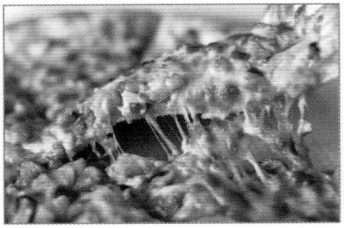

▲ Giving the cheese more emphasis makes the pizza look tempting.

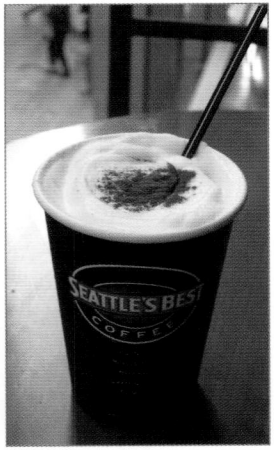

▲ A cup of coffee with a frothy topping looks rich and enticing.

A common mistake in taking photos of non-solid food is to place the camera so close that the broth or sauce gets splashed onto the lens. When taking such close-ups, keep the camera a safe distance away.

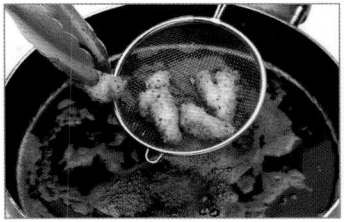

▲ Make sure that oil does not get on the lens.

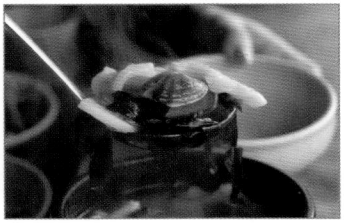

▲ Avoid splashes from soups or broths.

Vary the Angle and Composition

A well-composed photo showing part of the food can be more appetizing than a shot showing the food and the entire serving dish. In photography, less is often more, and you can create a stronger impact by showing just a portion of the food. The objective is to keep the point of interest on what matters most. This varies with the characteristics of the food, the table setting, and the background.

When taking photos of food (especially those with good form and color), use selective focusing to blur the background clutter. By opening up the aperture (small f-number) or using the Macro mode, you can focus on the food and blur the background.

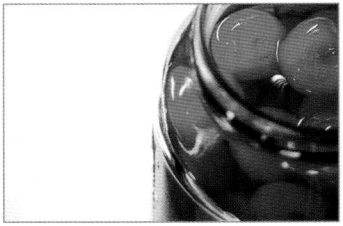

▲ Only a section of this jar of cherries was photographed to emphasize the redness of the cherries.

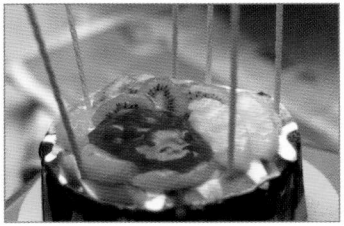

▲ A close-up showing the top of the cake emphasizes the splendid presentation and vibrant colors.

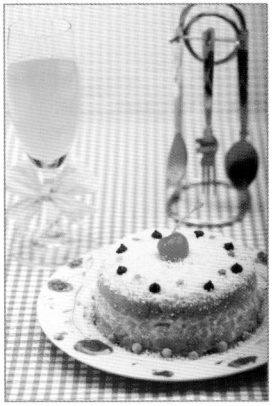

▲ Blurring the table gives emphasis to the food in the photo.

For food with little form or color, on the other hand, it is better to introduce accents, such as rising steam, or to keep decorative elements like crockery, table setting, and background in focus. In the shot on the right, coffee beans were used as accents for an otherwise dull shot.

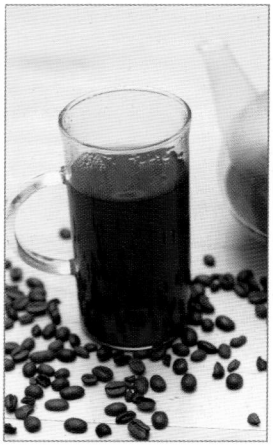

▶ Including coffee beans in the shot relays the message of freshness and use of quality ingredients.

As a guide, try to vary the food presentation, camera angle, and composition in your shots and also consider enhancing your shots using natural ingredients or artificial props.

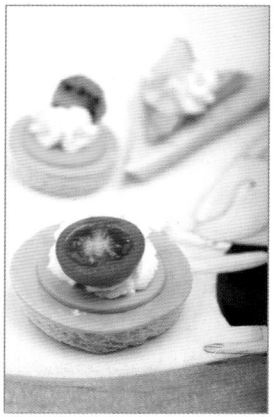

▲ Use a large aperture of *f*/2.0 or Macro mode to fade the table into the background.

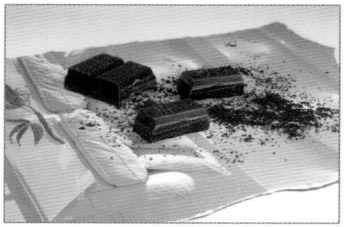

▲ A background sheet and a sprinkling of chocolate powder complete the look.

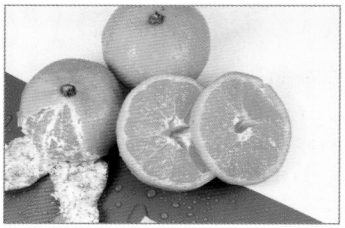

▲ Spraying water on the oranges adds a refreshing touch to the photo.

31 Taking Product Shots

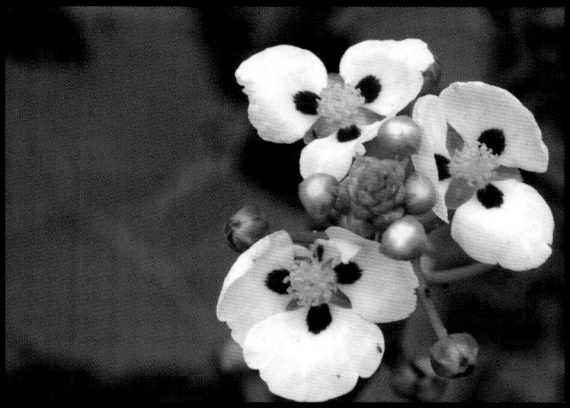

Although product photography is mainly a commercial field, you do not need expensive equipment to take reasonably good shots. Whether you are a small business owner or a consumer, you can use a digital camera to take interesting shots of products.

Use Natural Light

It is important to avoid direct sunlight when taking product photos outdoors. The best times for a shoot are between 9 a.m. and 10 a.m. or 4 p.m. and 5 p.m.

When shooting indoors, place the product on a table next to the window so that it will be illuminated by a soft natural light from the side. This technique gives excellent results. In fact, the play of shadow and light on the product can produce as good a result as any artificial studio lighting.

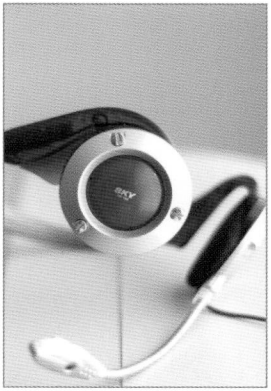

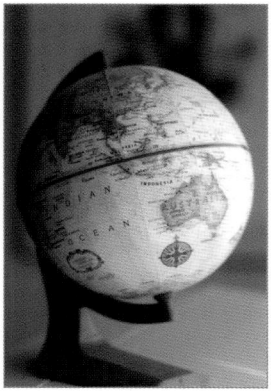

▲ Using natural light can give surprisingly good results.

Using a Background Sheet

If you have a messy background, cover it with a background sheet to create a simple background and keep the focus on the product. Even if you have an uncluttered background, you may wish to use a background sheet for its color and design to create an atmosphere that complements the product.

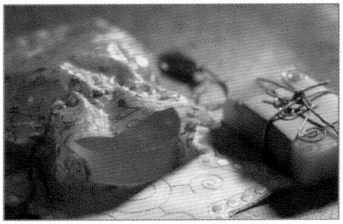

▲ The brown background sheet color-coordinates the products in this photo.

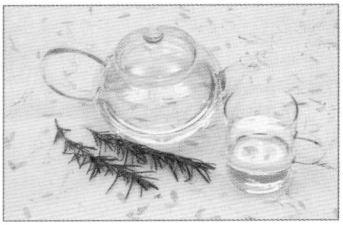

▲ A white sheet with patterns is used to emphasize the transparency of the tea set.

Use Household Lamps

Instead of using the camera's built-in flash, it is better to use an external light source, like a lamp. Although it won't be as bright as the flash, the light from the lamp can make the product look more natural and bring out the contours and texture of the product.

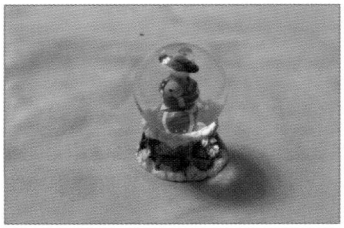

▲ Product photo taken without using a light source.

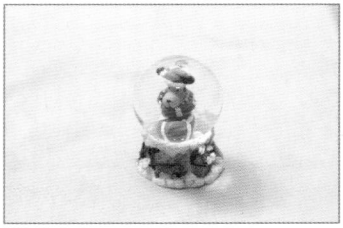

▲ Product photo taken using a lamp.

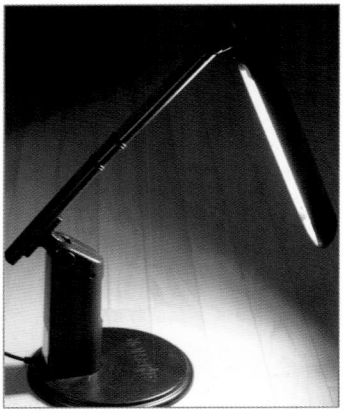

▲ You can use any lamp around the house.

Use a Tripod

When shooting product shots, you will spend most of your time changing the position of the product and the background elements to try out different compositions. To prevent fatigue, you should use a tripod. In addition, since neither household nor office lighting is as bright as studio lights, you will need a longer exposure time to take a product shot. As this increases the risk of camera shake and blurring, a tripod is helpful.

Increase the Exposure

Product photos need to be well lit and stand out from the background. If you use the Auto exposure specified by the camera, your photos will appear slightly dark. This is because the camera will average out the exposure for the scene to 18 percent gray. The solution is to override the Auto exposure and open up the aperture or slow down the shutter speed by 1 or 2 stops.

For cameras that have an exposure compensation feature, raise the exposure compensation by one or two levels before you take the photo. Alternatively, set the camera to the AEB, or Auto Exposure Bracketing mode. The camera will shoot at three different exposures in three continuous shots from which you can select the best photo.

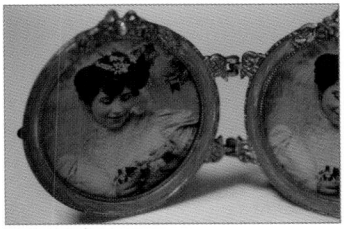

▲ Using Auto exposure in direct light without exposure compensation will make the photo slightly dark.

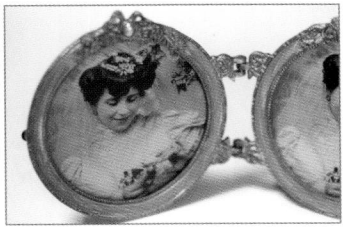

▲ Exposure raised by 1 stop.

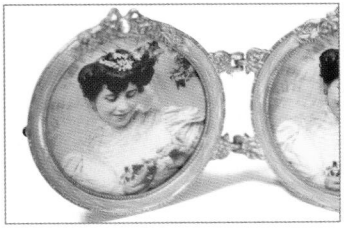

▲ Exposure raised by 2 stops.

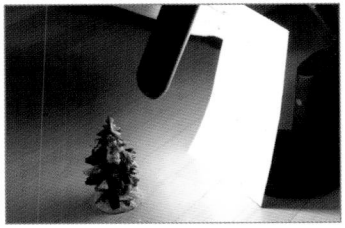

▲ Use a piece of paper to reflect the light from a lamp.

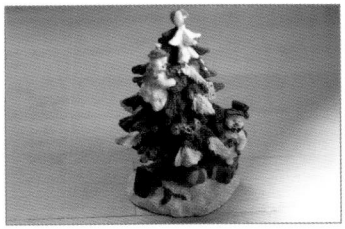

▲ Raise the exposure by 2 stops when using reflected light.

Built-In Flash

Do not use the camera's built-in flash when taking product photos, as this will create harsh shadows.

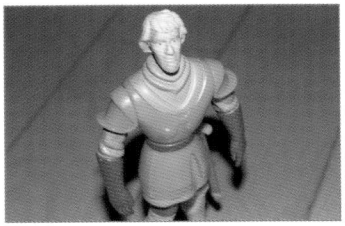

▶ Try to avoid shooting products with the embedded flash.

Use a Simple Still-Life Lighting Package

Shooting good product photos requires several large light sources and a background lamp. Such equipment is expensive and can be too bulky to store in regular households. For hobbyists, a simple still-life photography lighting package is a less expensive option and works just as well for small products and still-life setups.

A typical lighting package includes two small lamps and a diffusion box to soften the light and eliminate harsh shadows. These lights are small, making them easier to set up and store, and they can also be triggered wirelessly, making them suitable for use with digital cameras.

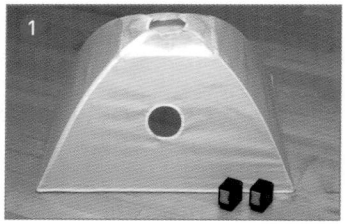

▲ The set includes two small lamps and a box for displaying the product.

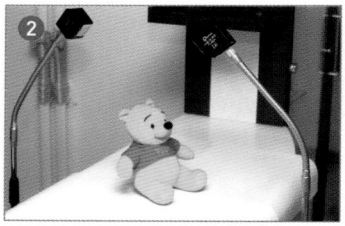

▲ Place the background sheet on a flat surface, place the product on top, and position the lamps.

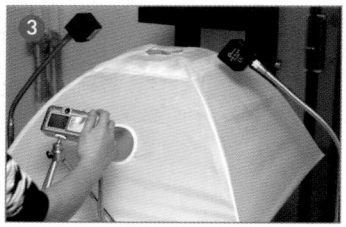

▲ After covering the product with a diffusion box and setting up the camera, use the flash to take the photo. The two lamps will flash at the same time.

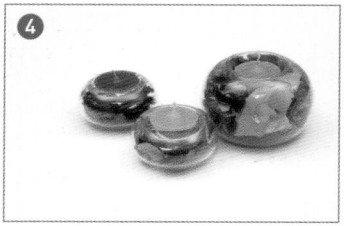

▲ No shadows will be cast on the white background.

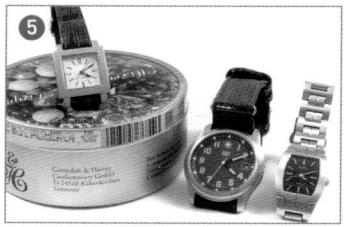

▲ Even objects with highly reflective surfaces can be photographed in this way without any problems.

32 Photographing Cars

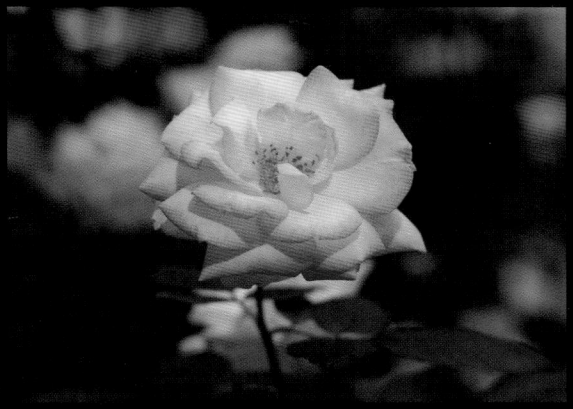

Cars are not only modes of transportation designed to get you quickly from one place to another; they are also objects of beauty and precision engineering. While vacationing in another country, you will probably see many makes and models that are not found back home. If you love cars, try taking photos of them with your digital camera.

Shooting Close-Ups

Although full shots are great, you should also try to take photos of a car at different distances and perspectives to add variety to your selection of photos. Study the form of the car, pick out its most attractive features, and fill the frame with it. For example, you may want to shoot a close-up of a specific area in order to emphasize the beauty of the car's contours or the power of its build.

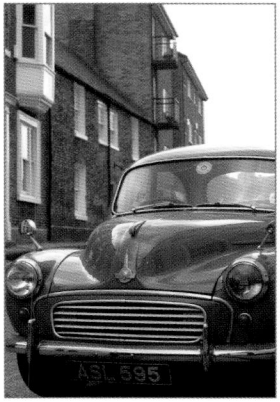

◀ Taking a close-up lets the viewer study the car's design elements in detail.

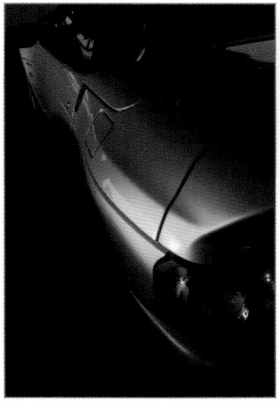

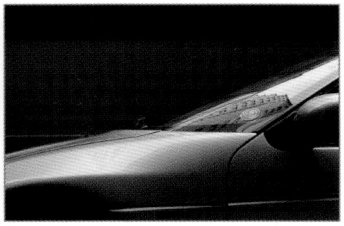

◀ ▲ These shots emphasize the sleek contours.

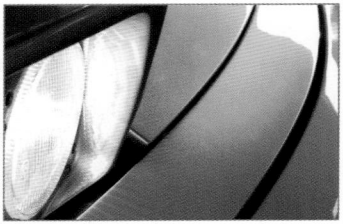

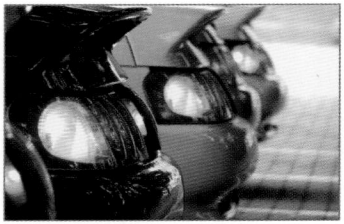

▲ Close-ups can turn images into an abstract study of form, color, and light.

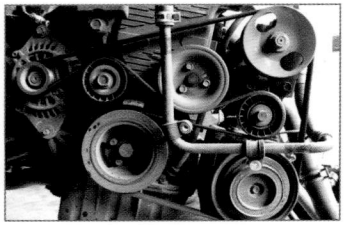

▲ Emphasize the power of the car by taking a close-up shot of the engine.

Weather and Time of Day

The weather and time of day affect not only the exposure but also the color and the mood of your image.

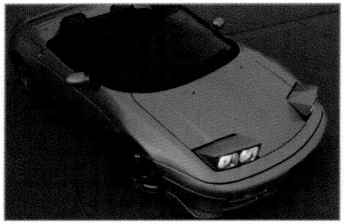

▲ Turn on the headlights when shooting at sunset to capture the fleeting sensation of day turning into night.

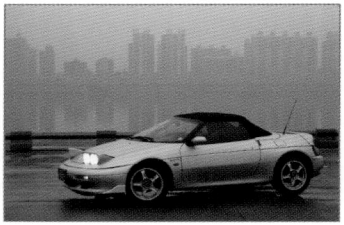

▲ Rain makes the car and the road highly reflective, giving it a sleek appearance.

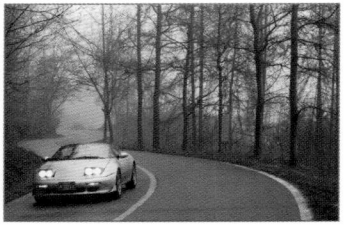

▲ The muted colors and foggy conditions at dawn provide contrast and highlight the car in the image.

Lens Type

When taking photos of cars, use a wide-angle lens to deepen the depth of field and keep the background in focus. Including the background will make the image more interesting, as it provides information about the car's owner and the locale.

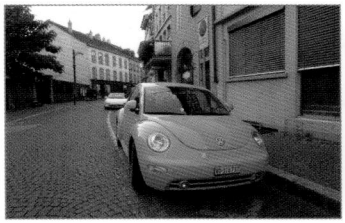

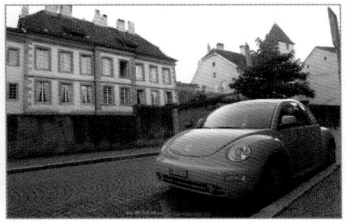

▲ Try taking a few compositions that include the background.

Camera Angle

Instead of taking a shot from the front, stand slightly to the side to add dimension and perspective to the photo. Try to find an interesting angle; stand, squat, or lie down if you have to.

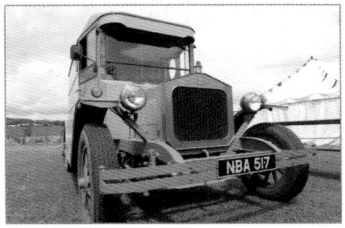

▲ Classic cars always make nice subjects for photos.

Shutter Speed

You can use either a fast shutter speed to freeze the motion of a car or a slow shutter speed to blur the traffic around it.

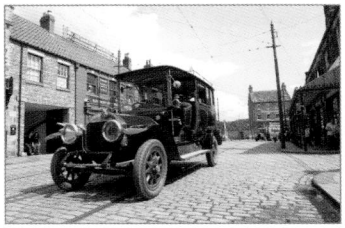

▲ Use a fast shutter speed (1/200 second) or the Sports Scene mode to freeze a moving car.

33 Photographing Architecture

When taking photos of building exteriors, you need to decide whether to include the entire building or just a section of it.
The sheer size and height of some buildings makes it hard to include the entire structure without barrel distortion. However, by keeping a few things in mind, you can take spectacular photos of any structure, from your own house to massive architectural wonders.

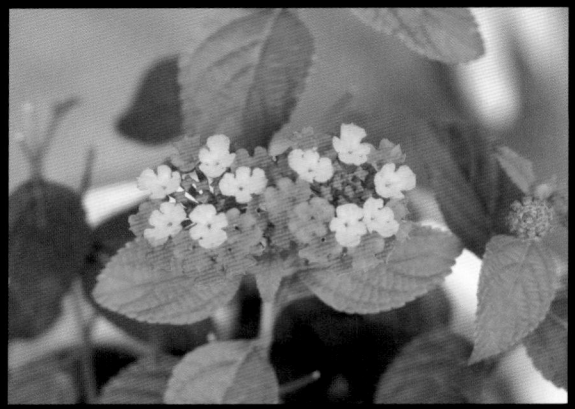

Use a Telephoto Lens

Most people tend to leave too much space in their image by including too much of the background or the building. Remember that although the wide expanse before you may look inspiring and majestic, the subjects will look insignificant and even diminutive when printed. If you are standing some distance away, you need to avoid shooting such broad, generalized views by using a telephoto lens to fill the frame with the subject. If you do not have a good telephoto lens, you should get closer to the building and photograph a major feature of the building.

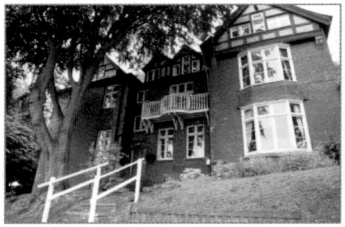

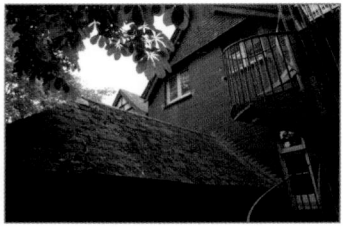

▲ Fill the frame and you will start seeing a distinct improvement.

Introduce Foreground Objects

Where possible, include some meaningful objects or people in the foreground of your building shot to give it more depth, dimensionality, and thematic interest.

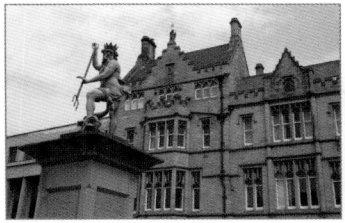

▲ A statue is included to give the photo a central focus.

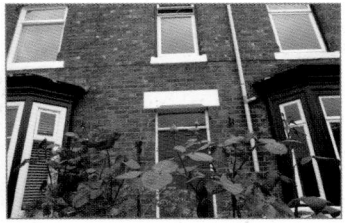

▲ By introducing a soft element in the form of the flower, you can make an imposing apartment building appear more warm and welcoming.

Avoid Distortion

A wide-angle lens with a focal length of 35 mm or less tends to create distortion at the photo edges and warp the straight edges of buildings. Distortion becomes more obvious with shorter focal lengths and taller buildings.

To snap a photo that will reproduce an image of the building without distortion, the lens must have a focal length of 50 mm or more (telephoto). When shooting with a telephoto lens, a building can be captured as it is without any distortion, but you will have to shoot from farther away to fit more of the subject in the frame.

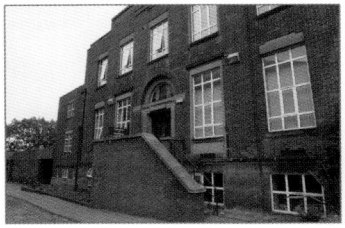

▲ ▶ Buildings can look distorted when shot with a wide-angle lens.

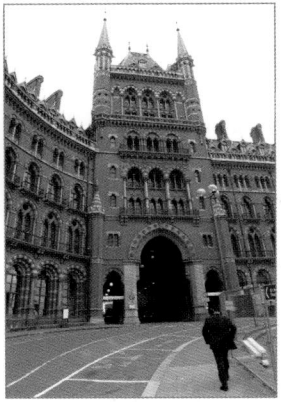

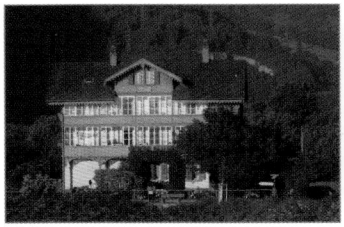

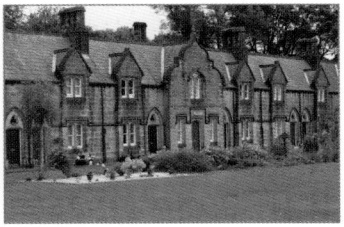

▲ Using a telephoto lens to shoot from a vantage point at a distance of half the height of the building will reduce distortion.

Vary the Composition

You can make your photo album livelier by using different compositions, angles, and props. Here are some ideas:

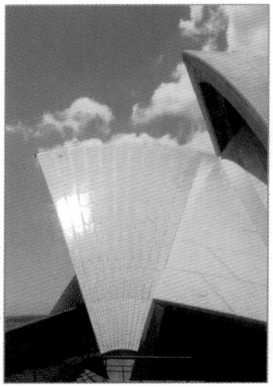

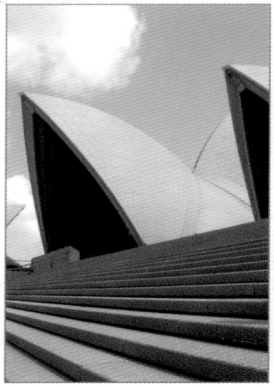

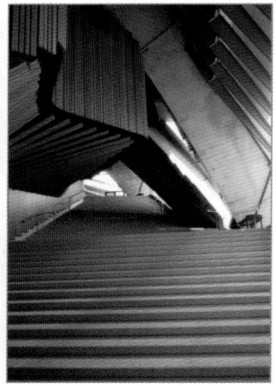

▲ Using leading lines and different camera angles creatively can produce many rewarding shots.

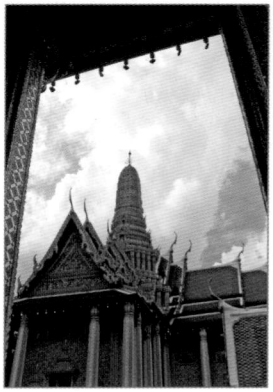

▲ When shooting at or from buildings, try using the doors, arches, or windows to frame the subject.

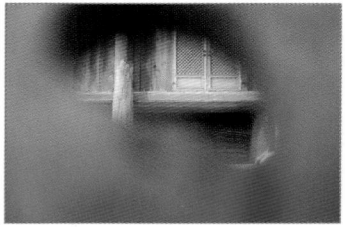

▲ Shoot through a colored sheet with a hole or any other objects to selectively focus on the building.

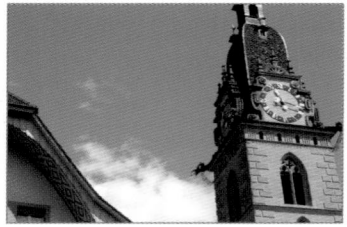

▲ This image is kept simple by shooting only a small section of both buildings. The focus is on the form of the buildings rather than on the structures in their entirety.

34 Taking Photos in a Museum or Art Gallery

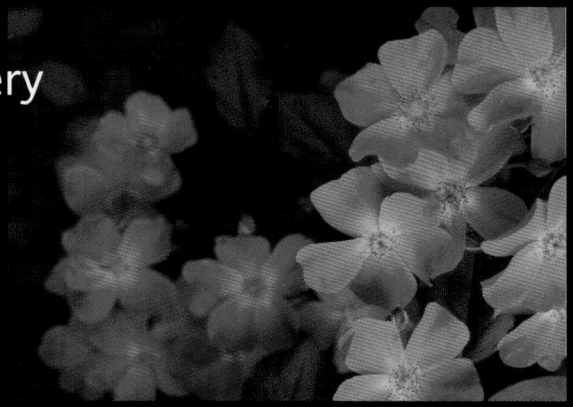

Even if you are not a history buff or an avid art lover, you are likely to visit museums or art galleries at one time or another.
While this section specifically addresses taking photos at museums and art galleries, these same techniques can also be applied for taking photos under other indoor conditions.

Glare and Reflection

Most displays in a museum are encased in glass, which can create reflections and glare in your photos if you use the flash. To overcome this problem, stand at a distance from the glass casing and shoot with a telephoto lens, without using a flash.

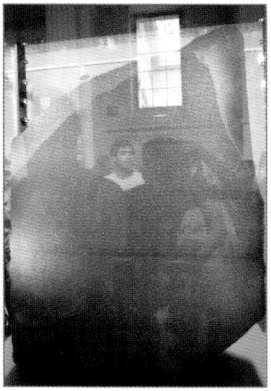

▲ You can't get a clear view of the display if you use a flash.

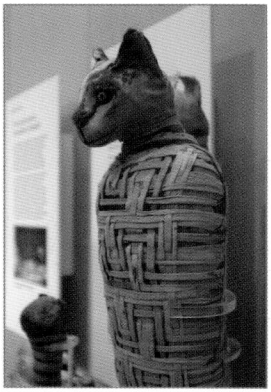

▲ Look for an angle with the least reflection.

Lighting

Since many museums are dimly lit indoor spaces, getting enough light for a good exposure becomes a problem. As most people set their cameras to Auto mode, the low-light conditions will trigger the flash. As you have just learned, this creates reflections in your image. To counteract this problem, deactivate the flash, set a slower shutter speed to let in more light, and hold the camera steady to prevent blurring. Another option is to take advantage of the natural light coming through the museum's windows.

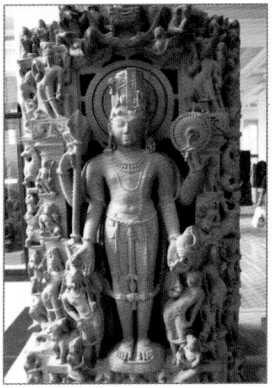

▲ Take advantage of the natural light.

No Flash Photography

Many museums have strict regulations against photography because your camera's flash (together with the flash from millions of other tourists) can damage an artwork over a period of time. A way of getting the right exposure under these conditions is to increase the camera's sensitivity (ISO) to light.

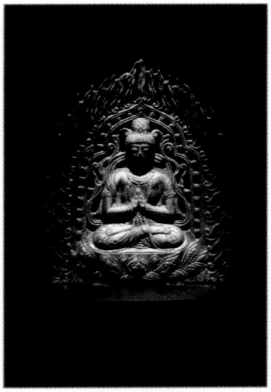

▲ Photo taken at high sensitivity without using flash.

White Balance

Most museums use either incandescent or halogen lamps, which will cast an orange tint over your images. To avoid this, you must adjust the white balance to match the color temperature of the museum lights. Simply pick the Museum Scene mode or the Incandescent White Balance mode before taking photos.

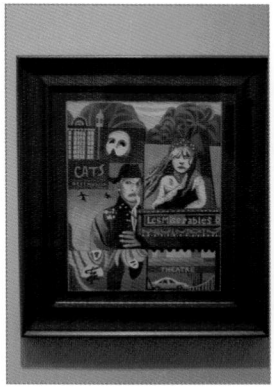

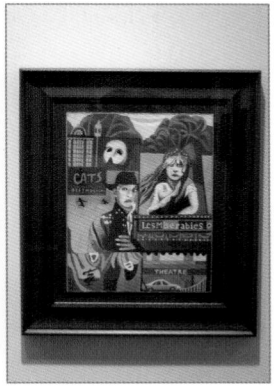

▲ The colors are more accurate (right photo) after adjusting the white balance.

Camera Distance

When photographing small displays, you should stand as close as you can to the glass case. For large sculptures, try to take close-up shots to eliminate the presence of other visitors and secondary objects from the background.

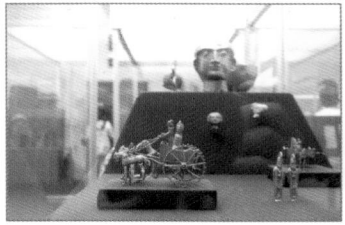

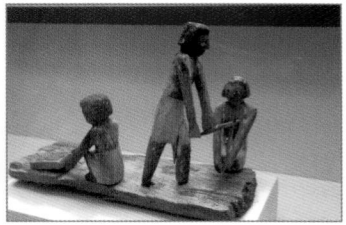

▲ You need to get really close to shoot small objects.

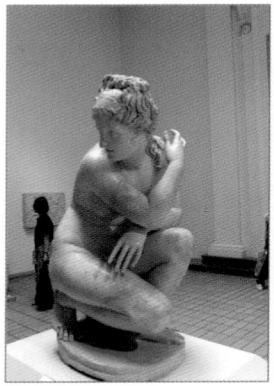

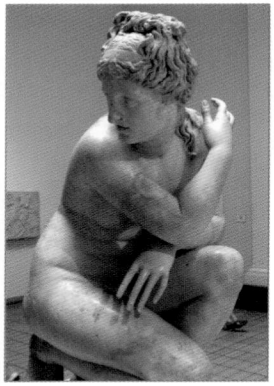

▲ Notice how the close-up focuses our attention on the sculpture and removes the distracting passersby.

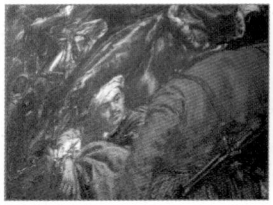

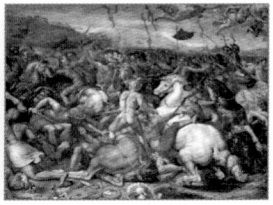

▲ Take borderless, close-up shots of a mural or a drawing for a postcard look.

Museum Building

Many museums are housed in grand old buildings that are artworks in themselves. On your next trip to a museum, study the architecture and you will find many photo opportunities.

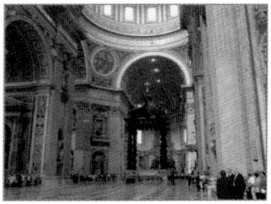

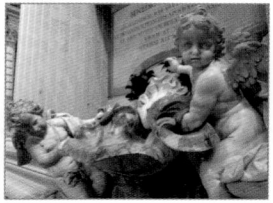

▲ The museum itself can be a work of art.

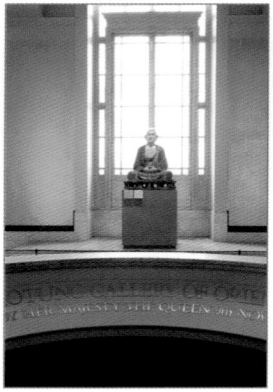

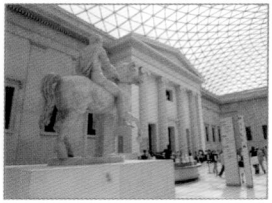

◀ ▲ You may also want to take a photo of the museum's exterior as a keepsake.

35 Photographing Pets

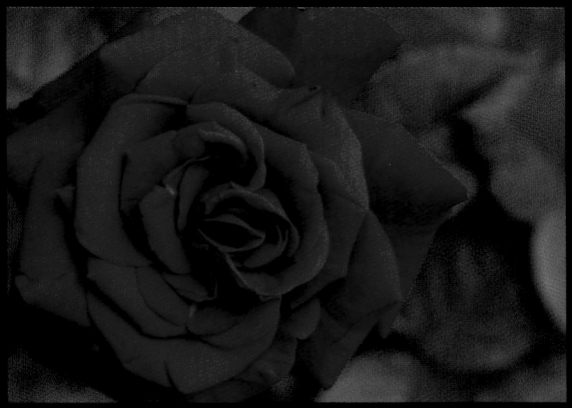

Pets are generally restless and move about constantly. Photographing pets can be tricky, because they won't pose for the camera and don't take instruction very well. Although it is difficult to take photos of pets, the results can be immensely satisfying.

Basic Techniques

▶▶▶ Use a Toy

Grab your pet's attention with its favorite toy or food. This will keep your pet amused long enough for you to take the photos.

▶▶▶ Avoid Flash

If you use a flash, the sudden burst of bright light can frighten your pet or make its eyes look red in the photo. To overcome this problem, try to avoid using flash where possible or, if you must, use the Red-Eye Reduction mode found in most digital cameras.

▶▶▶ ISO and Shutter Speed

By increasing the camera's sensitivity (higher ISO) or opening up the aperture, you can use a fast shutter speed to capture the movement of your pets. You can achieve the same result by using the Sports Scene mode.

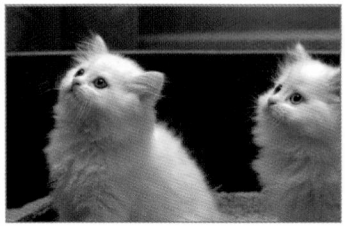

▲ A dangling, jingling toy did the trick with these two.

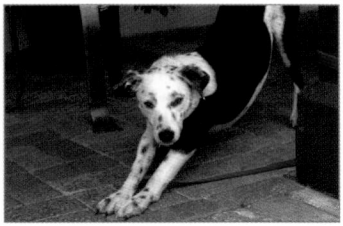

▲ You will need fast reflexes as well as fast shutter speeds to shoot your pet in action.

Advanced Techniques

▶▶▶ Continuous Shots

You never know when your pet will assume the look or gesture you want to photograph. To be sure that you don't miss the magic moment, use the Continuous Shot feature to take several successive shots and then choose the best from the lot.

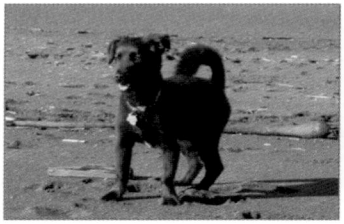

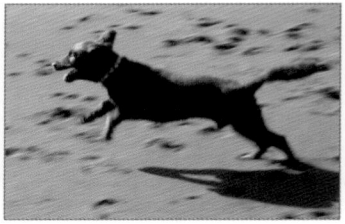

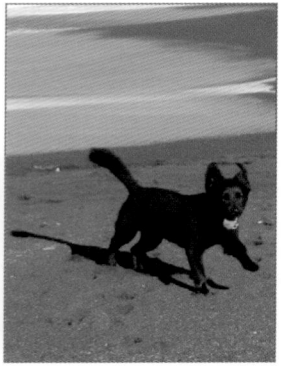

▲ For randomly moving subjects like pets, it is advisable to use the Continuous Shot feature.

▶▶▶ Selective Focusing

Open up to the maximum aperture (or use the Portrait mode) and use the selective-focusing technique to blur the background and keep the focus on your pet.

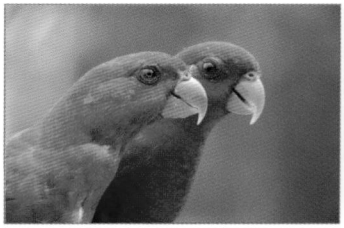

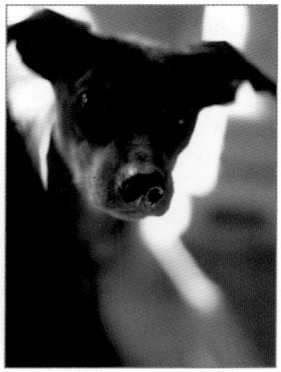

▲ Selective focusing has the effect of making the background and your pet look soft and fuzzy.

▶▶▶ Close-Ups

Try taking close-ups to communicate a sense of intimacy and familiarity.

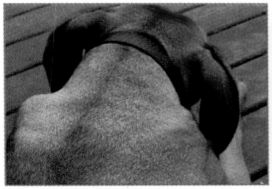

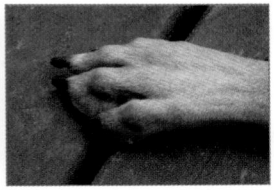

▲ You don't have to include your pet's face or its entire body in your photos. Try taking close-ups from a different angle or focus on a specific area.

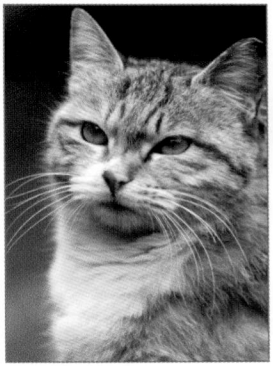

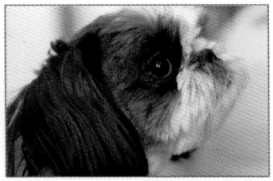

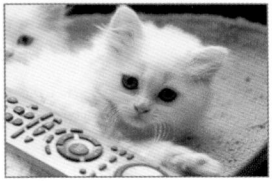

▲ Use close-up shots to capture the expression on your pet's face.

▶▶▶ Experiment!

You can take photos of your pet in countless ways. Here are a few ideas to help you get started:

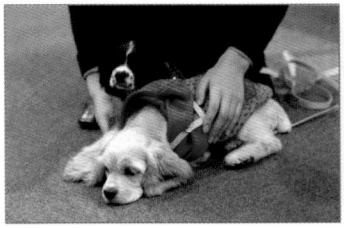

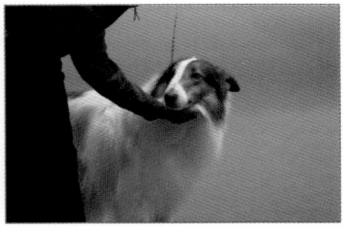

▲ Photograph your pet interacting with others to show its personality.

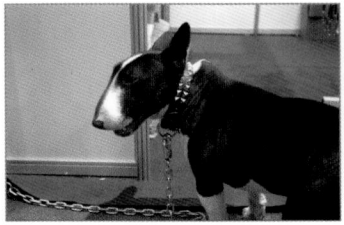

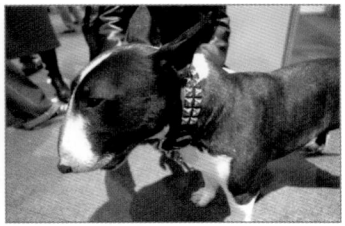

▲ Use a wide-angle lens (right) to take zany shots of your pet.

36 Animal Shots in the Zoo

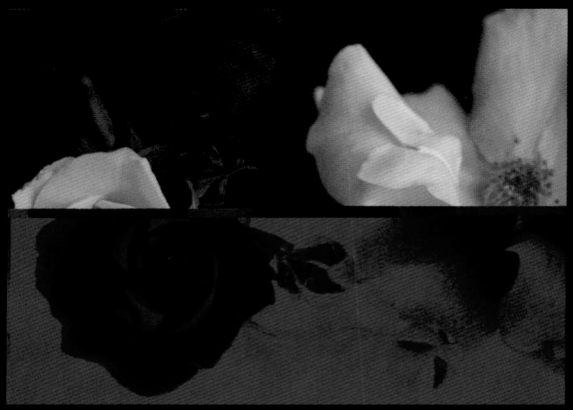

Though it might be ideal to take pictures of animals in the wild, these opportunities are rare in everyday life. Also, photographing wild animals requires very expensive professional equipment. This section applies the basics of animal photography to taking shots of animals in the zoo.

Use a Telephoto Lens

Though there may be exceptions, animal photos are generally shot with the longest focal length (telephoto status of zoom lens). As a regular digital camera's optical zoom has its limit, the photographer may use digital zoom as well. As digital zoom enables enlargement of over 100×, it may let you capture extreme close-ups. Unfortunately, the image quality decreases as digital zoom is used, as it is in effect the same as magnifying a photo in editing software.

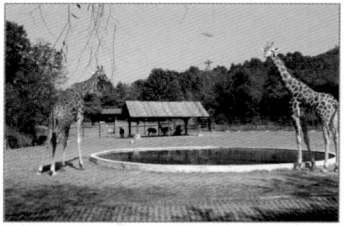

▲ Shot at 50 mm focal length.

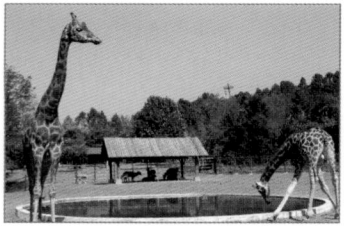

▲ Shot at 85 mm focal length.

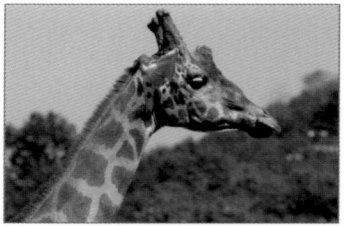

▲ Shot at 300 mm focal length.

When you do not have a suitable telephoto lens, another way to zoom is to use the crop function. Digital cameras with a high number of pixels are better at performing this function. As more color pixels means better resolution, you can easily crop the small parts and enlarge them.

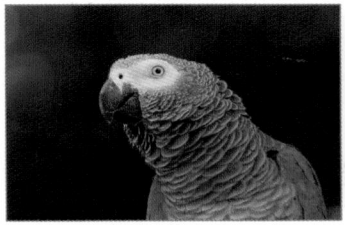

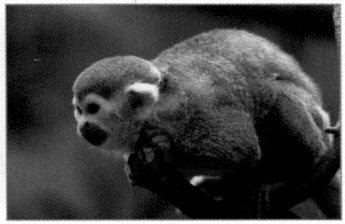

▲ Animals shots are more focused when you use a telephoto lens and dark backgrounds.

Use a Fast Shutter Speed

Another hurdle in photographing animals is that animals do not pose for the camera. Also, they move quickly, so it is hard to focus and easy to accidentally produce blurred pictures.

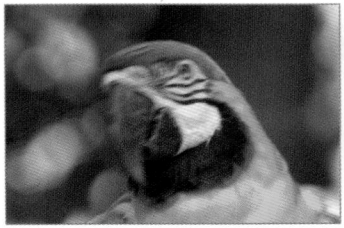

▲ A blurred photo taken with a slow shutter speed (1/60 sec).

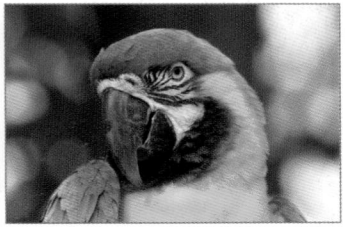

▲ A well-focused picture with a fast shutter speed (1/250 sec).

Generally, when you hold your camera with your hand, the slowest shutter speed you need to take a blur-free photo is [1/focal length] second. That is, if you take a picture with a 50 mm lens, the shutter speed should be at least 1/50 of a second, and with a 200 mm lens, it should be at least 1/200 of a second. However, when you take photos of moving animals, much faster shutter speeds are needed.

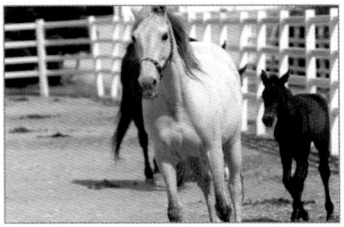

▲ Take a dynamic photo of animals using a fast shutter speed.

Close-up Photos of Animals

While full-body shots of animals are fine, close-ups of eyes, ears, beaks, or horns, for example, can also produce good pictures. Start with pictures of the overall body, and then observe closely to discover the unique characteristics of each animal. In order to take close-up photos, you need a lens with a long focal length.

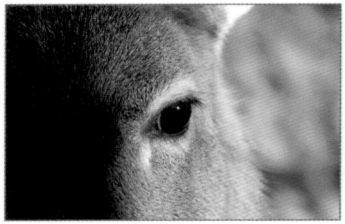

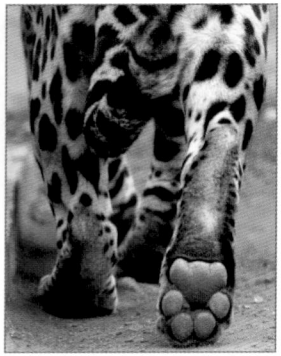

▲ Take various close-ups of animals.

Animal Photos with Wild Ambience

As a zoo has confined settings, it is hard to take animal photos that have the same appeal as wildlife shots. Animals that are behind glass walls or thick bars are particularly difficult to photograph.

When you take a picture of an animal behind bars, you have to put your lens right next to the bars to keep them from appearing in your photos. In particular, the bars tend not to appear if you shoot the photos in telephoto setting with an open iris. Try various settings to see what produces the best shot.

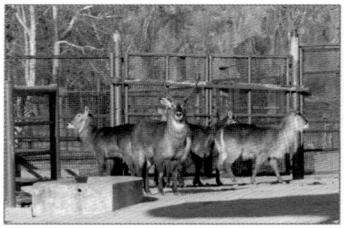

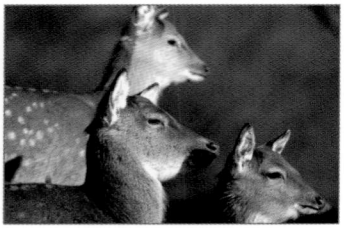

▲ Keep the bars out of the picture by using a telephoto lens and opening the iris.

Backgrounds are important if you want to give a wildlife touch to your photographs. Try to take pictures with natural elements in it, avoiding artificial structures such as bars or fences.

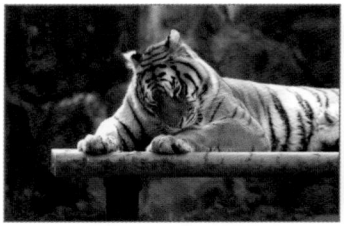

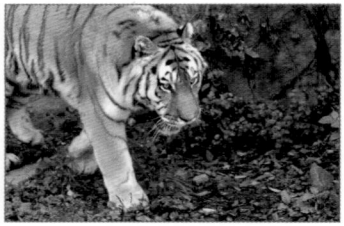

▲ Try to add a wildlife touch by shooting trees or grasses, instead of artificial structures.

- √ When taking pictures of objects such as food or products, capture the defining characteristic, consider taking a close-up of part of the object, and use decorative elements and a background sheet if necessary.
- √ Spray water (on fruits) or lightly glaze oil on a food item (cooked dishes) to make a more appetizing photo.
- √ Try taking product shots by a window for a soft, natural lighting effect.
- √ Use household lamps instead of the flash for a more balanced lighting effect. If the light from the lamp is too harsh, bounce it off a piece of white paper.
- √ When taking product shots, use a tripod, as you will need to adjust the subject placement often.
- √ Use a still-life lighting package if you often take product shots.
- √ Use a telephoto lens to shoot architecture from a distance of approximately half the height of the building, to avoid distortion at the edges.
- √ In a museum or art gallery, shoot at an angle without using flash if shooting through glass, increase the sensitivity if there is insufficient light, adjust the white balance to compensate for the lighting hue, and shoot close-ups to exclude other tourists from the shot.
- √ When taking pictures of pets, use a toy to engage the pet; turn off the flash, and use a fast shutter speed, the Sports Scene mode, or the Continuous Shot function.

40 Digital Photography Techniques

Chapter 6

After the Photo Shoot

In this last chapter, you will learn how to connect, transfer, manage, and store the images taken with your digital camera on the computer. We will also look at some common options for printing your shots, explore the problem of color matching across devices, and discuss the appropriate image resolutions for your print size. In the last technique, you will learn how to use Photoshop Album to create your own photo gallery for the Internet.

37 Transferring Images to the Computer

If your camera uses CompactFlash, Memory Stick, SmartMedia, or any other removable storage media, you can pop it out of your camera and use a card reader or adapter connected to your computer to transfer the files. Alternately, you can transfer images by linking your camera to your computer using a serial cable or USB cable. Yet another transfer method is through infrared. But since most new digital cameras use USB, we will only focus on this transfer method in this section.

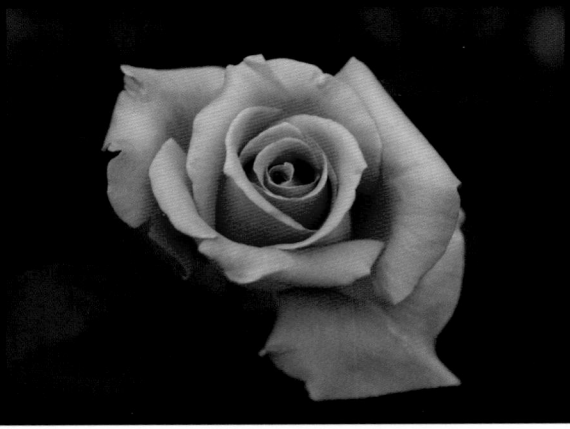

Installing a Device Driver

Before you transfer images using a USB (Universal Serial Bus) cable, you need to install the camera's device driver on your computer. A device driver is software that enables a computer to communicate with other devices. The device driver for your digital camera usually comes with it on a diskette or CD-ROM. If your PC runs on Windows 98, the device driver needs to be installed manually. See the steps below.

1. Insert the Device Driver CD-ROM into the CD-ROM drive. An installation program will load automatically. Select USB Driver for Windows 98 from the menu.

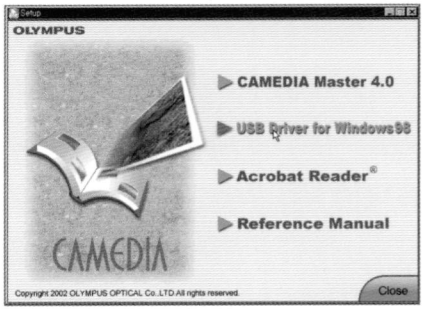

tip For PCs running Windows 2000/ME/XP, the installation is done automatically.

② A dialog box will appear. Click Continue to start the installation process. Most installers require you to restart your computer before completing the installation process. After the computer is restarted, connect the camera to the computer and the installation will complete automatically. Read your camera's manual for more information on the installation of your device driver.

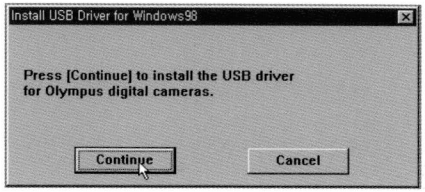

Connecting the Digital Camera to a Computer

① Plug the flat connector of the USB cable into the computer's USB port, as shown.

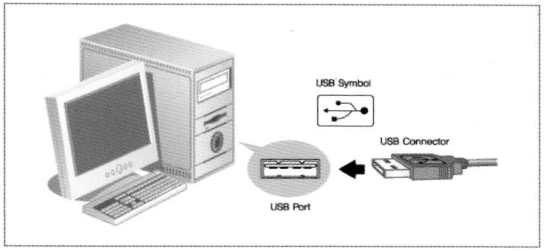

② Flip the camera's USB connector cover open and plug the square end of the USB cable into the camera's USB connector, as shown. Keep the camera lens cover on at all times.

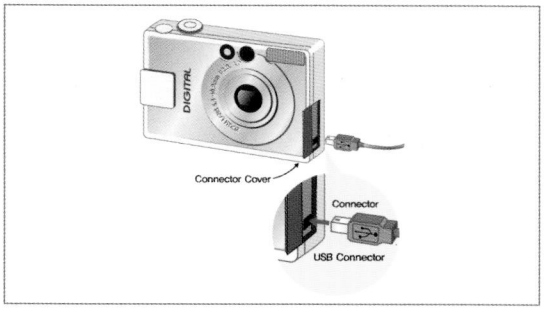

③ If the device driver is installed, the following dialog box will appear automatically. You can transfer images to the computer by using the Scanner and Camera Wizard.

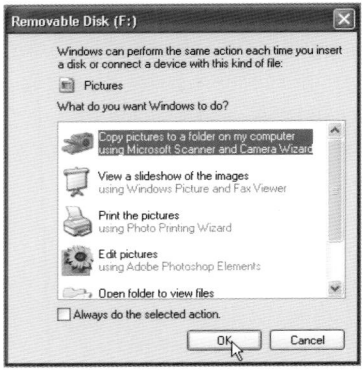

Ⓥ Using Dedicated Software Programs to Transfer Images

Some digital cameras require the use of dedicated software programs to transfer and manage images. For such cameras, you need to install the program before connecting them to the computer. As the steps vary from camera to camera, read the camera's manual for more information.

Use a Reliable Power Source

Before transferring data to the computer, make sure your camera's battery is fully charged.

Transferring Images to a Computer

The Scanner and Camera Wizard is a program that comes with your Windows operating system. It helps you transfer data from scanners and digital cameras to your computer. Once the camera is plugged into the computer, the wizard will recognize the digital camera as a removable storage media. The digital camera will then appear as an icon on the Scanners and Cameras window. You should activate Windows Explorer and start transferring the images to the computer. Once transferred, you can copy, move, rename, and erase the images through Windows Explorer. The folllowing steps show you where to locate the transferred images:

① Run Windows Explorer and click on Removable Disk.

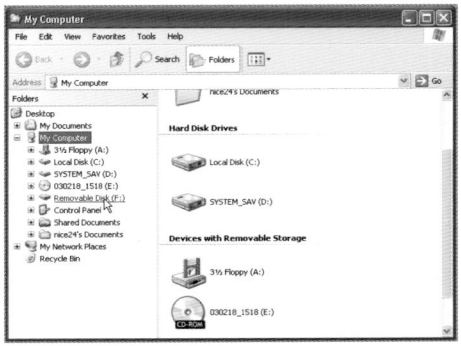

② A list of images stored in the camera's portable memory disk will be displayed. You can use Windows Explorer to manage the image files in the same manner as you would any other files on your computer.

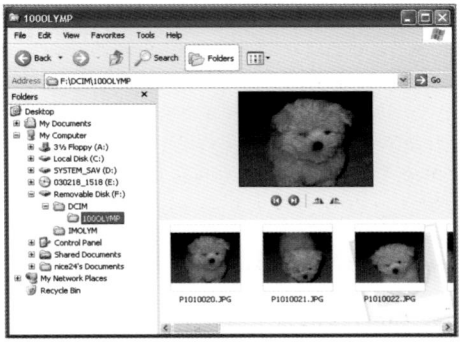

Special Directory for Images

Some cameras will save the images into a special directory. If such is the case, click on the folder where the images are stored to view the files. Read your camera's manual to final out about the special directories that images are automatically saved to.

Detaching a Camera from a PC

Once the images have been transferred, you have to disconnect the camera from the PC safely. Here's how:

▶▶▶ Windows 98 Users

① Right-click on Removable Disk in the My Computer window and choose Eject.

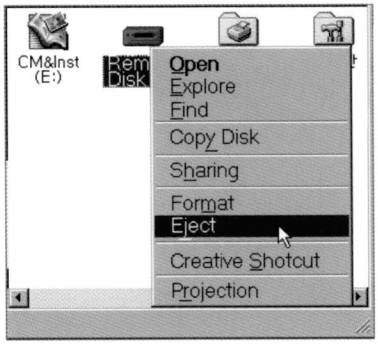

② The camera light, which shines green to indicate that the camera is connected to a PC, will turn off. Disconnect the cable from the camera and the computer.

▶▶▶ Windows 2000/ME/XP Users

① Click on Safely Remove Hardware from the taskbar and choose Safely Remove USB Mass Storage Device-Drive.

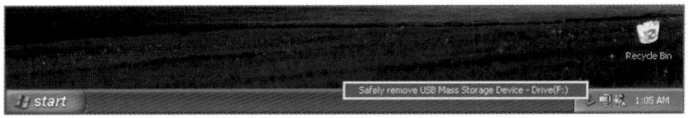

② When the Safely Remove Hardware dialog box appears, click on the Stop button. Disconnect the cable from the camera and computer after the Safe to Remove Hardware message is displayed.

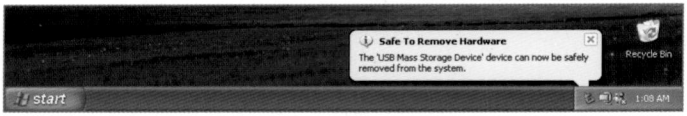

38 Organizing and Managing Images

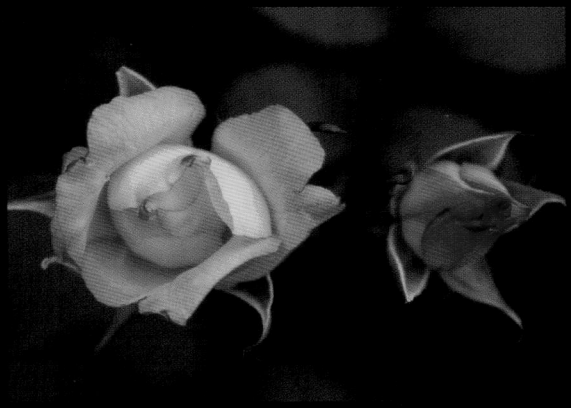

The best part of owning a digital camera is that you can take as many photos as you want without worrying about the additional expense of film and developing fees. Ironically, this can be too much of a good thing. With a large library of images, you may end up unable to locate the image you want. It is important that you organize and manage your images well.

Renaming Images

A digital camera automatically assigns the images you take with file names like DSCN0030.jpg. As you can see, the names are meaningless and do not describe the images at all. This becomes a problem when you have to look for a particular image from the tens or hundreds that you have shot. To make it easier to identify the images, you should rename the images in a way that is meaningful to you. Let's see how you can do this:

1. First, transfer the images to your computer. Select the images you want to keep and delete the rest.

2. Rename the selected images. For example, a shot of a temple from a trip to Japan in 2003 could be labeled as japan-2003-kyoto-temple1.jpg. The file name should get more descriptive toward the end. If the image were named temple1-kyoto-2003-japan.jpg, it would have been listed by the generic "temple" first and the more specific location, "kyoto," second.

3. Save the images in a folder named in the same descriptive way. You may want to keep notes or other information about the images that you take in the same folder.

4. Back up your images on CD-ROMs. Label the CD-ROMs. For example, Japan 2003 Photo CD 6.

Using ACDSee

There are many programs designed to help you manage and edit your photos. In this section, we will look at ACDSee, a popular digital camera program for PCs. The main advantage of ACDSee is its easy-to-use image viewer. It allows users to view images in three different ways: Folder Tree, Thumbnail, and Preview. You can download the ACDSee 9.0 Free Trial from the http://www.acdsee.com site.

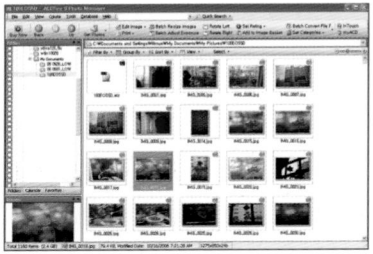
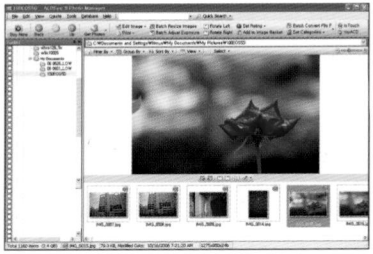
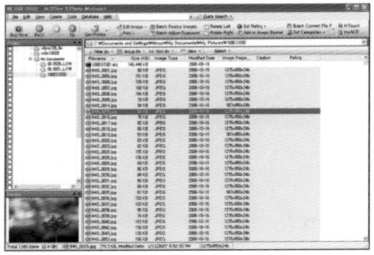

▲ User-friendly Thumbnail and Preview functions.

▶▶▶ The menu at the top contains the following options:

- Acquire: Imports images from a digital camera or scanner.

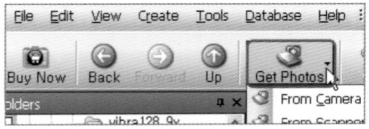

▲ Imports images when Acquire icon is clicked.

- Edit: ACDSee not only ables you to view a file, but allows you to make various changes and edits.

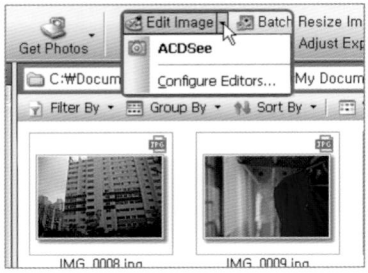

▲ Click Edit to touchup and enhance your images.

- Create: Create a slide show, compact disc, or other HTML documents.

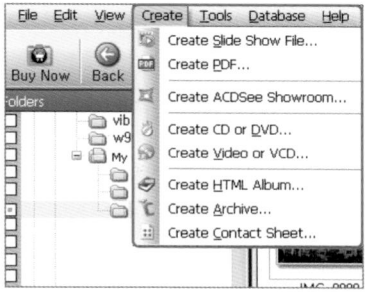

▶ You can make unique projects with the Create function.

▶▶▶ Properties

Information about an image, which may be useful for future reference, is stored in the Metadata tab.

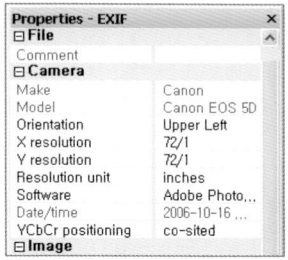

▲ Image information is stored in the Metadata tab.

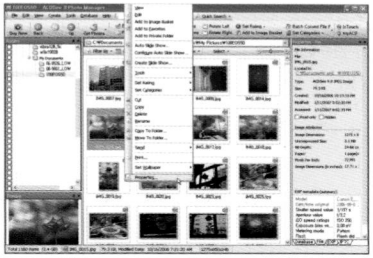

▲ Select an image, right-click, and choose Properties.

▶▶▶ Batch Rename

Use the Batch Rename tool to rename a batch of images at the same time.

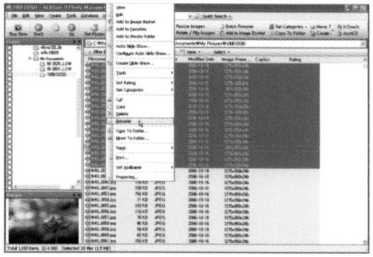

▲ Select the images and right-click Rename.

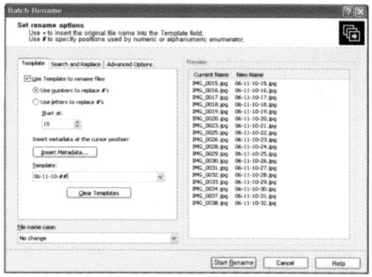

▲ With the wildcard function, ###, numbers in running order are applied automatically to the selected images.

▶▶▶ Image Rotate

Vertical images can be easily rotated with the Image Rotate function.

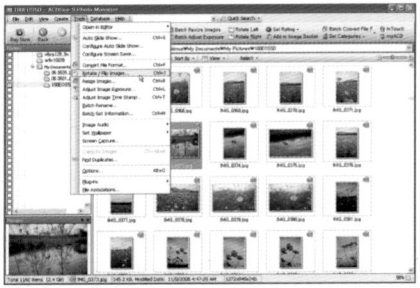

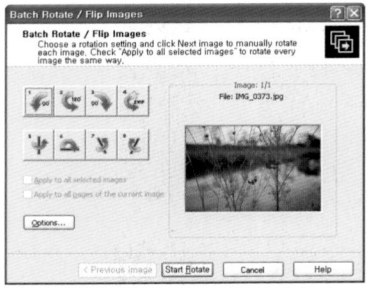

▲ Using the Image Rotate function.

▶▶▶ Resize

You can adjust the size and resolution of an image using the Resize function in the menu.

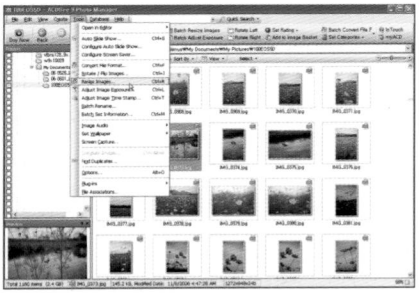

▲ Choose the Resize icon from the menu.

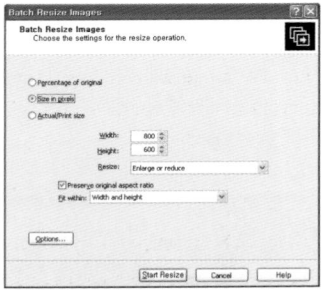

▲ Change the image resolution.

39 Developing Photos

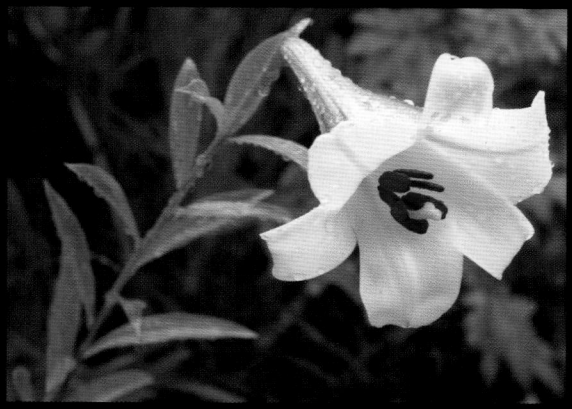

A big advantage of digital cameras over film cameras is that you can choose to print only the images you want and do it right at home. In fact, you can print anywhere if you own one of those small, portable photo printers. As image-editing software, consumer photo printers, and paper become better and more affordable, it has become possible for average consumers to produce high-quality prints that match those from a photofinisher.

Printing at Home

▶▶▶ Using a General Document Printer

You can use normal 8 1/2 × 11 inch paper or photo paper specially made for printing photographs. Although photo paper is expensive, you can produce quality prints on it that come close to the quality of normal photographs. When using a general printer, you can use image-editing programs such as Windows XP's Photo Printing Wizard or Adobe's Photoshop to print.

Editing the Image

You can use the ACDSee 9 Photo Manager to make simple changes before printing the image.

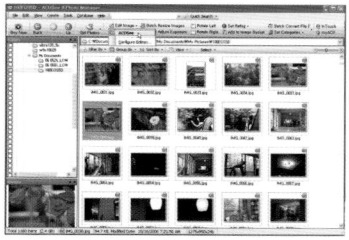

▲ Run the ACDSee program and click on Edit Image.

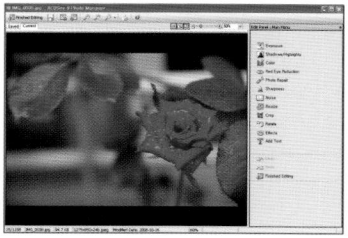

▲ An Edit Panel appears on the right hand side of the edit window.

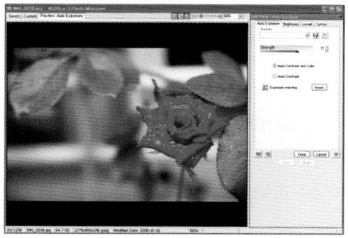

▲ Click the Exposure button from the Edit Panel to correct the exposure or brightness.

● Using Photo Printing Wizard to Print

① Select an image, right-click, and choose Print.

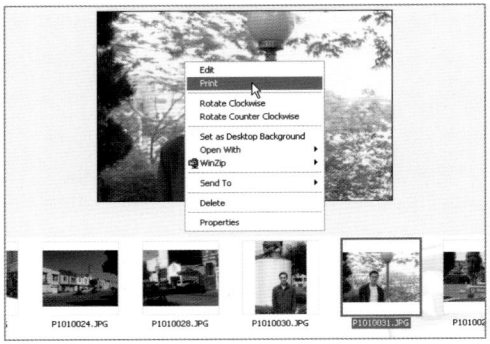

② Photo Printing Wizard will begin.

If you are not selecting any special options, keep clicking on Next until you reach the layout option screen. Choose a layout and click on Next. Your photo will start printing soon.

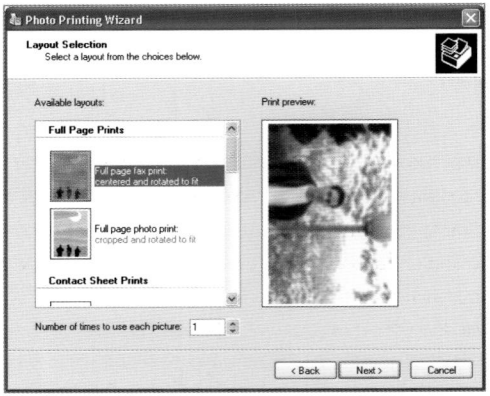

● Using Photoshop Elements to Print

Before you start printing, you have to set an output resolution. Generally images used for the Web have a resolution of 72 dpi. However, to get a reasonably good print on photographic paper, the images should have a resolution of 200 to 300 dpi.

▶▶▶ Using a Photo Printer

When using photo printers, you do not need a computer to print, which makes the process a lot simpler. You can print photos by simply inserting your camera's memory card into the photo printer. These days, even low-priced photo printers offer good value in terms of cost and performance, so shop around if you intend to buy a photo printer. Read your printer's manual to learn more about the printing process.

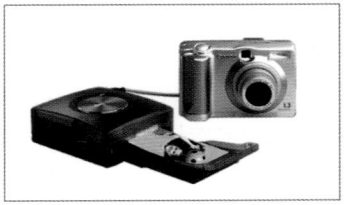

▲ Canon's photo printer

Calibrating the Monitor and the Printer

Monitors display colors on the screen by using a mix of red, green, and blue (RGB) lights, while printers print colors in a mix of cyan, magenta, yellow, and black (CMYK) inks. Due to the difference in the way that color is recorded and output from these devices, the range of colors produced by both color models do not correspond accurately to each other or overlap completely.

So, if you notice that the colors in your image look significantly different when printed, you may need to match the colors on your monitor to your printer. This process of matching color across devices is called calibration. You can calibrate your devices using a color matching software, but this requires patience and experimentation or you may end up with worse prints than before.

Alternately, you can look at the printed copy and try to change the colors on the monitor for a more accurate print. But this means that your image will print differently on another printer. Before you calibrate your devices, check to see if the color difference is due to the paper quality, ink purity, or the lighting conditions. It is easier to fix these problems than to calibrate colors.

Sending Prints to Professional Printers

Even though you can print your images at home, you may still want to send your non-urgent prints to a photofinisher for a couple of reasons. For instance, if you want to print hundreds of shots, you may find that it takes too much time and effort to print them at home. You can also get better and larger prints at a photofinisher, as they have more sophisticated equipment and they can also correct the color of your images. At these photofinishers, you can print high-quality photos and enlargements of more than 10 × 15 inches in size. For the best prints, make sure that you discuss your expectations with the printer and are specific about the results you want.

Another option is to use a web-based print service, but you will need to register as a member first. Online providers usually provide 50MB to 100MB of storage space for each account. Customers have to upload the images and specify sizes when they place an order. The provider then prints the photos and delivers them by mail or express delivery in about three to five days. The cost is about the same as printing from film negatives. An added benefit is that you can also use the allocated storage space as your own image archive to share your photos with friends.

Additional options include printing your images at Fuji Film's FDI Stations, if they are found in your neighborhood, or at general photo studios, which are beginning to offer such services as well.

Adjusting the Aspect Ratio

Most images shot by digital cameras have an aspect ratio of 4:3, although some have a ratio of 3:2. Aspect ratio refers to the ratio of the image's height and width. However, the aspect ratio of most prints is different from the images' aspect ratio. Prints usually come in the ratio of 3:5, 4:6, 5:7, 8:10, 11:14, or 10:15.

So, if an image with an aspect ratio of 3:2 is printed on a photographic paper with an aspect ratio of 10:8, part of the image will be cut off. Since 3:2 = 12:8, the image will be cut off lengthwise on one or both sides.

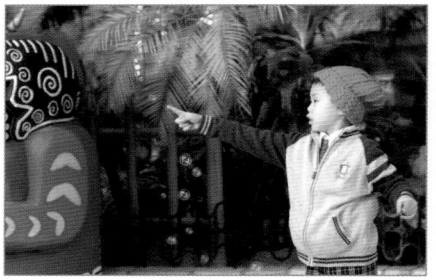

▲ Original image with a ratio of 3:2.

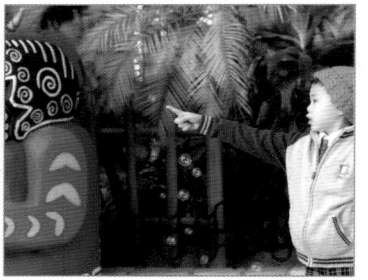

▲ Photo gets cut off when printed on 8 × 10 inch photographic paper.

▶▶▶ Full Image Option

One way to prevent your images from being cut off is to order your prints in Full Image option. This option preserves the image ratio but leaves a margin on both sides of the photo. The actual size of the photo may shrink a little.

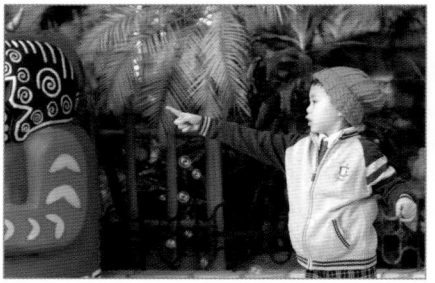

▲ Original image with a ratio of 3:2.

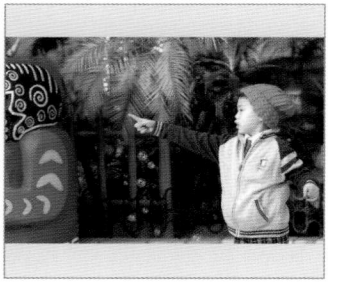

▲ Printed in Full Image option on 8 × 10 inch paper.

▶▶▶ Photoshop Element's Crop Function

You can use the crop function in Photoshop to crop the image so that it will fit on 8 × 10 inch paper when printed. This method is recommended because you can crop the image according to your own preference and resize the image to fit the print size. Some printers support a Trim and Print service where users can crop their own images before printing.

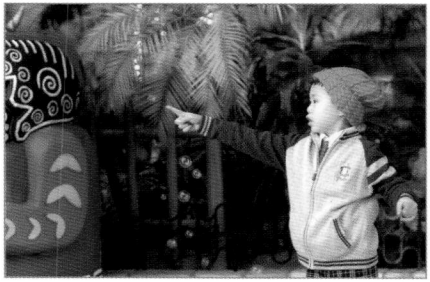

▲ Original image with a ratio of 3:2.

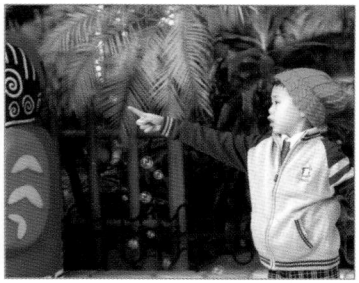

▲ Printed image after being cropped to fit a ratio of 8:10.

Recommended Resolutions

To get a good-quality print at a certain size, you should make sure that your original image resolution is high enough for that particular print size.

Paper Size (Inches)	Recommended (Minimun) Resolution	Number of Pixels on Digital Camera
3 × 5	1024 × 768	850,000
4 × 6	1280 × 1024	1,400,000
5 × 7	1600 × 1200	2,100,000
8 × 10	2048 × 1536	3,340,000
11 × 14	2272 × 1704	4,130,000

40 Web Photo Gallery

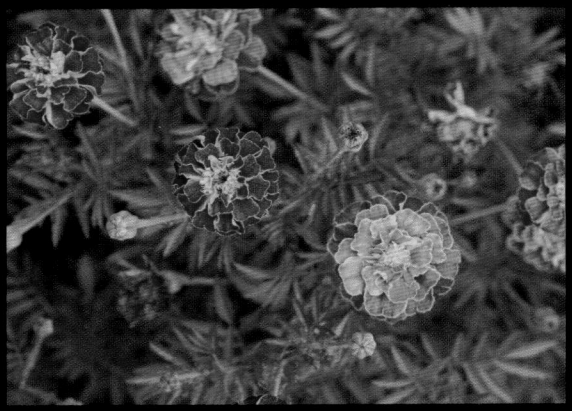

If this technology is new to you, you may assume that it is difficult to create, manage, and operate an online photo gallery. However, numerous software and Web-based programs make it easy to share and organize your photos online. This section will demonstrate one such program—Photoshop Elements 5.0—which can be downloaded as a 30 day trial version from the www.adobe.com website.

① Once you install and run Photoshop Elements 5.0 on your computer, a Welcome Screen will appear as shown below. Click on View and Organize Photos.

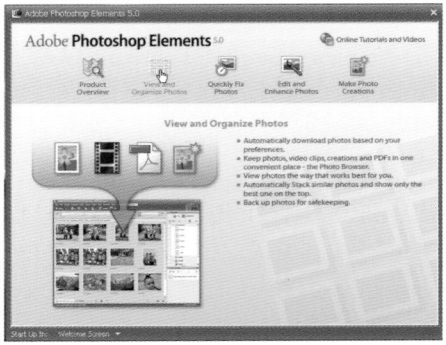

② The Organizer window will appear. Click on File > Get Photo > From Files and Folders to open the image files you wish to include in the web photo gallery.

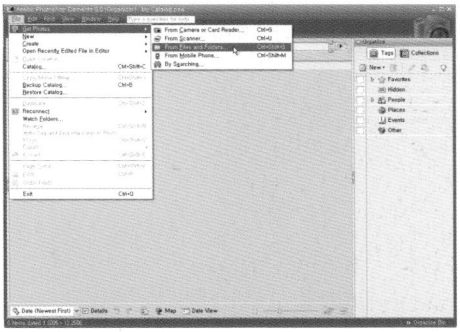

③ Once the Get Photo From Files and Folders window appears, select the desired images, then click the Get Photo button.

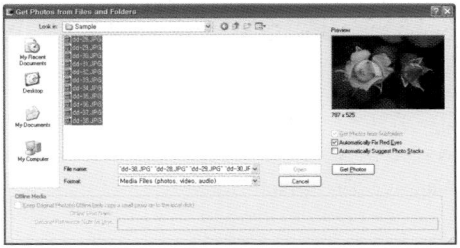

④ The selected image files will appear in the Organizer window.

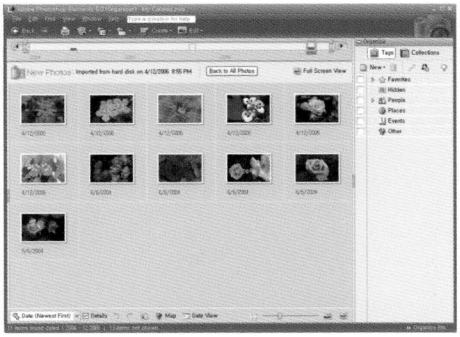

⑤ Click on the Create button after you have selected all the image files. Then select Photo Galleries.

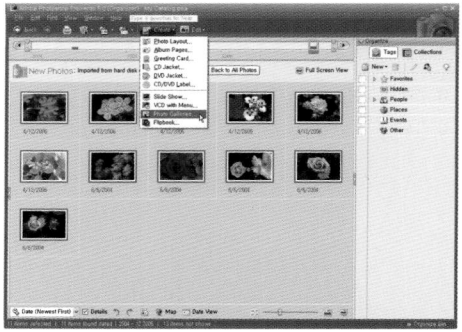

⑥ Photoshop Elements Photo Galleries Wizard window will appear. Confirm that Type pull-down menu is set to Web Galleries, then select a specific formatting for your gallery.

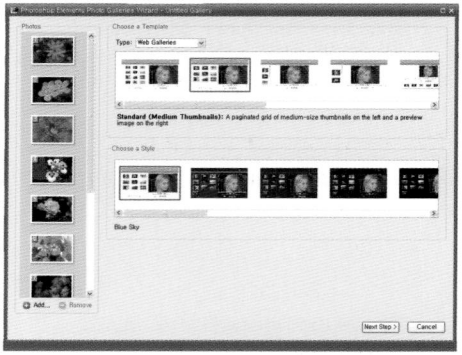

⑦ Under Choose a Style, scroll to the right to select Patina Style, as shown in the image. Click on the Next Step button.

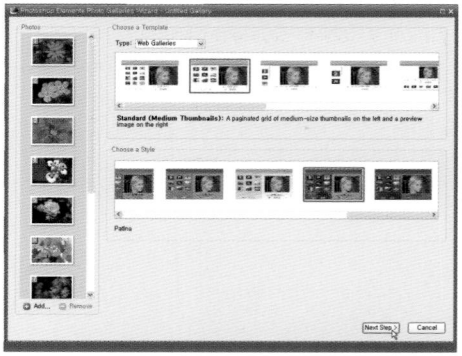

⑧ When the window appears, input the data in the menu on the left.

If you drag the scroll bar down, there are options to change the color of the background, title bar, etc.

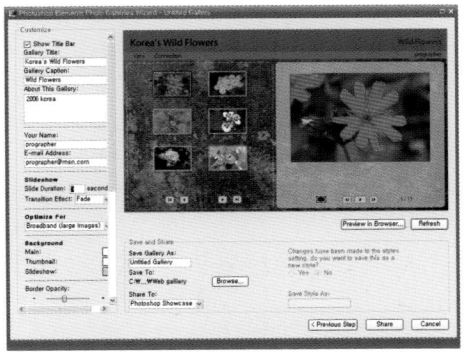

⑨ To assign a folder where your photo gallery will be saved, click on the Browse button under the Save and Share option.

tip You can preview the photo gallery that you have created in your web browser by clicking the Preview in Browser button.

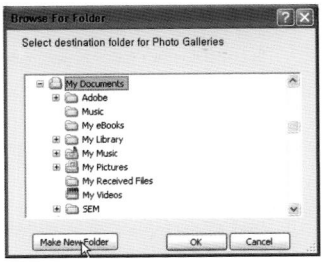

⑩ Once all the options have been set, click the Share button. The Share Photo Gallery window will appear, as seen below. Input your personal data to create an account, then click the Next button.

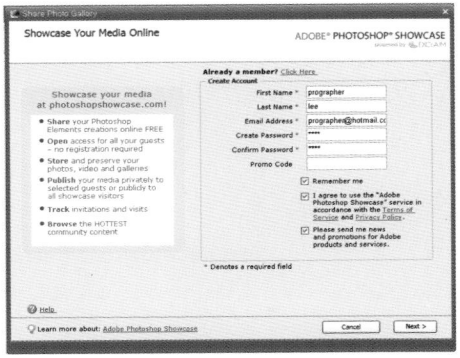

⑪ Input the desired name for your gallery, then click Next. When the Invite window appears, input the email addresses of the people you want to view your album, or select the box to make your gallery public. Personalize your email message, then click Next.

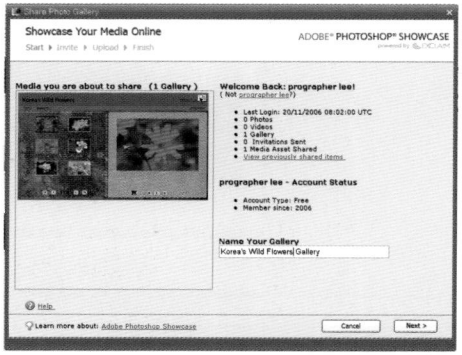

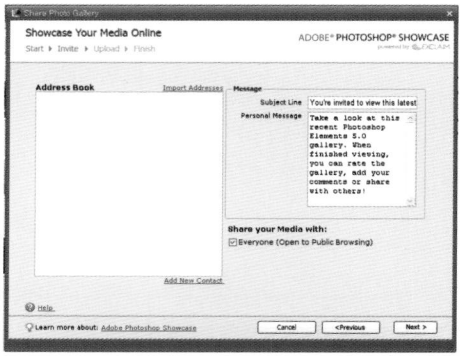

⑫ If your computer is online, your photo gallery will begin uploading. Once uploading is complete, a window will appear as shown below. Click on the View This Gallery button.

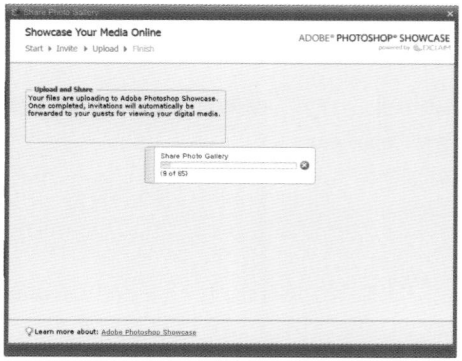

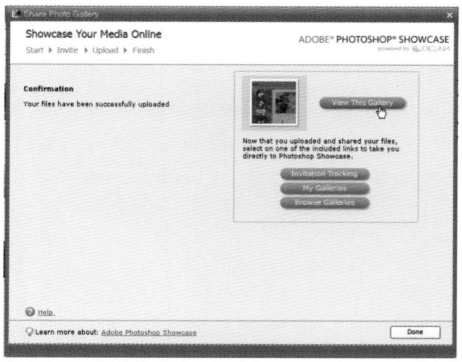

(13) Internet Explorer or your web browser will appear. By clicking on your project, you can view your gallery.

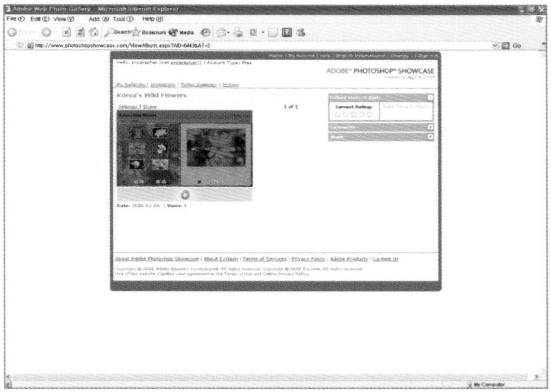

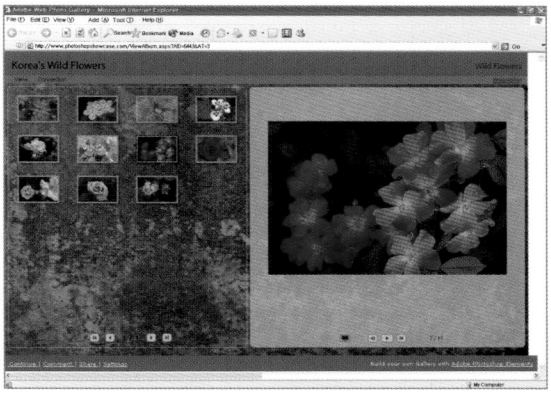

Chapter 6 | After the Photo Shoot

- √ Install a device driver for your camera, if you have't already done so.
- √ Connect your camera to the computer and transfer your images using the Scanner and Camera Wizard program in the Windows operating system.
- √ Use ACDSee or other similar programs to manage and edit your images.
- √ Use ACDSee or other similar programs to rename your images.
- √ Print your images using a general document printer at home, send them to a photofinisher, or upload them to a web-based print service.
- √ Set up your own photo gallery with Photoshop Elements 5.0 or other similar programs.
- √ If you are interested in editing your images, you may wish to check out our book *40 Digital Photo Retouching Techniques with Photoshop Elements*.

Index

A

accessories, 21–23
ACDSee, 192–194
action shots, 86–88, 125
angle of light, 62
angle of view, 44
animals (photographing), 180–182
Anytime Flash mode, 68
aperture, 14, 42, 49
Aperture Priority mode, 50
architecture (photographing), 170–172
art gallery (photographing in), 173–176
artificial light, see *flash*
aspect ratio, 198
Auto Exposure Bracketing, 84
Auto Flash mode, 117
autofocus, 40
automatic cameras, 18
Auto White Balance mode, 90

B

babies (photographing), 112
background, 78, 101–102
backlighting, 63
bags, 22, 140
barrel distortion, 80
batteries, 17
beach photography, 26
Best Shot Selector, 85
black-and-white photography, 72–75
blower, 25
blurring (reducing), 32–36
bracket, 68
bracketing exposures, 84
buildings (photographing), 170–172
buying a digital camera, 27

C

calibrating the monitor and printer, 197
camera angles, 105, 114, 131, 169
camera bags, 22
camera care, 24–26
camera shake, 32–36
camera-to-subject distance, 104
card reader, 23
cars (photographing), 167–169
CCD, 8, 10, 11, 20
center-weighted metering, 64
CF card, 16
Character scene mode, 106
children (photographing), 109–112
close-ups, 76–80, 98, 112, 167
Close-Up Scene mode, 107
Cloudy White Balance mode, 91
CMOS, 9
color and skin tone, 118
color cast, 71, 89–90
color temperature, 89
CompactFlash card, 16
comparing with film cameras, 8–10, 72
composition, 53–58, 131–132
compression, 39
computers and digital camera, 173–191, 187–190
connecting and transferring images, 187–189
continuous shots (taking), 81–85
Continuous Shot function, 15, 38, 81–85, 110, 178
conversion lens, 23
cropping, 199
cross star filter, 123
Custom White Balance mode, 92

D

Daylight Sync Flash mode, 70
degrees Kelvin, 89
depth of field, 45, 50
device driver, 186
documents (photographing), 75, 80
diaphragm, see *iris diaphragm*
diffusers, 70
digital cameras (introduction), 6–26
distortion, see *barrel distortion*

E

editing an image, 195–197
exposure, 14, 48–52, 78, 84, 143
exposure compensation, 48, 65
exposure meters, 64, 143
eyes (focusing on), 99

F

f-numbers, 49
Fast Action Scene mode, 109
file formats, 12
fill flash, 134
Fill Flash mode, 63, 68
filling the frame, 56
filters, 22, 120–123, 143
Fine White Balance mode, 91
fireworks (photographing), 147

Fireworks Show Scene mode, 52
flash, 15, 67–71
blurring, 32-36
external flash units, 23, 67–68
portraits, 113–116
products, 163–166
still-life lighting package, 166
Flash Cancel mode, 69
flash distance, 15, 67
Flash modes, 68–70
Flash Off mode, 69
flowers (photographing), 79
Fluorescent White Balance mode, 91
focal length, 13, 43, 44, 76
focal range (macro photography), 77
focus, 106
focus lock, 40, 41
focusing range, 14
food photography, 160–162
frames per second, 81

G

general document printer, 195
graininess, 15, 110
grip cameras, 19
group photos, 103

H

holding the camera, 33
horizontal orientation, 56, 131
hot shoe, 23, 67–68

I

image resolution, 12, 37
image size and quality, 37–39
Incandescent White Balance mode, 91
insects (photographing), 79
interference (avoiding), 54
Internet, see *Web Photo Gallery*
Interval mode, 84–85
iris diaphragm, 8, 14, 42
ISO, 15, 49, 110

J

JPEG, 12
JPEG compression level, 12

L

landscape photography, 130–156
Landscape Scene mode, 43
LCD screen, 16, 20
leading lines, 57
lens adapter, 23, 120
lens brush, 25
lens cloth, 25
lens element, 8, 42
lens terminology, 43
lenses, 13, 42–47
blurring, 32
cleaning, 25
minimum focusing distance, 76
rotating, 20
see also *aperture*
light-metering methods, 64
lighting, 62–66, 77, 83
landscape, 130–134
macro photography, 76
portraits, 113–116, 121
products, 163–166
still-life lighting package, 166
see also *flash*

M

Macro mode, 76–77, 79–80, 161
macro photography, 76–80
managing images, 191–194
manual cameras, 19
matrix metering, 64
megapixels, 11
memory cards, 16, 21
Memory Stick, 16
microdrive card, 16
movies, 15
Multi-Shot 16 feature, 85
museum (photographing in), 173–176

N

neutral density (ND) filter, 122
Night Flash mode, 69
Night Landscape Scene mode, 43, 52
night photography, 144–147
noise, 146

O

omni-bounce, 71
optical zoom, 13
organizing images, 191–194

P

panoramas, 152–156
parallax error, 16
Party Scene mode, 141
people, 96–126
perspective, 44
pets (photographing), 177–179
photo gallery, *see web photo gallery*
photo printer, 196
Photoshop Elements, 196, 199
pixels, 11, 19, 20, 37

points of view, 57, 58, 114
polarizing filters, 22, 121, 143
portraits, 113–116
Portrait Scene mode, 141
preparing to shoot, 30–31
printing, 195–197
product photography, 163–166
professional printers, 197
properties of light, 89

R

rainy days, 139–141
RAW, 12
Red Eye Reduction Flash mode, 69
reflectors, 71
resolution, 37–39
Rule of Thirds, 54

S

semiautomatic cameras, 14
sensitivity, 15
scene (choosing), 130
Scene modes, 14
Backlight, 63
Character, 102
Close-up, 76–80, 98–99
Fast Action, 109
Fill Flash, 63
Fireworks Show, 52
Indoor, 117, 163, 174
Landscape, 50
Macro, 76–77, 79–80, 161
Night Landscape, 43, 52
Party, 141
Portrait, 50, 98, 106
Sports, 52, 83, 109, 141, 177
SD card, 16
selective focus, 106–108, 111, 133
self-portraits, 113–116
Sepia mode, 72
shutter, 8
Shutter Priority mode, 52
shutter speed, 14, 36, 51, 84, 86, 109, 142
single-lens reflex (SLR) cameras , 108
Slow Sync Flash mode, 69
SmartMedia card, 86
snowy days, 142–143
soft filter, 122
Sports Scene mode, 86, 142, 177
spot metering, 66, 78
starburst filter, 123
still-life lighting package, 166
storage media, 16, 23
strobe, 23
structure and basic functions, 11–17
subject placement, 53
sunrises, 66, 148–151
sunsets, 66, 148–151

T

telephoto lens, 46–47
TIFF, 12
time of day, 66
tourist attractions, 135–138
traffic light trails, 49, 146
transferring images, 188
travel photography, 135–138
tripods, 22, 35, 78, 116

U

urban landscape, 143
UV filters, 22

V

vacation photos, 135–138
vertical orientation, 55, 131
viewfinders, 16

W

water, and camera care, 26, 127–129
waterproofing cameras, 139–140
weather, 65, 168
web photo gallery (setting up), 200–205
white balance, 89–94, 119
White Balance modes, 90–92, 119
wide-angle lens, 44–45, 46
window (photographing through a), 138
winter, and camera care, 26

X

xD-picture card, 16

Z

zoom, 13
zooming effect, 43

Acknowledgments

I would like to thank ED, Lasid, Thomas, and Simona for modeling for the pictures and also thank all the individuals who contributed photographs for this book.

Picture Copyright © Angelica: page 38(a, b, c), 58(a, b, c, d)

Picture Copyright © Brianne Agatep: page 179(a, b)

Picture Copyright © Carl Keyes: page 134(f), 142(b), 143(a), 150(d)

Picture Copyright © Chongseok Cheong: page 79(b)

Picture Copyright © Derick Miller: page 86(a), 99(b), 112(c)

Picture Copyright © FotoArte-Krakow (www.fotoarte.com.pl): page 124(a), 125(a, b, c)

Picture Copyright © Jeongbin Lee: page 80(a)

Picture Copyright © Jeongmin Lee: page 79(a)

Picture Copyright © Judy Fung: page 57(e), 136(a), 151(a, b, c)

Picture Copyright © Lak Yau Hui: page 15(a, b, c), 46(a, g, h), 50(a, b), 54(e), 57(a, b), 101(c), 130(a), 131 (a, b), 135(a, b), 136(c, d), 137(b), 138(b, e), 143(b, c), 145(c), 172(d), 178(d)

Picture Copyright © Larry M. Gottschalk: page 115(e), 132(a), 133(c), 134(c, e), 146(c), 177(b)

Picture Copyright © Mariann Barsolo: page 178(a, b, c)

Picture Copyright © Seonghyun Kim: page 167(b, c), 168(a, b, c, d, e, f)

Picture Copyright © Suzie Lee: page 111(c)

Picture Copyright © Thom Dyson: page 150(e)

Picture Copyright © Tracey J. O'Brien: page 172(a, b, c)

All other pictures Copyright © John Kim

BOCA RATON PUBLIC LIBRARY, FLORIDA
3 3656 0550186 0

775 For

40 digital photography techniques